Hamka and Islam

Khairudin Aljunied

Hamka and Islam

Cosmopolitan Reform in the Malay World

SOUTHEAST ASIA PROGRAM PUBLICATIONS
an imprint of
Cornell University Press
Ithaca and London

Cornell University Press gratefully acknowledges a grant from the National
University of Singapore that aided in the publication of this book.

First published 2018 by Cornell University Press

Printed in the United States of America

Library of Congress Cataloging-in-Publication Data
Names: Aljunied, Syed Muhd. Khairudin, 1976– author.
Title: Hamka and Islam : cosmopolitan reform in the Malay world / Khairudin
    Aljunied.
Description: Ithaca : Southeast Asia Program Publications, an imprint of Cornell
    University Press, 2018. | Includes bibliographical references and index.
Identifiers: LCCN 2017055046 (print) | LCCN 2017056754 (ebook) |
    ISBN 9781501724589 (pdf) | ISBN 9781501724596 (epub/mobi) |
    ISBN 9781501724565 (cloth : alk. paper) | ISBN 9781501724572
    (pbk. : alk. paper)
Subjects: LCSH: Islamic renewal—Malay Archipelago. | Hamka, 1908–1981. |
    Faith and reason—Islam. | Islam—20th century.
Classification: LCC BP63.M35 (ebook) | LCC BP63.M35 A45 2018 (print) |
    DDC 297.09598/0904—dc23
LC record available at https://lccn.loc.gov/2017055046

CONTENTS

PREFACE

This book is, in many ways, a product of my journey with one of the most towering figures in the history of Islam in the Malay world: Haji Abdul Malik bin Abdul
Karim Amrullah (better known as Hamka). It is a journey that grew from an internal
crisis and the will to reform myself, with Hamka as a companion in the twists and
turns and confusing mazes of life, in the search for my own identity as a Muslim and
a human being.

The journey began when I was just a young student. Barely in my twenties and
trying to find meaning in my own faith through the study of Sufism, I encountered a
copy of *Tasauf Modern* (*Modern Sufism*) at a local library. I can still remember how difficult it was to read the book. Written in 1930s Malay, printed on dark brown paper,
and worn out perhaps from a large number of borrowings, the book was a mixed bag
of poetic analogies, personal anecdotes, and moralistic injunctions laced with intellectual insights about what leading a spiritual life amounted to and the happiness that
comes with it.

I must admit that I did not read *Tasauf Modern* cover to cover. The style was somewhat too archaic for my liking then. But the book—and Hamka—never quite left my
mind and heart. *Tasauf Modern*, as I see it now with the benefit of age and learning, was
not meant to be read at one go. It is to be read piecemeal, to be reflected on, and put
into practice, as one seeks to be a better person. And so began my own personal and
intellectual acquaintance with Hamka in the many years that followed. He appeared
as an outspoken defender of Malay-Muslim rights in my doctoral thesis on the Maria
Hertogh controversy. This was a legal tussle over a Dutch-Muslim girl, which culminated in 1950 in the outbreak of the first-ever ethnic riots in Singapore. He emerged
once again as an ideologue in my study of Malay radicals in British Malaya who relentlessly agitated for freedom for their homeland. Hamka—to steal some words from
another influential Muslim thinker of our time, Muhammad Asad—"came over me
like a robber who enters a house by night; but unlike a robber, it entered to remain
for good."[1]

Soon enough, I returned to Hamka's books when I needed sagacious quota-
tions for public lectures. As I ventured deeper and deeper into his wide range of
writings—covering not only Sufism but also philosophy, history, ethics, theology, and
morality—I began to discern more about what the author stood for and about his
concerns, dreams, and hopes for Muslims in the Malay world. In the pages that follow, I offer my own interpretation of one central aspect of Hamka's lifelong writing
career: his thoughts about reforming the Muslim mind. As a scholar from Singapore
and currently based in the United States, I analyze Hamka's project of reform from
the perspective of a critical-reflexive Muslim. There is no denying that I appreciate the

---

[1] Muhammad Asad, *Islam at the Crossroads* (Petaling Jaya, Malaysia: The Other Press, 1999), xix.

company that Hamka has given me all these years. Like many Muslims in the region, I remain his admirer and an avid reader of his oft-reprinted books. And yet I maintain an analytical stance toward his ideas, visions, and propositions. I distance myself from his lapses. I engage critically with the limits of his ideas. This book is, in essence, an attempt to think with Hamka and beyond Hamka. I hope my readers will read it in that light.

Many people gave me their moral and material support to make this book possible. Jeff Hadler urged me to work on the book project on Hamka merely a few months before he was diagnosed with cancer. Although we managed to exchange only several e-mails before he succumbed to his illness, his perceptive suggestions played a big part in shaping my thoughts. James Rush and Kamaludeen Nasir gave deeper insights that I took to heart during the writing process. Shaharudin Mohd Ishak lent his copy of *Tafsir Al-Azhar* and shared some of his own ideas during our weekly breakfast sessions. I thank Hafiz Othman, Desyanto Marbun, Isngadi Marwah Atmaja, Pusat Studi Uhamka, and Suara Muhammadiyah for their help with the photographs for this book. Shuaib Silm located many of the Arabic-language sources. For that I am eternally grateful.

Rommel Curaming and Siti Norkhalbi worked hard to make the visiting professorship at the University of Brunei possible and a fruitful experience for my family and me. The few months were enriched by discussions with Professor Osman Bakar, Mulyadhi Kartanegara, Wan Zawawi Ibrahim, Bachamiya Hussainmiya, and Henk Maier. Frank Dhont, Muhammad Mubarak, Baihaqy, Marwan, Adli, Khairul Nazif, and Hasif added spice to the life there. The families of Sharifah Nurul Huda Alkaff and Amran Mohamad welcomed me warmly into their homes. They made my time in Brunei memorable.

While at the University of Muhammadiyah Yogyakarta (UMY), I learned much from conversations with Pak Abdul Madjid, Nurwanto, Naufal Rijalul Alam, Sadam Shodiq, Hilman Latief, Suroor, Rofiudin, and Wahyu. Smiling and polite all the time and never failing to be on time, Isnan Fauzi drove me around to places I needed to go for research and to experience life, and he also pointed me to Yogya's great food. Aditya Pratama at Suara Muhammadiyah helped generously in locating some rare editions of Hamka's books and sharing his perspectives. Participants of the seminars on Hamka that I delivered at UMY asked many challenging questions that made me reconsider my own presumptions.

The National University of Singapore afforded me the much-needed time to finish the final revisions of this book. I am indebted to the dean of the Faculty of Arts and Social Sciences, Robbie Goh, for his support and understanding. Jonathan Brown, the director of Georgetown University's Prince Alwaleed Bin Talal Center of Muslim-Christian Understanding, arranged for my appointment as professor and the Malaysia chair of Islam in Southeast Asia. Ermin Sinanovic helped much to ensure that I settled well in Washington, DC. *Jazakallahu Khairan Kathira!*

I thank the two anonymous reviewers of this book for their constructive comments and criticisms. They improved the text in ways that I otherwise could not have done. My editor at Cornell University Press, Sarah Grossman, has been supportive throughout the project, guiding and encouraging me from the proposal up through the publication stage. She and her dedicated team refined the text and smoothed the rough edges to make the final version of the book far more readable and sharper than the original.

Various parts of this book have appeared elsewhere in academic journals. I thank the editors of *Indonesia, History of Religions, Public Historian,* and *Islam and Muslim-Christian Relations* for permission to reproduce these articles, which I have heavily revised for this publication.

My parents, Noah and Norasiah; siblings; and close friends have never failed to shower their advice on me and give me much-needed motivation. Marlina deserves a Super-Mum award for tolerating my hectic writing schedule. She has single-handedly taken care of our six children during my frequent travels and late nights at work. This book is for her, as always.

ABBREVIATIONS

Masyumi   Partai Majelis Syuro Muslim Indonesia (Council of Indonesia Muslim Associations)

MUI   Majelis Ulama Indonesia (Indonesian Ulama Council)

PSII   Partai Sarekat Islam Indonesia (Islamic Association Party of Indonesia)

UDHR   Universal Declaration of Human Rights

Hamka and Islam

INTRODUCTION

Hamka's Cosmopolitan Reform

> Paradigms may change, the frameworks of global governance may change too. And Muslims are an inescapable part of these shifting configurations. But the light that shines in the hearts of those infused with the spirit of Islam, with the soul of Islam, will not change. It may be suppressed for some time, but it lingers. It lingers like a fire trapped beneath a husk. When the time comes, it emerges. Take notice that the husk would soon be scorched by the burning flames.
>
> With certainty in the continued existence of this spirit [of Islam], the global Muslim community in general, and in Indonesia in particular, confronts the future!
>
> Hamka, *Keadilan Sosial Dalam Islam*
> (Social Justice in Islam) (1966)

Although written many decades ago, the passage above anticipates the changes that are taking place in the Islamic world today. Now more than ever before, Muslims in almost all corners of the globe are calling out for reform. They are asking whether Muslim elites and thinkers have been effective in diagnosing and addressing the ongoing upheavals and crises in the Middle East, North Africa, and South Asia. Frustrated by the inability of traditional Islamic scholars to respond to the manifold challenges of modernity and disillusioned with successive authoritarian regimes that have torn Muslim societies asunder, an emerging crop of Muslim activists and thinkers are crying out for change. They desire a total transformation of Islamic thought and practice. These reformers advocate a reexamination of age-old methods of teaching and transmitting Islam. In the words of Tariq Ramadan, an influential figure in this renewed wave of thinking about Islam, Muslims are in need of "radical reform." This is a brand of reform that builds upon innovation in the reading of sacred texts in Islam alongside a "full and equal integration of all available human knowledge."[1]

Similar calls for reform and change can be heard in the Malay world, a region that houses the largest Muslim population on the planet and yet is all but neglected by most analysts of Islam.[2] The more than three hundred million Muslim inhabitants in the Malay world—Brunei, Indonesia, Malaysia, Singapore, South Thailand, and South Philippines—share common elements of the same language and culture,

---

[1] Tariq Ramadan, *Radical Reform: Islamic Ethics and Liberation* (Oxford: Oxford University Press, 2009), 33.

[2] For discussions of the neglect of Islam in the Malay world in Islamic studies, see Greg Fealy, "Islam in Southeast Asia," in *Contemporary Southeast Asia*, ed. Mark Beeson (Basingstoke, UK: Palgrave, 2009), 158–73.

with Islam as the dominant religion.[3] One figure who has cast a long shadow on the history of Islamic reform in the Malay world is Haji Abdullah Malik Abdul Karim Amrullah (1908–81), more commonly known as Hamka. Described as the most prominent twentieth-century Muslim intellectual hailing from that region, Hamka beguiled thousands of avid listeners with his lectures.[4] He wrote more than a hundred popular and scholarly Islamic books, as well as several successful novels. His literary career spanned a wide range of topics, including history, theology, philosophy, Islamic jurisprudence, and spirituality. The attractiveness of Hamka's writings and speeches can also be attributed to his ability to reconcile opposing ideas about culture, modernity, and Islam. The late Nurcholish Madjid (1939–2005), who was one of Indonesia's intellectual giants, observed, "His [Hamka's] ideas are accepted by a wide spectrum of Muslims, principally the Muslim community in Indonesia who identify themselves as 'the modernist group' or the 'reformist group.'"[5]

Hamka's writing is omnipresent in the Malay world. His books, such as his commentaries on the Qur'an, are used widely in Muslim schools and tertiary institutions.[6] Some popular titles, such as *Ayahku*, *Falsafah Hidup* and *Tasauf Modern* (Modern Sufism), are now in their ninth editions. These books are found in all major libraries in the Malay world, with a select few of these libraries featuring special collections in Hamka's name.[7] To cap it all, Hamka's acknowledged contributions to popularizing Islam have recently been memorialized in a museum located in his hometown, Tasek Maninjau, Sumatra.[8] In Semarang, Java, a road has been named after him: Jalan Prof. Dr. Hamka." His large body of work has outgrown him and taken on a life of its own, and it has become part of the shared scholarly heritage of Muslims in the region. Indeed, Hamka is that rare modern Islamic thinker who is the subject of hundreds of scholarly monographs, articles, and editorial commentaries touching on various aspects of his ideas, activism, and vision. A towering figure in the eyes of many Muslims in the Malay world, he has also attracted a fair share of criticism. Notable volumes by Junus Amir Hamzah, Nasir Tamara, M. Yunan Yusuf, Md. Sidin, Sidek Baba, Abdul Rahman Abdul Aziz, Shamsul Nizar, Abdul Rauf, and

---

[3] Leonard Andaya, *Leaves of the Same Tree* (Honolulu: University of Hawai'i Press, 2008), and Anthony Milner, *The Malays* (Oxford: Wiley-Blackwell, 2008).

[4] Michael Feener, "A Re-examination of the Place of al-Hallaj in Southeast Asian Islam," *Bijdragen tot de Taal-, Land- en Volkenkunde* 154, no. 4 (1998): 585, and Jeffrey Hadler, "Home, Fatherhood, Succession: Three Generations of Amrullahs in Twentieth-Century Indonesia," *Indonesia* 65 (1988): 125.

[5] Nurcholish Madjid, *Tradisi Islam: Peran dan Fungsinya dalam Pembangunan di Indonesia* (Jakarta, Indonesia: Paramadina, 1997), 123–24.

[6] Sartono Kartodirdjo, *Indonesian Historiography* (Yogyakarta, Indonesia: Kanisius, 2001), 25–26. The list of works on Hamka in Malay and Indonesian languages deserves a bibliography of its own and would take up too much space to be listed in full here. Among the universities that use Hamka's books as course texts are International Islamic University of Malaysia, Institut Wasatiyyah Malaysia, and Universitas Muhammadiyah Prof. Dr. Hamka.

[7] See "Profil Perpustakaan Hamka," Perpustakaan Prof. Dr. Hamka, accessed June 5, 2017, https://hamkalibrarymugu.wordpress.com/about.

[8] Fauziah Muslimah, "Berkujung Museum Rumah Kelahiran Buya Hamka Di Tepian Danau Meninjau," accessed June 10, 2017, http://www.gomuslim.co.id/read/destinasi/2016/11/27/2344/berkunjung-ke-museum-rumah-kelahiran-buya-hamka-di-tepian-danau-maninjau.html.

M. Alfan provide us with a wide range of approaches that scholars have used to engage with, and provide critiques of, Hamka's ideas.[9]

Hamka has been censured as a scholar without any formal training or real expertise in any fields of Islamic knowledge. Although he wrote on a range of Islamic topics, his critics maintained that he was never recognized by the *ulama* (scholars) in the Malay world as a specialist in one of these topics. His stories were said to be direct adaptations of Arabic and European fictional classics in which he had merely tailored the characters and contexts to reflect the places that he was most familiar with.[10] Hamka's lack of attention to facts and accuracy, his poor referencing style, and the absence of proper acknowledgments of the sources that shaped his ideas and conclusions have also made him the target of many scholars. Both his admirers and his detractors viewed him as a man in a hurry—a polymath who did not take the trouble to polish his writings, who moved hastily from one subject to another, publishing them quickly, perhaps too quickly, so much so that many of his writings lack coherence and logical rigor. The end result is that most of his books are filled with errors.[11] Despite this broad and diverse range of responses to his work from local and contemporary scholars, Western-language scholarship has captured only isolated aspects of his reformist thought.[12] There is only one book-length study by an American historian, James R. Rush, that looks primarily at Hamka's Islamic background and

---

[9] Junus Amir Hamzah, *Hamka sebagai Pengarang Roman* (Djakarta: Megabookstore, 1964); Nasir Tamara, Buntara Sanusi, and Vincent Djauhari, eds., *Hamka Di Mata Hati Umat* (Jakarta: Pustaka Panjimas, 1984); M. Yunan Yusuf, *Corak Pemikiran Kalam Tafsir Al-Azhar* (Jakarta: Panjimas, 1990); Md. Sidin Ahmad Ishak, ed., *Pemikiran dan Perjuangan Hamka* (Kuala Lumpur: Angkatan Belia Islam Malaysia, 2001); Abdul Rahman Abdul Aziz, *Pemikiran Etika Hamka* (Kuala Lumpur: Utusan Publications, 2002); Shamsul Nizar, *Membincangkan Dinamika Intelektual dan Pemikiran Hamka tentang Pendidikan: Seabad Buya Hamka* (Jakarta: Kenchana, 2008); Sidek Baba, ed., *Pemikiran Hamka* (Kuala Lumpur: Dewan Bahasa dan Pustaka, 2008); Abdul Rauf, *Tafsir Al-Azhar: Dimensi Tasawwuf* (Selangor, Malaysia: Piagam Intan, 2013); M. Alfan Alfian, *Hamka dan Bahagia: Reaktualisasi Tasauf Di Zaman Kita* (Bekasi, Indonesia: Penjuru Ilmu Sejati, 2014). Recent journalistic commentaries on Hamka are found in Rahmat Nur Hakim, "Lewat Islam, Hamka dan Pramoedya Ananta Toer pun Berdamai," June 29, 2016, accessed June 6, 2017, http://nasional.kompas.com/read/2016/06/29/05050041/Lewat.Islam.Hamka.dan.Pramoedya.Ananta.Toer.pun.Berdamai and Dr. Mohd Asri Zainul Abidin, "Pesan Hamka: Panggil saya Muslim," June 8, 2014, accessed June 6, 2017, https://m.malaysiakini.com/columns/265033.

[10] Adries Teeuw, *Modern Indonesian Literature* ('s-Gravenhage, Neth.: Martinus Nijhoff, 1967), 71.

[11] James R. Rush, *Hamka's Great Story: A Master Writer's Vision of Islam for Indonesia* (Madison: University of Wisconsin Press, 2016), 15.

[12] The majority of Western-language scholarship on Hamka analyzes his fictional and biographical works. Among prominent ones that touch primarily on Hamka are Deliar Noer, "Yamin and Hamka: Two Routes to an Indonesian Identity," in *Perceptions of the Past in Southeast Asia*, ed. Anthony Reid and David Marr (Singapore: Heinemann, 1979), 249–262; Karel Steenbrink, "Hamka (1908–1981) and the Integration of the Islamic *Ummah* of Indonesia," *Studia Islamika* 1, no. 3 (1994): 119–47; Hadler, "Home, Fatherhood, Succession," 122–54; Conrad William Watson, *Of Self and Nation: Autobiography and the Representation of Modern Indonesia* (Honolulu: University of Hawai'i Press, 2000), 106–29; Wan Sabri Wan Yusof, "Religious Harmony and Inter-faith Dialogue in the Writings of Hamka," *Intellectual Discourse* 13, no. 2 (2005): 113–34, and Rosnani Hashim, "Hamka: Intellectual and Social Transformation of the Malay World," in *Reclaiming the Conversation: Islamic Intellectual Tradition in the Malay Archipelago*, ed. Rosnani Hashim (Selangor: The Other Press, 2010), 87–205. One of the critics of Hamka was Andries Teeuw, who wrote that "Hamka cannot be considered a great author by any standards." See Andries Teeuw, *Modern Indonesian Literature* (Dordrecht, Neth.: Foris Publications, 1986), 2.

his acumen as a master writer and storyteller and reveals how he contributed to the making of Islam in Indonesia through his oeuvre.[13]

This book seeks to expand the scope of existing studies on Hamka by bringing to light his conceptualization and theorization of social problems in Muslim societies as well as the solutions he offered for dealing with these challenges. While Rush portrayed Hamka as an Indonesian scholar who was absorbed with issues affecting his home country, this book situates him as a shaper of Islam in the Malay world in general, a writer whose works have significantly influenced the study of Islamic reformism outside the region. As his son Rusydi succinctly put it, Hamka was a man of letters from and for Muslims in the Malay world. He was a child of the Minangkabau society in Sumatra, but his writings and speeches were directed toward a wide audience with the aim of bringing about religious reform on a regional scale.[14] Deliar Noer drives home this point by stating that "Hamka was a Muslim first and an Indonesian second. Indeed, for many Indonesian Muslims in the second and third decades of this [twentieth] century, attachment to the Muslim community [*ummat Muhammad*] was felt more intensely than to Indonesia as a nation."[15]

Hamka himself ensured that his name traveled far beyond Indonesia's borders. Many of his books were published in both Malaysia and Singapore and were read, sold, and debated in Brunei and South Thailand. From the 1950s onward, he accepted many speaking tours in neighboring countries and wrote books strictly for Malaysian and Singaporean audiences. One such book was titled *Kenangan kenangan-ku di-Malaya* (My Memories in Malaya). In it Hamka expressed his hopes for an independent Malaysia and shared his encounters with, as well as critiques of, Malayan Muslim thinkers and politicians. He openly admitted that in the 1930s, he had written primarily in the Malay dialect that was commonly used in Malaya. Because of this, his books were more warmly received there than in Java.[16] Another Singapore-published pamphlet was a polemic against the *mufti* (expounder of Islamic laws) of Johor, Syed Alwi bin Tahir al-Haddad. Hamka believed that al-Haddad was spreading falsehoods about the reformist movement in Malaya.[17]

Hamka's conscious efforts to gain recognition overseas paid off, in both monetary and symbolic terms. He gained much income from royalties of various editions of his books and was often paid handsomely during speaking tours across the Malay world. In 1974, Hamka received an honorary doctorate from the National University of Malaysia.[18] The popular Malaysian magazine *Al-Islam* covered the event, detailing Hamka's scholarly career. The magazine's editor underscored the significance of the honorary degree by querying, "When will Indonesian universities confer the same award on its own son [Hamka]? Why are countries such as Egypt and Malaysia foremost in conferring such recognition on him? They are more familiar with Hamka than Indonesians themselves."[19]

---

[13] Rush, *Hamka's Great Story*.

[14] Rusydi Hamka, *Hamka: Pujangga Islam Kebanggaan Rumpun Melayu* (Selangor: Pustaka Dini, 2002).

[15] Noer, "Yamin and Hamka," 253.

[16] Hamka, *Kenangan kenangan-ku di-Malaya* (Singapore: Setia Darma, 1957), 6.

[17] Hamka, *Teguran Suci dan Jujur Terhadap Mufti Johor* (1958; repr., Selangor: Pustaka Dini, 2009).

[18] Universiti Kebangsaan Malaysia, *Majlis Konvokesyen Kedua* (Bangi, Malaysia: UKM, 1975), 3.

[19] Editorial, "Sambutan rakyat Indonesia terhadap Dr Hamka," *Al-Islam* 9 (1974): 12.

It follows then that Hamka ought to be positioned as an *ummah* (global Muslim community)-oriented Muslim scholar with strong ties throughout the Malay world rather than as an Indonesian thinker per se. This is not to say that Indonesia was of secondary importance to Hamka. Hamka saw Indonesia as a strategic launchpad from which to reach out to Muslims in the Malay world. A comprehensive survey of his long list of publications shows that there is a fair balance between the works he wrote that were largely Indonesian in nature and those that addressed issues affecting the ummat and the Malay world. Hamka's most influential book, the thirty-volume *Tafsir Al-Azhar* (The Al-Azhar Exegesis), is not centered on Indonesian themes; instead, it is much wider in its reach and focus.

Hamka's reformist thought, showcased in works such as *Tafsir Al-Azhar*, thus escaped the attention of most Western-language scholars. As Mun'im Sirry sharply observed, "Like other reformers, Hamka was concerned primarily with how to reform people's religious life."[20] Still, Hamka's venture to reform Muslim minds and his attempts at transcending the ideological limitations of his time remain understudied and insufficiently understood. I employ the term "cosmopolitan reform" to describe Hamka's reconstruction of Islam in the Malay world and his adoption of ideas and influences from intellectuals and scholars globally. First, it refers to Hamka's work, distilling and harmonizing what was best from the many streams of Islamic thought—traditionalist, rationalist, modernist, reformist, Salafi, and Sufi—to provide fresh reinterpretations of Islam. More than an erudite writer, Hamka was a master synthesizer. He melded different Muslim intellectual traditions, placing radically different thought systems in tension and in a dialogue with one another. He held the firm belief that Muslims should not confine themselves to a single school of thought, proclivity, or ideology, for such parochial tendencies had caused unnecessary divisions while stifling the formulation of innovative and cutting-edge ideas.

This was clearly exhibited in his exegesis of the Qu'ran, which is reflective of his broad-minded attitude toward different streams of Islamic knowledge.[21] What Hamka called for was a cosmopolitan approach to the rich legacy of Islamic knowledge and sciences, urging Muslims to find inspiration from the differing outlooks of a broad cross-section of Muslim thinkers. Hamka held that only with a wide exposure to and perceptive adoption of all bodies of knowledge within Islam, whether from the various schools of jurisprudence, theological doctrines, approaches to Qur'anic exegesis, or strands of philosophy and mysticism, could Muslim minds be broadened and divisions within the Muslim community be blurred toward unity in thought and action.[22]

Hamka's vision of cosmopolitan reform also entailed a judicious selection and creative appropriation of relevant aspects of European and other non-Muslim epistemologies and ideas to afford in-depth diagnoses and to propose viable antidotes for the many problems confronting Muslims. Citing the Prophetic tradition that states "Wisdom is the lost property of the believer, so wherever he finds it then he has the right to it," Hamka encouraged Muslims to be informed in many disciplines. Muslims ought to be well versed in all branches of human knowledge in order for them to keep

---

[20] Mun'im Sirry, *Scriptural Polemics: The Qur'an and Other Religions* (New York: Oxford University Press, 2014), 87.

[21] See Wan Sabri Wan Yusof, "Hamka's 'Tafsir al-Azhar': Qur'anic Exegesis as a Mirror of Social Change" (PhD diss., Temple University, 1997).

[22] Hamka, *Renungan Tasauf* (Jakarta: Pustaka Panjimas, 2002), 62–64.

up with the demands of modern life. This spirit of openness toward wisdom from all civilizations and nations, regardless of faiths or creed, is not new to Islam. Hamka explained that the greatness of Muslims of the past hinged upon such an inclusive attitude. The decline of Muslims during the dawn of modernity, he argued, was born out of their unwillingness to learn from competing civilizations, which led in turn to intellectual stagnation throughout the Islamic world:

> It would be unrewarding for the modern generation of Muslims to accept all of the opinions of Al-Ghazali in an age where there is a wide selection of philosophi-cal ideas. We must consider the currents of philosophical thought since ancient Greece, till the advent of Islamic philosophy, to the time of the scholastic philoso-phers, up until the coming of modern Western philosophical thought. . . . We should be aware that all of these thinkers were not without weaknesses, because they were human beings and the absolute truth lies only in God's revelation. But our encounters with a flawed idea should not hinder us from reflecting upon it.[23]

Finally, I use the term "cosmopolitan reform" to underscore Hamka's attempt to over-come extremist, communalist, bigoted, and gendered tendencies that defined many of the societies in the Malay world. Hamka believed that modern Muslims should be just toward everyone in society and should consider men and women to be of equal value in the task of improving Muslim civilization. Muslims should observe respect-ful dialogue and empathy toward humankind while recognizing their own limita-tions. Extremism and bigotry breed exclusionary attitudes and the inability to accept change. Communalism creates gulfs and widens the gaps between Muslims and non-Muslims. Gendered paradigms as well as jaundiced practices have resulted in the mar-ginalization of both men and women in Muslim societies. To engage in cosmopolitan reform, in Hamka's formulation, is to internalize the ideal of moderation and a sense of common humanity and to be open to change while also respecting people of dif-ferent sexes, ethnicities, worldviews, classes, nations, and cultures. Hamka explained cogently that Islam "is for the world, not for the Arabs as such. Inviting the world [to Islam] requires us to be open-minded, to be embracing, to view the whole world as part of a universal brotherhood. If our hearts are filled with hatred, fraternity among all of humankind cannot be sowed in this world."[24]

In sum, Hamka's cosmopolitan reform was aimed at encouraging Muslims in the Malay world to think and act in a more inclusive, fairer, and more pluralistic man-ner without having to compromise the basic precepts and universal aims of Islam. Defined in this way, cosmopolitan reform is not unique to Hamka. Muslim intellectu-als and thinkers in other parts of the world have exhibited such an approach to reform, even when their concerns were different from Hamka's.[25] The idea of cosmopolitan reform therefore provides a useful heuristic tool for understanding the thought pro-cesses and breakthrough ideas of other twentieth-century Muslim reformers. Some

---

[23] Hamka, *Membahas Kemusykilan Agama* (Selangor: Pustaka Dini, 2009), 28.

[24] Hamka, *Prinsip dan Kebijaksaan Da'wah Islam* (Kuala Lumpur: Pustaka Melayu Baru, 1981), 47.

[25] For an excellent survey of modern Islamic reformers and reformist thought, see Shireen T. Hunter, ed., *Reformist Voices of Islam: Mediating Islam and Modernity* (London: M.E. Sharpe, 2009), and Ibrahim M. Abu-Rabi, ed., *The Blackwell Companion to Contemporary Islamic Thought* (Malden, MA: Blackwell, 2006).

examples of Muslim reformers whom Hamka referenced in his works were Muhammad Iqbal (1877–1938), Rashid Rida (1865–1935), Mahmud Shaltut (1893–1963), Ali Shariati (1933–77), Malek Bennabi (1905–73), and Muhammad Natsir (1908–93), among others. These thinkers' ideas of reform—or more specifically, cosmopolitan reform—inspired Hamka to formulate his own take on the reconstruction of Islam in the Malay world. As one cosmopolitan reformer among many in the Islamic world of the twentieth century, Hamka was thus both a man of his time and a man ahead of his time.

Studying a thinker as prolific as Hamka has methodological challenges. I have chosen to draw upon the history of ideas, as developed by Quentin Skinner and Dominic LaCapra. Skinner emphasized the "need to situate the texts we study within such intellectual contexts and frameworks of discourse as enable us to recognise what their authors were *doing* in writing them. To speak more fashionably, I emphasise the performativity of texts and the need to treat them intertextually."[26] In what follows, I will bring to the fore the various contexts and currents of thought that shaped Hamka's own thinking. I will show how he engaged with the prevailing ideas of his day and age and how he utilized various Islamic and non-Islamic traditions and philosophies to reconstruct Islamic thought. The following pages will also highlight Hamka's use of various discursive techniques to gain the attention of his readers and to destabilize his intellectual opponents' perceptions of Islam.[27]

Dominic LaCapra, in turn, highlights the different ways by which a historian of ideas can read the work of extremely prolific scholars. The first is by showing "continuity among texts ('linear development')"; second, by exposing "discontinuity among texts (change or even 'epistemological break' between stages or periods)"; and third, by bringing to the fore "dialectical synthesis (the later stage raises the earlier one to a higher level of insight)."[28] LaCapra problematizes these three ways of reading texts and sees them as seductive traps that writers can fall into while trying to make sense of genres of written work, yet I find that Hamka's works do exhibit a "dialectical synthesis" of past ideas with new ones. He was remarkably consistent about his views regarding the reformation of Islamic thought and society, progressively adjusting his scholarly positions as he encountered new knowledge. Hamka's corpus ought to be read dialogically and cumulatively "like a single text writ large."[29]

I have structured this book to consider Hamka's exposition of six central issues through the prism of cosmopolitan reform. Chapter 1 explores Hamka's argument for the harmonization of reason and rationality and the need to move beyond *taqlid* (blind obedience) and fatalistic thinking on the road to reforming Malay-Muslim thought. Hamka introduced the concept of "guided reason," a type of reasoning guided by the sacred sources of Islam, by good character, and by changing contexts, as well as by new forms of knowledge for Muslims to adapt effectively to a modernizing world.

---

[26] Quentin Skinner, *Visions of Politics*, vol. 1 (Cambridge: Cambridge University Press, 2002), vii (my emphasis).

[27] Henk Maier, for example, describes Hamka's writing style as "of a breathtaking grace, mellifluous and silvery, perfectly suitable for recitation." See *We Are Playing Relatives: A Survey of Malay Writing* (Leiden, Neth.: KITLV Press, 2004), 335.

[28] Dominic LaCapra, *Rethinking Intellectual History: Texts, Contexts, Language* (Ithaca: Cornell University Press, 1983), 55.

[29] Ibid.

Linked to the concept of guided reason is the notion of moderation. Chapter 2 examines Hamka's clarification of what moderation entails and what its antithesis is. He explained that the ruptures of modernity and the failure of Muslims to utilize their God-given intellectual gifts had brought about various forms of extremism that had bedeviled Muslims globally. However, he stressed that Muslims must also be cognizant that the media and some scholars had used extremism as a trope to obscure and paint a dark picture of Islam. To resolve extremist tendencies and correct negative images of Islam, Hamka enjoined his readers to appreciate and live up to the notion of *keseder-hanaan di dalam segala perkara* (moderation in all things), a concept he drew from Plato (424–348 BC) but redefined through the lens of Prophet Muhammad's teachings.

To Hamka, "if only human beings are moderate [in all things], their lives would not be ridden by anxieties" that lead to injustice toward themselves and society.[30] Chapter 3 develops this theme by focusing on Hamka's thoughts about the importance of social justice in the Malay world. He urged Muslims to reclaim the Islamic conception of social justice and incorporate what was best of capitalist, socialist, and communist conceptions of social justice. The Islamic conception is guided by the practical concepts of *khalifatullah fil'ard* (vicegerents of God on earth), *amanah* (sacred trust), *shura* (mutual consultation), and *maslahah* (general welfare). It has been and can still be fully realized if elites, activists, intellectuals, and ordinary Muslims alike study how Muslims in the past lived as ethical human beings. Chapter 4 expands on the issue of social justice between different groups in the Malay world by focusing on Hamka's project of "recasting gendered paradigms." This involves reinterpreting, reconceptualizing, and reconfiguring various dominant understandings about the roles, functions, and responsibilities of women in Islam as reflected not only in the Qur'an and the *adat* (traditional customs) but also in modern discourses about feminism. Hamka questioned the inflexibility of classical and literalist Islam, the limitations of the modernist paradigm, and the approaches of proponents of an emerging group of secular thinkers toward gender issues.

How can Muslims become ethical human beings? Hamka's answer is that this can occur through the agency of Sufism. Nonetheless, he believed Sufism in the Malay world was corrupted and weakened by superstition and wayward beliefs. In chapter 5, I highlight Hamka's efforts to restore Sufism through his clarification of its origins and his delineation of the teachings of pure Sufism as well as the intellectual and spiritual contributions of Sufi scholars to Islam. He enjoined Sufis in the Malay world to modernize themselves, admonishing them and their *murshids* (spiritual guides) to inject the positive aspects of spirituality into the lives of ordinary Muslims. The last chapter explicates the "reformist histories" that Hamka wrote as an extension of his concern with Sufism. These historical works were driven by his conviction that history could be utilized as a tool to reform the minds of ordinary Muslims. Hamka utilized a historicist mode of explanation that was centered upon the "belief that the truth, meaning, and value of anything, i.e., the basis of any evaluation, is to be found in its history; and, more narrowly, the antipositivistic and antinaturalistic view that historical knowledge is a basic, or the only, requirement for understanding and evaluating man's present political, social, and intellectual position or problems."[31]

---

[30] Hamka, *Falsafah Hidup* (Kuala Lumpur: Pustaka Antara, 1977), 216.

[31] Dwight E. Lee and Robert N. Beck, "The Meaning of 'Historicism,'" *American Historical Review* 59, no. 3 (1954): 577.

I critically examine a few threads of Hamka's reformist histories. First, these histories link the Arab world of Islam with other centers of the faith in Africa, Asia, and Europe into one seamless and synergistic whole, as part of Hamka's hope to create awareness among Muslims in the Malay world that they belonged to a millennium-old civilization and that they had interacted easily with non-Muslims throughout the history of Islam. The second thread of Hamka's reformist histories underscores the agency of grassroots reformers in determining the course of Muslim history. Many lessons can be learned from their attempts to overcome the obstacles that were stacked up against them. The third distinctive strand of Hamka's reformist histories is his effort to motivate contemporary Muslims in the Malay world to make positive transformations by showing how courageous Muslims upheld social justice in the past.

A brief biography of Hamka is in order here to help us appreciate the genesis of his project of cosmopolitan reform and the various circumstances that shaped his thoughts. There are three factors that structured Hamka's approach to Islamic reform. The first resulted from his personal life struggles; the second was related to the impact of the societal conditions of his time; and the third had to do with shifts in the thinking about Islam and Muslim societies—coming in the form of reformist and modernist pulses—at both the local and global levels. These circumstances drove him to carve out his own unique interpretations of Islamic reform in the Malay world.

Hamka was born into the matrilineal world of Minangkabau, Sumatra, on 17 February 1908. A scion of an illustrious line of Muslim religious scholars, Hamka was first taught by his father, Abdul Karim Amrullah (1879–1945), a strict disciplinarian who demanded full compliance from his first son. His daily lessons included learning the rudiments of the Arabic language and memorization of the Qur'an. At the age of eight he was sent to a village *dinniyyah* (religious) school. He studied there for a few years and was then enrolled in the *thawalib* (senior students) school, where he learned and memorized classical Islamic texts. Boredom and daily frustrations with the dismal state of this traditional Islamic school caused him to drop out soon afterward.[32] From then on, Hamka was practically self-taught, building his reputation as an autodidact who spent his time reading books at private libraries owned by his father's students, including Zanuddin Labay el-Yunusi. Disenchanted with his home region of Minangkabau and always wanting to escape the influence of his overbearing father, Hamka traveled to Java in 1924 to observe at close range the rapid growth of Muslim social movements such as Sarekat Islam and Muhammadiyah. Three years later he was already on a ship to Mecca to further his studies and carve out an independent life, only to return to Minangkabau just six months later to establish himself as a popular writer of novels and religious books. Hamka had initially planned to stay in Mecca and dreamed of following in his father's footsteps and becoming a religious scholar. He was, however, advised by an Indonesian consul in Mecca, Agus Salim (1884–1954), to shelve the idea. Agus remarked in the local Minangkabau dialect, "You should go back home. There are more important tasks in the field of activism, studies, and other

---

[32] Deliar Noer, *The Modernist Muslim Movement in Indonesia, 1900–1942* (Kuala Lumpur, 1973), 44–45.

struggles that you will encounter in Indonesia. This country is a place of worship. It is not a place to study. You are better off developing yourself in your own country."[33]

Similar to his contemporary, the South Asian scholar-activist Abul A'la Maududi (1903–79), from whom he drew much inspiration,[34] Hamka continued to be a self-taught throughout his life, harnessing his superb memory and writing skills to write on any religious topic that piqued his interest. He was part of what Michael Laffan has vividly described as the "alternative religious-print network" in Southeast Asia that "was bound to a religious centre, Cairo, where politics had firmly entered the realm of the popular Muslim imagination."[35] Hamka's house was filled with books written by reformist and modernist thinkers from Egypt, Lebanon, Saudi Arabia and India. Although he was fluent only in the Malay-Indonesian and Arabic languages, Hamka's wide collections of books included translated works of European authors, especially books concerned with philosophy, theology, and gender issues.[36]

In Hamka's family many different visions of Islam were represented. This diversity of thought inspired him to try to bridge the contending paradigms of Islam. His great-grandfather and grandfather were both proponents of Sufi practices and subscribed to the Naqshbandiyyah Sufi order, which had a strong following on the island Sumatra as well as in other parts of the Malay world. By comparison, Hamka's father, Abdul Karim Amrullah, was an ardent opponent of Sufistic tendencies and one of the leading proponents of Islamic modernism in modern Indonesia. Together with Mohammad Djamil Djambek, Sheikh Abdullah Ahmad, and Sheikh Thaib Umar, all of whom were studying and teaching in Mecca for over a decade under the tutelage of Sheikh Ahmad Khatib (1860–1916), Abdul Karim Amrullah formed a formidable anti-Sufi faction that invited strong reactions from Sumatra's traditionalist Muslim leaders.[37]

Very early in his life Hamka realized that, if left to fester, the differences between Sufis and anti-Sufis could tear the Muslim community in the Malay world apart, leaving it susceptible to other powers and influences that would threaten the faith of Muslims.[38] Such intellectual skirmishes in his own family, the ebb and flow of Sufism in the region, and Hamka's encounters with many syncretic mystical movements that began to take hold in the hearts of Muslims in the Malay world drove him to reinterpret and write about Sufism from a modernist and reformist point of view. His book *Tasauf Modern* (in some versions titled *Tasauf Moderen*, published in 1939 and still in print today) established Hamka as "one of the most important figures in the popularisation of Sufism amongst Indonesia's modernizing elites," according to Julia Howell.[39]

---

[33] Hamka, *Kenang-kenangan Hidup* (Jakarta: Gapura, 1951; Shah Alam, Malaysia: Pustaka Dini, 2009), 101.

[34] Seyyed Vali Reza Nasr, *Maududi and the Making of Islamic Revivalism* (Oxford: Oxford University Press, 1996), 19.

[35] Michael Francis Laffan, *Islamic Nationhood and Colonial Indonesia: The Umma below the Winds* (New York: Routledge, 2003), 10.

[36] Hamka, *Kenang-kenangan Hidup*, 175–83.

[37] Zaim Rais, *Against Islamic Modernism: The Minangkabau Traditionalists' Responses to the Modernist Movement* (Jakarta: Logos Wacana Ilmu, 2001), 32.

[38] Hamka, *Said Djamaluddin Al-Afghany: Pelopor Kebangkitan Muslimin* (Djakarta: Penerbit Bulan Bintang, 1970), 174.

[39] Julia D. Howell, "Indonesia's Salafist Sufis," *Modern Asian Studies* 44, no. 5 (2010): 1031. See also Martin van Bruinessen, "The Origins and Development of Sufi Orders (*Tarekat*) in Southeast Asia," *Studia Islamika* 1, no. 1 (1994): 13.

Despite their ideological differences, Hamka's progenitors nevertheless shared a common practice that troubled Hamka throughout his life: they were polygamists and frequently divorced. Hamka was born into a polygamous family and grew up as a neglected child in a divorced household. Although his father had a reputation as a scholar and reformer whose condemnations of local customs and folk Islam had led traditional Muslims to label him *sesat* (wayward),[40] he subscribed to the local culture of marrying nearly a dozen wives. He maintained four at one time, in keeping with Islamic laws, and divorced them when domestic conflicts arose. Religious elites in Minangkabau in the early twentieth century regarded this as an accepted practice. Hamka's paternal grandfather had eight wives, who bore him forty-six children.[41] The 1930 national census conducted by the Dutch colonial authorities confirms the prevalence of polygamy. According to this census, 8.7 percent of the marriages in Minangkabau were polygamous. This was more than four times the percentage in Java and Madura, where 1.9 percent of marriages were reportedly polygamous.[42]

Widespread polygamy went hand in hand with high rates of divorce in the Malay world. In his study of marriage dissolution in the twentieth century, Gavin Jones found that divorce among Malays usually occurred within the first five years of marriage. Many interlocking factors can explain the high rates of divorce in Indonesia and Malaysia, including early marriage, the economic independence of women, spousal incompatibility, social safety nets made available to divorcees by their kith and kin, the ease of remarriage, and the problems that arose from polygamy.[43] Discussing the frequency of divorce in Aceh in the 1930s, Edwin Loeb wrote in a rather hyperbolic way that it was normal for an Acehnese woman to marry ten to fifteen times.[44] Broken marriages, along with the imposition of colonial and feudal rule, brought about stark injustices in local societies. Predictably, Hamka's writings were colored with issues of justice and injustice, as evinced most strikingly in his book *Keadilan Sosial dalam Islam* (Social Justice in Islam). He was probably one of the few male Muslim scholars in the history of the Malay world to write extensively on the subject of Muslim women. While other Malay-Muslim thinkers, such as Syed Shaikh Al-Hadi (1867–1934) and Agus Salim (1884–1954), wrote about the conditions and circumstances of Muslim women in the region,[45] none of the writers prior to Hamka wrote so much about the subject or made it their

---

[40] *Sesat* in that context meant those ideas and practices that did not conform to the prevalent understandings of Islam that were shaped by a mixture of Shafi'i law, Asharite theology, and local manifestations of Islamic piety. See Roy F. Allen, "Social Theory, Ethnography and the Understanding of Practical Islam in South-East Asia," in *Islam in South-East Asia*, ed. M.B. Hooker (Leiden, Neth.: Brill, 1983), 50–91.

[41] Azra Aryumardi, *Historiografi Islam Kontemporer: Wacana, Aktualitas dan Actor Sejarah* (Jakarta: Gramedia Pustaka Utama, 2002), 262.

[42] Saskia Wieringa, "Matrilinearity and Women's Interests: The Minangkabau of Western Sumatra," in *Subversive Women: Women's Movements in Africa, Asia, Latin America and the Caribbean*, ed. Saskia Wieringa (London: Zed Books, 1995), 252.

[43] Gavin Jones, *Marriage and Divorce in Islamic South-east Asia* (Kuala Lumpur: Oxford University Press, 1994), 218–234.

[44] Edwin M. Loeb, *Sumatra: Its History and People* (Vienna: Institut fur Volkerkunde der Universitat Wien, 1935), 238–39.

[45] See Ibrahim Abu Bakar, *Islamic Modernism in Malaya: The Life and Thought of Sayid Syakh Al-Hadi, 1867–1934* (Kuala Lumpur: University of Malay Press, 1994), and Solichin Salam, *Hadji Agus Salim: Hidup dan Perdjuangannja* (Djakarta: Djajamurni, 1961).

lifelong intellectual pursuit. Hamka's book titled *Kedudukan Wanita Di Dalam Islam* (The Position of Women in Islam), which was first published in 1929 and is now regarded as a classic, served to counter masculinist ideas about gender, culture, freedom, and modernity from within the Islamic tradition.[46]

By the time he was twenty, Hamka was already a strong proponent of what would become the largest modernist Muslim organization in Indonesia, the Muhammadiyah. His father, siblings, and other relatives also played important roles in the spread of Muhammadiyah branches across West Sumatra, "an Amrullah family affair," as Jeffrey Hadler describes it.[47] At the same time, Hamka was earning his living as a writer of essays published in the popular Islamic weekly *Pedoman Masyarakat* (Society's Compass). He later collected these weekly essays and published them in a few acclaimed self-help Islamic books. *Lembaga Budi* (Foundation of Character), *Falsafah Hidup* (Philosophy of Life), and *Lembaga Hidup* (Foundation of Life) were best sellers throughout Indonesia in the 1930s and 1940s.

It was also during this period that Hamka established himself as an admired novelist, or in the Indonesian language, a *pengarang roman*.[48] *Si Sabariyah*, *Dibawah Lindungan Ka'abah* (Under the Protection of Ka'bah), *Kerana Fitnah* (Because of Defamation, later republished as *Terusir*, Cast Aside), *Tenggelamnya Kapal van der Wijck* (The Sinking of van der Wijck), and *Merantau Ke Deli* (Sojourning to Deli) were realist fictions of the travails of Muslims in a modernizing era, written in the years before the outbreak of the Second World War.[49] He became more involved in political activism at this time. With the encouragement of his brother-in-law, Sutan Mansur, he joined Partai Sarekat Islam Indonesia (PSII), which was agitating for the independence of Indonesia. Predictably, this brought him to the attention of Dutch colonial officials.[50]

The Japanese Occupation (1942–45) was a major turning point in Hamka's life. He openly collaborated with the Japanese, advising them on the management of Muslim affairs. This work bought him and his family a comfortable life in the city of Medan, but the gains of collaborating turned out to be short-lived. He was marginalized by many Muslim leaders, who accused him of selling out his religion to reap quick benefits from the Japanese occupiers. Fearing reprisal at the end of the war, and cast aside by his close associates in Muhammadiyah, Hamka returned to West Sumatra in 1945. The outbreak of the Indonesian revolution, which lasted from 1945 to 1949, was a golden opportunity to redeem himself in the hearts and minds of the Muslim public. He was an energetic propagandist and mobilizer for the revolution, escaping near-death situations on a few occasions while finding the time to publish several books that touched on revolutionary themes.[51] During these four years and thereafter, Hamka defined himself as one of the foremost public Muslim intellectuals based in Jakarta, the capital city of the new Republic of Indonesia.

---

[46] Hamka, *Kedudukan Wanita dalam Islam* (Selangor: Pustaka Dini, 2009).

[47] Jeffrey Hadler, *Muslims and Matriarchs: Cultural Resilience in Indonesia through Jihad and Colonialism* (Ithaca: Cornell University Press, 2008), 164.

[48] Yunus Amir Hamzah, *Hamka sebagai Pengarang Roman* (Jakarta: Puspasari Indah, 1993).

[49] Hamka, *Dibawah Lindungan Ka'bah* (Djakarta: Balai Pustaka, 1936); Hamka, *Kerana Fitnah* (Djakarta: Balai Pustaka, 1938), and *Merantau ke Deli* (Djakarta: Djajamurni, 1962).

[50] Alfian, *Muhammadiyah: The Political Behavior of a Muslim Modernist Organization under Dutch Colonialism* (Yogyakarta, Indonesia: Gadjah Mada University Press, 1989), 280–81.

[51] Hamka, *Kenang-Kenangan Hidup*, 364.

Figure 1 Hamka writing in the 1950s. Courtesy of Pusat Studi Uhamka.

As a result of his established reputation as an author, a religious scholar, and an activist during the Indonesian revolution, Hamka was appointed as a high-ranking official by the Ministry of Religious Affairs under the Sukarno administration from 1951 until 1960. This position enabled him to travel globally, including a four-month visit to the United States, which he documented in a two-volume travelogue. He was certainly impressed by some of what he saw in the United States, even though he was dismissive of the moral laxity among men and women and troubled by the treatment of African Americans. The aspects of the United States that especially enthralled him were respect for democracy, the staggering number of institutions of higher education, and scientific and technological innovations such as nuclear energy. Hamka thought that these were indicative of an advanced state of cultural and intellectual development. He felt that Muslims in Indonesia, and the Malay world in general, had a lot of work to do to catch up. They could do so if they adopted a proud and confident attitude.[52]

In the decades that followed Hamka rolled out dozens of books on a variety of subjects, including general history and politics (the nine hundred-page *Sejarah Umat Islam*, *History of the Muslim Peoples*, was written during this era), the history of Sufism, a biography of his father, and his own autobiography. But the bulk of his works from the 1950s onward dealt with matters of faith and reason, among which was *Filsafat Ketuhanan* (Philosophy of Divinity). He published several other volumes that addressed religious questions posed by the Muslim public. Hamka began to cut back on the writing of fictional works in order to devote more time to writing an exegesis of the entire Qur'an, an ambitious project that had long been delayed because of his hectic schedule. In between periods of writing, he met community leaders, religious scholars, social activists, and politicians daily at his home. He responded to countless interviews by newspapers and periodicals, spoke to radio and television channels, and served as the grand imam of the newly established Masjid Agung Kebayoran Baru in South Jakarta. In 1960, the name of the mosque was changed to Masjid Agung Al-Azhar. The man behind the name change was none other than the prominent Egyptian scholar Sheikh Mahmud Shaltut (1893–1963), who convinced the Al-Azhar University to confer on Hamka an honorary doctorate in 1958.[53]

Hamka was soon elected to the Constitutional Assembly, or the Konstituante, as a representative of the Parti Islam Masyumi, and he served there from 1955 to 1959. In his work to bring Muslims closer to the Islamic faith, Hamka entered into an ideological battle against communists in Indonesia, who were increasingly belligerent in their attacks on Muslim movements and on Islam as a faith. At the same time, he made a deep impression on the minds of Muslims in the Malay world through public lectures and sponsored visits all around the region. Hamka was asked to mediate scuffles between Muslim modernists and traditionalists in Singapore and Malaya. In Brunei, he was an oft-invited speaker and was known to the locals as a celebrity preacher.[54]

Hamka and President Sukarno were close friends during the nascent days of the Indonesian revolution, but the relationship between them soured as both men developed diametrically opposite views of communism. Hamka maintained that communism and Islam could never be reconciled, while Sukarno promoted the fusion of nationalism, religion, and communism in what he termed *Nasakom* (*Nasionalisme, Agama dan Komunisme*). Things came to a head when Hamka began to openly criticize

---

[52] Hamka, *Empat Bulan di Amerika, Djilid*, vol. 2 (Djakarta: Tintamas, 1954), 66.

[53] The speech that Hamka delivered during the conferment of his honorary doctorate was published as follows: Hamka, *Pengaruh Muhammad Abduh di Indonesia; Pidato Diutjapkan Sewaktu Akan Menerima Gelar Doctor Honoris Causa Dari Universitas al-Azhar di Mesir Pada Tgl. 21 Djanuari 1958* (Jakarta: Tintamas, 1961).

[54] Hamka, *Kenangan kenangan-ku di-Malaya*; Hamka, *Teguran Suci & Jujur Terhadap Mufti Johor* and Iik Arifin Mansurnoor, "Islam in Brunei Darussalam: An Analysis of Their Interaction," in *Islam in the Era of Globalization*, ed. Johan Meuleman (London: Routledge, 2002), 65.

Sukarno's authoritarianism. Sukarno reacted by banning Hamka's mouthpiece, *Society's Compass*. Hamka was arrested in 1964 for his alleged involvement in antigovernment movements. The years in captivity turned out to be the much-needed time Hamka yearned for to complete his magnum opus—the thirty-volume *Tafsir Al-Azhar*.[55]

After two years in detention, Hamka was released by General Suharto, the leader of the military coup that toppled the Sukarno regime. The days Hamka spent behind bars were not as catastrophic as he had initially anticipated. His years as a prisoner became a badge of honor and a testimony to many Muslims that Hamka was among the many ulama in the history of Islam who had experienced the painful ordeal of incarceration by unjust regimes. But just as his life was stabilizing under the new government and he was becoming accustomed to his new role as the preeminent living Muslim scholar in the Malay world, his wife passed away in 1971. To get over his bereavement, Hamka had to continuously motivate himself to remain committed in the struggle to reform the minds of his fellow Muslims. His productivity in writing and publication was substantial in spite of these difficulties, and his contributions to Islam and Muslims were widely acknowledged.[56] As noted earlier, Hamka received a doctorate from the Universiti Kebangsaan Malaysia (UKM) in 1974. A year later, he was elected the first chairman of the Majelis Ulama Indonesia (MUI, the Indonesian Ulama Council), a position that he described as a balancing act between the rage of the people and pressure from the state.[57]

Hamka wanted the MUI to advise the government on matters pertaining to Muslim affairs and serve as a mouthpiece for the government on policies relating to Islam. The MUI would also facilitate intellectual discussions between the ulama and state bodies in addition to performing the task of becoming a conduit for the ulama to deliberate and issue *fatwas* (religious edicts) for the benefit of ordinary Muslims. Although sponsored by Suharto's New Order regime, dissenters against the state's brand of Islam within the MUI itself were not spared from the state's heavy hand. Hamka was the state's first victim.

Concerned about what he saw as the rising tide of Christianity in Indonesia and the unethical means that many missionaries used to convert Muslims, Hamka wrote passionately about the need to put the evangelicals in check. For Hamka, the last straw came when the government pressured the MUI to issue an edict allowing a joint celebration of Christmas and Eidul Fitri (signifying the end of the fasting month), since both festive days were in the same month. Hamka resisted the government's pressure and held that celebrating any non-Muslim religious events would endanger the faith of ordinary Muslims at a time when Christian missionary activity was at its zenith. He had, however, promoted good relations and cooperation with Christians in other spheres of life. A long and controversial debate ensued between him and the Ministry of Religion that culminated in his abrupt resignation in 1981.[58]

---

[55] Hamka, *Tafsir Al-Azhar*, vol. 1 (Singapore: Pustaka Nasional, 1983), 1.

[56] Irfan Hamka, *Ayah: Kisah Buya Hamka* (Jakarta: Republika, 2013), 213.

[57] Taufik Abdullah, "Hamka dalam Stuktur dan Dinamik Keulamaan," in Tamara, Sanusi, and Djauhari, *Hamka di Mata Hati Umat*, 419. See also Moch. Nur Ichwan, "*Ulama*, State and Politics: Majelis Ulama Indonesia after Suharto," *Islamic Law and Society* 12, no. 1 (2005): 48.

[58] Melissa Crouch, *Law and Religion in Indonesia: Conflict and the Courts in West Java* (London: Routledge, 2014), 88, and Nadirsyah Hosen, "Behind the Scenes: Fatwas of Majelis Ulama Indonesia (1975–1998)," *Islamic Studies* 15, no. 2 (2004): 147–79.

Already suffering from diabetes and other health problems, Hamka died of heart failure on 24 July that same year. He left a legacy of writings that inspired a new generation of Muslims to reconsider how Islam should be understood and how they could be guiding lights for their own societies and the world at large. As Hendrik Maier beautifully puts it,

> At his death in 1981, Hamka left an amazing number of books—histories, treatises, surveys, commentaries, exegeses, speeches, sermons, and lectures—all of them written in the service of Islam and God's glory and splendour. His eloquence, his writing skills, his enigmatic personality had made him a well-respected man, inside and outside Muslim circles. . . . An authoritative religious leader. A respected writer. A gifted speaker.[59]

It will be evident to the readers of this book that Hamka's commitment to Islamic reformism was a product of his personal experiences and social interactions, just as he was shaped by profound political transformations, economic vicissitudes, social revolutions, and acute ideological shifts in the Islamic world in the twentieth century. Indeed, few Muslim thinkers and intellectuals in the Malay world of Hamka's generation transcended dualistic categories such as "traditionalist vs. modernist," "literalist vs. progressive," "fundamentalist vs. liberal," and "Salafi vs. Sufi," which ground many studies of Islam and Muslims globally. This book maintains that Hamka demonstrated intellectual openness and inclusiveness toward a whole range of ideologies and philosophies to develop his own imaginary and vocabulary of Islamic reform. I call it cosmopolitan reform.

---

[59] Maier, *We Are Playing Relatives*, pp. 380–81.

CHAPTER ONE

OF REASON AND REVELATION

Muslims have debated vigorously over the place of reason and revelation in human affairs since the early days of Islam. The Mu'tazilites in the eighth century were the first to focus on reason as the key to understanding God's commandments and the wisdom of creation. While not denying the importance of revelation, they gave primacy to reason in the event of any contradiction between the two. Such a radical intellectual position generated strong responses and resistance from many mainstream Muslim scholars. Ahmad Ibn Hanbal (780–855), Abu Ja'far Ahmad al-Tahawi (853–933), and Abu al-Hasan al-Ashari (874–936) were among the influential ulama who wrote treatises that sought to harmonize reason and revelation in Islamic thought. In exchange for their rebuttal and exposé of the contradictions of Mu'tazilism, these scholars suffered persecution and even death until the decline of the Mu'tazilites in the tenth century.[1]

Another major shift in Islamic thought was noticeable from then on. The conservative ulama began to view the function of reason in religious discourses with suspicion. This move ushered in the widespread adoption of taqlid in many parts of the Arab-Muslim world, which subsequently stifled philosophical-scientific thought. Indeed, even if we accept Wael Hallaq's persuasive argument that the gates of *ijtihad* (independent reasoning) were not closed after the first five Islamic centuries, what is certain is that theological discussions on the place of reason and rationality were severely circumscribed in many parts of the Muslim world.[2]

Muslims in the Malay world were relative latecomers to the fold of Islam (from the eleventh–twelfth centuries onward), and they followed an intellectual path that was very different from the route taken by their Arab counterparts. Since the fourteenth century, Malay-Muslim scholars have written legal and philosophical treatises that have contributed to the intellectual dynamism of Islam in that region. However, the dawn of high colonialism in the eighteenth century stifled Islam in the Malay world, transforming it from an intellectually driven faith that shaped the statecraft and the social life of ordinary Muslims "to a private and personal religion [that] justified itself in secular terms [treaties, the colonial state]."[3]

This atrophy of Malay-Muslim thought reached a turning point in the late nineteenth and early twentieth centuries as new ideas about reason and rationality in Muslim societies appeared in response to the challenges posed by European colonialism and modernity. Jamaluddin Al-Afghani (1839–97), Muhammad Abduh (1849–1905),

---

[1] For a sophisticated exposition of Mu'tazilite thought, see Sophia Vaselou, *Moral Agents and Their Deserts: The Character of Mu'tazilite Ethics* (Princeton: Princeton University Press, 2008).

[2] Wael Hallaq, "Was the Gate of Ijtihad Closed?," *International Journal of Middle East Studies* 16, no. 1 (1984): 3–41.

[3] Azyumardi Azra, *The Origins of Islamic Reformism in Southeast Asia: Networks of Malay-Indonesian and Middle Eastern "Ulamā" in the Seventeenth and Eighteenth Centuries* (Honolulu: University of Hawai'i Press, 2004), 150.

and Rashid Rida, to name a few of the many Muslim reformists and revivalists, questioned prevailing Muslim views about reason while critiquing the dependence of scholars on preceding intellectual traditions. These ideas spread quickly across the Malay world during the age of the steamship and print.[4] Modernist movements led by activists such as Syed Shaikh Al-Hadi, Syeikh Tahir Jalaluddin (1869–1956), and Ahmad Hassan (1887–1958; also known as Hassan Bandung) promoted these ideas zealously, so much so that by the early twentieth century, the region became an arena of intellectual combat between traditionalists, who urged blind obedience to customs and authority, and reformists, who asserted the primacy of reason.[5]

This chapter examines Hamka's interventions in the debates concerning the marginalization of reason and revelation in Malay-Muslim thought. I shall develop the argument that Hamka engaged in the process of reclaiming "guided reason" (*akal yang berpedoman*) in Malay-Islamic thought.[6] Reclaiming guided reason involves a few closely interrelated themes that Hamka developed in many of his writings on Islam and Muslims. First, Hamka outlined the problem of intellectual stagnation that was ubiquitous in societies across the Malay world of his time. Religious groups that were skeptical of using reason to chart new understandings of Islam were responsible for this crisis. These groups displayed scholarly dependency and espoused an unquestioning attitude toward different forms of temporal authority as well as established views about their religion.

Second, Hamka strategically appropriated what Muhsin Mahdi has termed the "rational tradition in Islam" to argue for the restoration of reason to its rightful place within Malay-Islamic thought. By rational tradition, Muhsin Mahdi means two things:

> one that may be called extreme rationalism in which anything that is religious is denied as non-existent or is explained as being simply there to rule and corrupt society, and the other rationalism which more or less dedicates itself to trying to make sense—perhaps not rational in the narrow sense—of the non-rational phenomena of prophecy, revelation, the divine law and the problems that cannot easily be subjected to the laws of pure reason.[7]

Hamka belonged to the latter rational tradition. To convince his readers that reason and rationality were essential tools for understanding the sacred and the profane, he drew on the writings of a long line of Muslim thinkers beginning with medieval scholars such as Al-Ghazali (1058–1111), Ibn Rushd (Averroes; 1026–1198), and Ibn Taymiyya (1263–1328) and extending to modern-day reformists such as Muhammad Iqbal (1877–1938), Muhammad Abduh, and Muhammad Natsir.

---

[4] James L. Gelvin and Nile Green, "Introduction: Global Muslims in the Age of Steam and Printing," in *Global Muslims in the Age of Steam and Printing*, ed. James L. Gelvin and Nile Green (Berkeley: University of California Press, 2014), 1–21.

[5] Deliar Noer, *The Modernist Muslim Movement in Indonesia, 1900–1942* (Kuala Lumpur: Oxford University Press, 1978).

[6] Hamka used this concept in many of his writings in varied ways, one of which was in his popular textbook on Islamic studies, *Pelajaran Agama Islam* (Kelantan, Malaysia: Pustaka Aman Press, 1967), 21.

[7] Muhsin Mahdi, "The Rational Tradition in Islam," in *Intellectual Traditions in Islam*, ed. Farhad Daftary (London: I.B. Tauris, 2000), 52.

Third, while Hamka acknowledged and promoted reason and rationality, he was cautious in his approach toward speculative thought that went against the boundaries set by Islam. He was aware of an emerging group of Muslims who were swayed by secularist and Mu'tazilite arguments that reason was on par with revelation, if not superior to it. In the last section of this chapter, I will elaborate on the concept of guided reason, which describes Hamka's views of how Muslims should exercise reason and rationality. From his vantage point, reason had its limits, particularly in matters of faith and belief. It therefore must be guided by revelation through the sacred sources of Islam—Qur'an and *Hadith* (Prophetic sayings)—by good character, and by changing contexts, as well as by new understandings of how Islam should be practiced and lived. Peter Riddell aptly sums it up by stating that Hamka's approach to Islam was based on "rational argument, reference to scripture, relating his discussion to a modern context, defence of what he sees as orthodoxy, and attacking what he considers as non-orthodox teachings."[8]

Hamka used more than one word to describe reason. He used the word *akal* (also spelled *'aql* in Arabic) to refer to the faculty of reasoning and rationalizing; it also referred to the mind or the intellect. In addition, Hamka often used the word *fikiran* to mean thinking and rationalizing, and he sometimes coupled the two terms to form the compound word *akal fikiran*.[9]

THE STAGNANT MIND

Hamka was certainly not the first to bring the crisis of Muslim thought in the Malay world into sharp relief. Moenawar Chalil (1908–61), Ahmad Hassan, Syed Shaikh Al-Hadi, and Hamka's own father, Abdul Karim Amrullah, were among the local reformers who forcefully argued for a total reformation of the ways in which local scholars approached Islam. They rejected the backward practices that resulted from an uncritical approach to faith and beliefs. For example, Syed Syaikh Al-Hadi's controversial treatise *Kitab Agama Islam dan Akal* (The Treatise on Islam and Reason) demonstrated the wisdom behind obligatory rituals in Islam through sound reasoning. Al-Hadi argued that Muslims should perform these rituals with a clear understanding of the various sacred sources that support them. The best approach to Islamic rituals, he stressed, was to avoid blind obedience to religious authorities who taught Islam with incomplete proofs.[10]

Al-Hadi's approach to Islamic rituals fits squarely within the revivalist strand of thinking that was gaining much ground in the Muslim world of the late nineteenth and early twentieth centuries. Samira Haj notes, "Going back to the original authoritative sources, the Qur'an and the *Hadith*, revivalists claimed to want to free Islam from the dead weight of ineffectual and harmful accretions. They considered the conventional religious authority, which imbued taqlid, as unable either to recognize the serious problems raised by current practices or to provide proper guidance to the

---

[8] Peter Riddell, *Islam and the Malay-Indonesian World: Transmission and Responses* (Singapore: Horizon Books, 2001), 219.

[9] The word *fikiran* is the Malay adaptation of the Arabic word *fakkara*, which means to think and contemplate. The compound word *akal fikiran* is still common among Malays and was not Hamka's invention.

[10] Syed Shaikh Al-Hadi, *Kitab Ugama Islam dan Akal* (Penang, Malaysia: Jelutong Press, 1931).

community."[11] Hamka built on the reformist legacy of revealing the crisis of thought in Muslim minds. But rather than dealing with symptoms as exhibited in the practice of taqlid among Muslims in the Malay world, he directed his attention to the root of the problem: the stagnant mind (*akal yang beku*).[12]

By the stagnant mind, he meant a mind that was not able to think critically, logically, or rationally to address issues pertaining to life and faith. Muslims with stagnant minds came from all walks of life, from the scholarly class to the laity. They accepted everything that had been taught to them by their teachers and were unable to think creatively or to interrogate their inherited beliefs and traditions. This inability led to sloppiness and unoriginality in their writings, their speeches, and their conversations. "And when stagnancy [*pembekuan*] happens," Hamka asserted, "the understanding of religion becomes rigid and the light that shines from it becomes dim."[13]

Hamka added that Muslims with stagnant minds were dismissive of new ideas and manufactured falsehoods in order to defend their established beliefs. They were overly dependent on outdated texts and wary of any new interpretations that departed from traditional understandings. In line with Hamka's observations, Khaled Abou el Fadl highlights that there have been moments in Islamic history when the interpretation of texts became "intolerant, hateful, or oppressive."[14] In the Malay world of the twentieth century, the traditionalist Muslims were prejudiced toward any alternative elucidations of religious texts. They accused Muslim reformers in the Malay world of succumbing to disbelief (*kafir*) and heresy (*zindiq*), calling them Mu'tazilites who were destroying the pillars of Islam. The traditionalists attacked the reformers bitterly to the point of making spurious claims about their beliefs. Hamka saw these attacks as a sinister strategy used by those with stagnant minds because they did not know how to defend themselves with far-reaching knowledge, deep learning, and critical reasoning.[15]

Hamka went even further, arguing that Muslims with stagnant minds could be categorized into two main groups: those characterized by simple ignorance (*jahil basit*) and those characterized by compound ignorance (*jahil murakab*). Jahil basit persons were ignorant because they lacked experience and socialization. Since they were usually open to knowledge, learning, and reasoning, this group could be enlightened through teaching and reminding. Jahil murakab persons were ignorant yet too proud to learn anything from anyone. The second group was, to Hamka, more dangerous because their lack of intelligence coupled with pride would lead them astray along with others who followed their path.[16] The ignorance of the jahil murakab "may be likened to walls that would always hinder men from reaching their objectives, especially in thinking about pertinent issues."[17]

But what are the factors that contributed to the stagnation of the Muslim intellect? Hamka took aim first at the ulama. His arguments were drawn mostly from his

---

[11] Samira Haj, *Reconfiguring Islamic Tradition: Reform, Rationality and Modernity* (Stanford: Stanford University Press, 2009), 9.

[12] Hamka, *Teguran Suci dan Jujur Terhadap Mufti Johor*, 82.

[13] Hamka, *Filsafat Ketuhanan* (Melaka, Malaysia: Toko Buku Abbas Bandong, 1967), 12.

[14] Khaled Abou el Fadl, *The Place of Tolerance in Islam* (Boston: Beacon Press, 2002), 23.

[15] Hamka, *Teguran Suci dan Jujur Terhadap Mufti Johor*, 64 and 72.

[16] Hamka, *Falsafah Hidup* (Kuala Lumpur: Pustaka Antara, 1977), 68.

[17] Ibid., 255.

Figure 2 Young Hamka in his twenties wearing formal Arab dress. Courtesy of Pusat Studi Uhamka.

father, Abdul Karim Amrullah, who castigated the ulama for their regressive mentality.[18] Hamka equated the ulama during his time with the priests in Christian churches during the dark ages of Europe. They were dictatorial and claimed the sole right to interpret religious texts. They also blocked access to many areas of knowledge by issuing edicts that outlawed the teaching of philosophical sciences. Their justification for such moves was that the masses would be led astray if they were overly reflexive about their own faith. "But the hazards that came with the closing of the doors [to learning philosophical sciences] was intellectual lethargy and being lost in an age of change."[19] Most ulama in the Malay world, Hamka exclaimed, were "archaic" (*ketinggalan zaman*),[20] a stinging criticism that resonated with the views of the Egyptian thinker Rashid Rida (1865–1935) on the sterility of the ulama in the modern age.[21]

Hamka explained that the ulama did more than block access to knowledge. They also corrupted knowledge by not going beyond what had been taught by the preceding scholars. Instead of coming up with new ideas, he emphasized, they would merely "interpret the interpretations from the interpretations of [past] interpretations." And because of this, the *kyai* (religious teachers) memorized the words of others instead of thinking for themselves.[22] Hamka's critique of the kyai was obviously directed toward the followers of the Nahdlatul Ulama (Awakening of the Ulama), which was an organization of traditionalist Muslim scholars founded in 1926. Until the 1970s, the leaders of Nahdlatul Ulama upheld the practice of taqlid. They discouraged the use of reason in discussing matters pertaining to Islam and relied heavily on the interpretations of the religion by medieval scholars. Consequently, reformist and modernist writers in Indonesia tended to scathingly describe the Nahdlatul Ulama as "a herd of buffalo in tow."[23]

Hamka intensified his critique by averring that had the ulama used their reason, their interpretations of the Qur'an would have been more nuanced. In his exegesis, he gave the example of how the ulama misinterpreted verse 7 of the chapter "Al-Anbiya'" (The Prophets) in the Qur'an. The verse reads, "And We did not send before you any but men to whom We sent revelation, so ask the people of knowledge if you do not know." The ulama used this verse as a rationale for the closing of the Muslim mind. They contended that only the ulama of the past were qualified to comment on religious issues. Hamka argued otherwise. The key words in that verse, to him, were not "people of knowledge" (*ahladz zikri*), which the ulama advocated that all Muslims should follow blindly. The more important word was "ask" (*fas'alu*). Muslims must ask those with knowledge until they too became knowledgeable.[24]

That was not all. Hamka bared the tyrannical practices of the ulama, who demonized and persecuted anyone who questioned their authority. "Anyone who tried to

---

[18] Mun'im Sirry, *Scriptural Polemics: The Qur'an and Other Religions* (New York: Oxford University Press, 2014), 16.

[19] Hamka, *Pandangan Hidup Muslim* (Djakarta: Bulan Bintang, 1984), 75.

[20] Ibid.

[21] Muhammad Qasim Zaman, *Modern Islamic Thought in a Radical Age* (New York: Cambridge University Press, 2012), 6. Hamka drew a great deal of inspiration from the writings of Rashid Rida, especially the *Tafsir Al-Manar*, for his own thirty-volume *Tafsir Al-Azhar*.

[22] Hamka, *Pelajaran Agama Islam*, 466.

[23] Rumadi, *Islamic Post-Traditionalism in Indonesia* (Singapore: ISEAS Press, 2015), 61.

[24] Hamka, *Tafsir Al-Azhar*, 17:4545.

reason out a problem with his own intellect will be accused of being a Mu'tazilite. And sometimes, these accusations are used to achieve immediate political ends."[25] Contrary to their arrogant claims of being able to understand Islam more than ordinary Muslims did, the ulama manifested stupidity (*kebodohan*) and were responsible for stagnating Muslim minds. Indeed, for Hamka, this stupidity was the root of all intellectual diseases. The cure was to be found in the freedom to pursue knowledge and to exercise one's reason.[26]

Colonialism was another factor that contributed to intellectual stagnation. Hamka highlighted the colonial powers' strategy of co-opting the ulama. These ulama were then used to issue religious edicts that served to further weaken Muslim minds. The ulama who refused to work for the colonial rulers were equally guilty of allowing colonial ideologies to reign supreme by being passive instead of actively opposing colonialism. Many ulama "retreated as far as possible, became stagnant, and died before death came."[27] Hamka added that the defeatist posturing of these ulama had tainted their teachings. By teaching the Muslim masses to practice asceticism and shun worldly success, they gave the colonial powers a mandate to usurp authority and dominate Muslim lands.[28] The masses were left uneducated by both the ulama and the colonialists. They became weak because of the lack of knowledge and learning and practiced their religion based on taqlid and fanaticism. This situation lasted for three hundred years.[29]

Because Hamka was unclear as to who these passive ulama were, he mentioned no names. His argument flies in the face of research on the ulama in the Malay world during the colonial period. Although a substantial number of ulama supported and collaborated with colonial regimes, there were many others who were equally active in opposing the foreign powers. Procolonial and anticolonial ulama were found among both the reformists and the traditionalists. Some were involved in militant, nationalist, socialist, and radical movements up until the end of colonialism.[30] It is reasonable to surmise that Hamka was merely inventing scenarios through his writings in order to rouse the ulama to do more than they had done in the past.

Above all, Hamka blamed mystical Sufism for causing intellectual stagnation. Sufi masters taught their followers that they could be invulnerable to dangerous weapons and capable of performing amazing feats. They propounded Ibn Arabi's (1165–1240) ideas about giving unquestioning obedience and reverence to the descendants of Prophet Muhammad.[31] "Hence, the ordinary Malays who were already ignorant became even more ignorant . . . and a segment among them who respected or loved the family

---

[25] Hamka, *Pelajaran Agama*, 465–66.

[26] Hamka, *Renungan Tasauf*, 94 and 98.

[27] Hamka, *Pengaruh Muhammad Abduh di Indonesia*, 7–8.

[28] Ibid.

[29] Hamka, *Renungan Tasauf*, 65.

[30] Michael Laffan, *The Makings of Indonesian Islam: Orientalism and the Narrations of a Sufi Past* (Princeton: Princeton University Press, 2011); Shukri Ahmad, *Pengaruh Pemikiran Ulama di Semenanjung Malaysia Abad Ke-20* (Kedah, Malaysia: UUM Press, 2011).

[31] For a fuller discussion of Ibn Arabi's ideas about the family of the Prophet, see Claude Addas, "Ibn 'Arabi's Concept of *Ahl al-bayt*," *Journal of the Muhyiddin Ibn 'Arabi Society* 50 (2011), accessed 10 July 2017, http://www.ibnarabisociety.org/articles/muhammadan-house.html.

of the Prophet in line with the teachings of Ibn Arabi saw it as a pillar of religion and whosoever opposes this was regarded as apostatizing the pillar of religion."[32]

The betrayal of the ulama, the colonial states, and the Sufis culminated in the pervasive acceptance of taqlid and wrongful beliefs about *taqdir* (fate) among Malay-Muslims. Hamka devoted much of his writing to the problem of taqlid. He defined it as "following blindly other people's words, or whatever has been learned from teachers, to the point that one's mind becomes stagnant and inactive. And when stagnancy happens, the understanding of religion loses its glowing light. That has come to be known as taqlid! Taqlid is the enemy of the freedom to reason!"[33] Hamka believed that taqlid was pervasive during his time to a point that anyone who opposed it would be regarded as opposing Islam. Muslims who were educated in secular tertiary institutions avoided the ulama because of the imposition of taqlid. They were keen on knowing about Islam intellectually but were not allowed to engage in such discussions.[34]

Hamka's discussion of a few types of taqlid shows the influence of Ibn Qayyim Al-Jauziyah (1292–1350) on his thinking.[35] The first was taqlid toward leaders. Hamka called such taqlid "a dangerous ailment that has befallen the hearts of Muslims during the age of decline."[36] Muslim leaders, specifically Muslim kings in Malay world, called on the general populace to obey them according to God's decree. They described themselves as "the shadow of God in this world" (*zillu'llahi fil 'alam*)—a term borrowed from the Ottoman Empire—for many centuries and up until as recently as the 1980s.[37] The taqlid toward leaders who saw themselves as God's shadow would not have been possible without the work of the ulama, who issued edicts that called for blind obedience to their authority.

Hamka deliberated on another form of taqlid: blind obedience toward adat. Muslims in the Malay world subscribed to the idea that the traditional Malay customs should not be changed even if they were no longer relevant or were threatening the welfare of the common people.[38] Most Malays hesitated to question their customs for fear of being accused of being antisocial and a liability to society.[39] To Hamka, this fear was unfounded. Taqlid toward customs was not part of the Prophetic tradition. Instead, Prophet Muhammad's mission was to free the hearts of men from "slavery, from having locked minds, from thinking bluntly, and blind obedience that will kill reasoning."[40]

---

[32] Hamka, *Teguran Suci dan Jujur Terhadap Mufti Johor*, 87.

[33] Hamka, *Filsafat Ketuhanan*, 12.

[34] Hamka, *Teguran Suci dan Jujur Terhadap Mufti Johor*, 65.

[35] He equated the relationship between Ibn Qayyim and Ibn Taymiyya with Plato and Socrates. Both Ibn Qayyim and Plato studied attentively and extended the work of their great teachers. Hamka indeed greatly admired Ibn Taymiyya, whom he described as the Greatest Scholar (*Alim Besar*). See Hamka, *Tasauf: Perkembangan dan Pemurniannya* (Jakarta: Pustaka Panjimas, 1983), 92, and Rush, *Hamka's Great Story*, 27. See also Ibn Qayyim's work on the topic of *taqlid: On Taqlīd: Ibn al Qayyim's Critique of Authority in Islamic Law*, trans. Abdul-Rahman Mustafa (Oxford: Oxford University Press, 2013).

[36] Hamka, *Pelajaran Agama Islam*, 95.

[37] Marie-Sybille de Venne, *Brunei: From the Age of Commerce to the 21st Century* (Singapore: NUS Press, 2015), 273.

[38] Hamka, *Pelajaran Agama Islam*, 95.

[39] Hamka, *Filsafat Ketuhanan*, 11.

[40] Hamka, *Dari Lembah Chita-Chita* (Kuala Lumpur: Pustaka Melayu Baru, 1968), 18.

As for taqdir, Hamka cited a late nineteenth-century Muslim thinker, Abdul Rahman Al-Kawakibi (1855–1902), who observed how misconceptions regarding fate and destiny had led to the downfall of Muslims. Muslims lost the motivation to succeed and developed a fatalistic attitude because they felt that everything had been decided and determined by God.[41] These distorted ideas were the result of the mental stagnation that had become predominant since the coming of colonialism. Alternatively, Hamka was of the view that a proper appreciation of taqdir had brought success to the vast majority of Muslims in the Malay world in the precolonial period. Taqdir was a "source of encouragement" (*pendorong semangat*) toward manifold achievements. Muslims had become confident and capable of achieving great things when they conceptualized fate as something that was not only determined by God but also shaped by human beings through their own efforts. Hamka made clear that Muslims should "be in pursuit of fate, rather than avoiding it; carving [their] fate, and not running away from it."[42]

It follows, then, that Hamka was opposed to the Jabariyah school of thought in Islam. The Jabarites believed that people had no control over their own actions, that God had determined their fate, and that they should accept whatever happened to them, be it good or bad. This ideology had affected Muslims in the Malay world so much that they failed to use their reason to construct their own destiny.[43] In arguing against the Jabariyah ideology, Hamka seemed to come closer to the Mu'tazilite ideas about human freedom and responsibility. In actual fact, he drew what was relevant from the Mu'tazilites to develop his arguments on the issue of faith. Unlike Harun Nasution, who emerged as a defender of neo-Mu'tazilite thought in Indonesia of the 1980s, Hamka deployed Mu'tazilite concepts that remained within the boundaries of the mainstream rational tradition in Islam. The straddling between Mu'tazilite and mainstream Islamic discourses on taqdir made Hamka's writings persuasive to many different Muslim audiences, whether traditional, modernist, or reformist. As Fauzan Saleh points out, "Hamka's discussion of free will and predestination has shed a new light on the development of Islamic theological discourse in Indonesia. To a certain degree, it has been a key work in the attempt to transform Indonesian Muslim religious attitudes."[44] In the next section, I will discuss Hamka's ideas about the importance of reason in Islam as a way to undo the negative effects of taqlid and ideas of taqdir.

ON THE IMPORTANCE OF REASON IN ISLAM

In expounding on the importance of reason in Islam, Hamka drew a great deal of inspiration from the ideas of his mentor, Muhammad Natsir, as well as from Ibn

---

[41] Hamka, *Pelajaran Agama Islam*, 409. For Al-Kawakibi's stinging attacks against the fatalist outlook of Muslims in the nineteenth century, see Charles Kurzman, ed., *Modernist Islam: A Sourcebook, 1840–1940* (New York: Oxford University Press, 2002), 153.

[42] Ibid., 410.

[43] Hamka, *Pelajaran Agama Islam*, 414.

[44] Fauzan Saleh, *Modern Trends in Islamic Theological Discourse in Twentieth Century Indonesia* (Leiden: Brill, 2001), 172; Fauzan Saleh, "The Belief in *Al-Qada'* and *Al-Qadr* in Indonesian Islamic Discourse," *Studia Islamika* 8, no. 3 (2001): 144.

Rushd and Ibn Taymiyya.[45] Arguing in the same vein as these thinkers, Hamka stated that the intellect is God's greatest gift to man. It is the crucial instrument that differentiates man from the rest of God's creations. Animals do not have the same capacity as humans to reason out what they do. They function mainly through instinct. Should human beings fail to use their reason, they can become worse than animals.[46]

One of the implications of such a standpoint is the rejection of the theory of evolution. "The theorist of evolution," Hamka wrote, "argues that man originated from apes. Even if we accept this argument, why is it that mankind has progressed millions of steps forward, while the apes still remain where they are? Who is the one that gives man the powers of reasoning? This is what religion wants us to believe: Reason is the gift of God to His chosen creation, which is mankind. But the faculty of reasoning is not a given, it needs to be nurtured."[47]

Hamka likened the faculty of reason that was given to humans and no other beings to the electrical generator. The generator has to be filled with water to facilitate the movement of all its energy-producing parts. Research, experimentation, and experience were the elements that sharpen human reason while making it creative and dynamic.[48] Through the faculty of reason, humans could also develop the capacity to judge. In other words, reason was a delineator that aided Muslims to sift truth from falsehood and to carry out their religious duties conscientiously. Hamka elaborated on this point at length: "The power of intellect facilitates the individual in understanding reality, [the intellect] keeps him away from ignorance, and disciplines him in respect of rules and regulations, to obey commands and to abstain from that which is prohibited. He is able to discern goodness and practice it, [he is able to] recognize what is bad and thus refrain from doing it."[49] A person with strong powers of reasoning could foresee the expected consequences of his or her actions.[50]

Appealing to religious texts to bolster his argument, Hamka stated that the Qur'an encourages people to use their reason as a tool to reflect on God's majestic creations. It is through sound reasoning that humans can unveil the mysteries that lie within nature.[51] Further, the Qur'an permits its adherents to reflect and think deeply about practically anything.[52] Hamka illustrated this point by citing the chapter "Ar-Rum" (The Romans), verse 22, in the Qur'an. The verse reads, "And among His signs is the creation of the heavens and the earth and the diversity of your languages and your colors. Indeed, in that are signs for the learned." Hamka argued that the verse is testimony to God's encouragement for humankind to study and research, that is, for people to use their intellect in the fullest sense. With reason, humans have

---

[45] M. Yunan Yusuf, *Corak Penafsiran Kalam: Tafsir al-Azhar* (Jakarta: Pustaka Panjimas, 1990), 90. Hamka was so impressed with Muhammad Natsir's works that he wrote a book titled *Falsafah Hidup*, which was derived from Natsir's classic work *Islam sebagai Ideologie* (Jakarta: Penjiaran Ilmu, 1950).

[46] Hamka, *Tafsir Al-Azhar*, 9:2717; Hamka, *Pemimpin dan Pimpinan* (Kuala Lumpur: Pustaka Melayu Baru, 1973), 2.

[47] Hamka, *Pelajaran Agama Islam*, 225.

[48] Hamka, *Renungan Tasauf*, 1.

[49] Hamka, *Falsafah Hidup*, 48.

[50] Hamka, *Pelajaran Agama Islam*, 225.

[51] Ibid., 56.

[52] Hamka, *Tafsir Al-Azhar*, 19:5074.

formulated many disciplines of knowledge, ranging from the hard sciences to philosophy, all of which enable them to uncover what Hamka called "The Grand Design" of God's creations.[53]

Through these detailed explanations of the nature and functions of reason, Hamka expressed his hope that Muslims in the Malay world would restore reason to its rightful place in their minds and daily lives. He felt that for too long Muslims had been stifled by taqlid and taqdir, as discussed above. They had also been too dependent on the selected ideas of Al-Ghazali, who deemphasized human agency. Among the grave mistakes committed by Muslim scholars in the Malay world was their sidestepping of Ibn Rushd, whose ideas were centered on causalities (*sebab akibat*) and philosophical-scientific thinking.[54] Hamka's negative assessment of Al-Ghazali is one-sided and misplaced or else excessively biased. Al-Ghazali did not deny causality. He was in full support of the scientific spirit insofar as such a spirit did not lead to the denial of the agency of God in human life.[55]

At any rate, Hamka opined that the influence of Ghazalian thought had ushered in a preoccupation with superstitions and myths among Muslims. They believed in ghosts and other beings that they felt could cause harm in their daily lives. Hence they placed more attention on the paranormal and epiphenomenal than on rational issues. Muslims in the Malay world, for example, believed that saints from anywhere in the world would pray in Mecca every Friday. Until the twentieth century, many Muslims remained convinced that the great Abdul Qadir Jailani (1077–1166) led prayers among the fish in the sea. While Muslims were steeped in their superstitious beliefs, the Europeans learned from Muslim scholars such as Ibn Rushd. This provided the pretext for Western colonization of Muslims in the Malay world.[56] Hamka's leap of inference between Western adoption of Ibn Rushd's ideas and colonization of the Malay world works well rhetorically but is historically tenuous. Ibn Rushd's philosophy, also referred to as Averroism, found its way to Europe in the thirteenth century, while formal colonization of the Malay world began only in the sixteenth century. In chapter 6, I will elaborate on Hamka's frequent use of "leapfrogging legacies," that is, the error of connecting events in different time periods without explaining the complex developments that took place in between.

More crucially, Hamka gives the analogy of two kinds of Muslims in the Malay world in his time. The first were those who lived without any sense of direction because they did not use their reason. They lived their lives without achieving anything for themselves, and they were forgotten on the very day they died. The second group included those who utilized their reason and intellect fully even though it resulted in their being ostracized by their own community. This group of Muslims was not in fear of death. They spent their lives studying nature and sharing their findings with others. "The first group," Hamka concluded, "added to the existing number of human beings. The second group created history. They research, verify and experience [things around them]. The fruits of their investigations and examinations defined their lives."[57]

---

[53] Ibid., 21:5506.

[54] Hamka, *Pelajaran Agama Islam*, 235.

[55] Lenn Evan Goodman, "Did Al-Ghazali Deny Causality?," *Studia Islamica* 47 (1978): 83–120.

[56] Hamka, *Pelajaran Agama Islam*, 244.

[57] Hamka, *Dari Lembah Chita-Chita*, 64–65.

And yet, Hamka was also aware that reason could be used in wrongful ways, as evinced by Muslims who graduated from Western institutions. They tended to doubt many aspects of their faith and values. A great number of them "confessed their skepticism about the existence of God, or they do not believe in God at all."[58] Because this group lacked a basic grounding in Islam and because they learned about Islam from thinkers who knew it not as a practice but as something to be critiqued and proven to be false, they were unable to accept Islam as their way of life. Islam thus became merely a part of their cultural identity. Religious beliefs, according to this group of Westernized Muslims, would appeal only to those who "have not developed sophistication in thought or intellect [*yang belum mempunyai kecerdasan fikiran atau intelek*]."[59]

Hamka singled out the communists as those who were deeply influenced by Western thought. His diatribe against them replicated the approach taken by many Muslim scholars and activists in the 1940s who were concerned about the multipronged communist strategy of inducing the Muslims in Indonesia to embrace their ideology after World War II.[60] The communists accused religious people of being feudalistic and claimed that they (the communists) were free from the shackles of religious beliefs and superstitions. They claimed that reason could be restored in the minds of Muslims only if they were able to free themselves from the grip of their age-old beliefs.[61] To make matters worse, very few among the religiously trained thinkers in the Malay world could engage with these Western-educated Muslims. In particular, Hamka censured Indonesian Muslims who were trained in Islamic studies in the medium of the Arabic language. He believed they were unable to explain the gist of the religion of Islam, specifically the articles of faith in the Indonesian language. This problem arose because they were not encouraged to write in the local language and sometimes were unable to do so.

Hamka was certainly hyperbolic in discussing the ineffectiveness of Islamic-educated scholars. Many of these scholars actually wrote about Islamic topics in the local languages and called for the rethinking of various aspects of Muslim thought.[62] The gap between the Western- and Islamic-educated Muslims was caused not by linguistic inefficiencies but by the inability of the Islamic-educated scholars to write cogently in a manner that could appeal to a larger audience. Hamka was probably among the few, if not the first, to write intelligibly and in an impactful way. He promulgated the notion of guided reason as a means to reach out to Western-educated Muslims.

GUIDED REASON (*AKAL YANG BERPEDOMAN*)

Before discussing Hamka's ideas of guided reason, it is important to address his lengthy elaborations on the limits of reason and the problems that could arise from unguided reason. Wan Sabri Wan Yusof, in his study of *Tafsir Al-Azhar*, found that

---

[58] Hamka, *Pelajaran Agama Islam*, vii–viii.

[59] Hamka, *Pelajaran Agama Islam*, 45.

[60] Katharine E. Mcgregor, "Confronting the Past in Contemporary Indonesia: The Anticommunist Killings of 1965–1966 and the Role of the Nahdatul Ulama," *Critical Asian Studies* 41, no. 2 (2009): 195–224.

[61] Hamka, *Pelajaran Agama Islam*, 45.

[62] R. Michael Feener, *Muslim Legal Thought in Modern Indonesia* (Cambridge: Cambridge University Press, 2007).

Hamka devoted much space in his writings to discussing the role of reason and rationality. Hamka did not, however, overemphasize reason. "Revelation [*wahy*]," according to Hamka, "is the one force responsible for guiding reason."[63] I argue further that in Hamka's view human beings could think, imagine, and explore all sorts of knowledge about the world with the faculty of reason. But reason alone could not comprehend God and the purpose of creation. Reason would not be able to uncover the supernatural (*ghaib*). Here, Hamka's position corresponded with the predominant Asharite school of thought in the Malay world that viewed human reason as manifestly limited when it came to understanding the divine.[64] The limits of human reason were evidenced in the unsolved mysteries of the universe even though thousands of libraries had been established all over the world. Hamka gave the example of research on the moon. We still know so little about it despite the rapid developments in human thought, science, and technology.[65]

Moreover, even though science had evolved into previously unimaginable terrains, humans could only manipulate nature and not create anything out of a vacuum. Hamka explained,

The more advanced our thinking and knowledge become, the more we are amazed by the strange and incredible laws or order that is found in nature. Our knowledge can only uncover the laws of nature. But we are unable to create something better than nature itself. We can only devise new arrangements, without departing radically from the original laws of nature. From whichever doors we may enter! Be it through logic or through higher mathematics. From geometry or chemistry, and from anywhere else.[66]

Reason is therefore limited because human beings are endowed with other faculties such as the soul (*rohani*) that enable them to perceive things the intellect cannot easily discern. The soul is able to enter into realms the intellect is unable to comprehend. One of the realms is dreams, which many scholars have tried to explain, but no concrete conclusions have been reached about why dreams occur and why some dreams can seem so real. In Hamka's estimation, the soul complements reason in that it provides humans with the ability to recognize certain truths that the intellect cannot fathom.[67]

Reason is not only limited; if left unguided, it can also lead people to a partial understanding of life and faith. Hamka discussed the problem of extremism that could taint reason. The most compelling case in point was that of the Mu'tazilites. They incorporated Greek philosophical thought into the heart of theological debates in Islam. Many Mu'tazilites became extreme and went so far as to declare that reason was superior to revelation and that the philosophers were equal in standing

---

[63] Wan Sabri, "Hamka's 'Tafsir al-Azhar,'" 201.

[64] Richard C. Martin and Mark R. Woodward, with Dwi S. Atmaja, *Defenders of Reason in Islam: Mu'tazilism from Medieval School to Modern Symbol* (Oxford: Oneworld, 2003), 32; Hamka, *Pelajaran Agama Islam*, v.

[65] Hamka, *Tafsir Al-Azhar*, 21:5580.

[66] Hamka, *Filsafat Ketuhanan*, 14–15.

[67] Hamka, *Dari Lembah Chita-Chita*, 17.

to the prophets.[68] The same problem of extremism was found among the atheists. They questioned the nature of God and the functions of revelation, concluding that whatever cannot be reasoned and proven through scientific means should not be believed.[69]

Hamka held that the chief reason why the Mu'tazilites and many thinkers and scientists in the twentieth century developed such extreme ideas was their pride and arrogance (*bangga dan sombong*).[70] These thinkers sought to limit God's eternal power and wisdom within the boundaries of the finite human mind. Some of them concluded that humans were no longer in need of God or of revelation because the expansive knowledge that they had accumulated was enough to resolve all human problems. With reason and knowledge, the world could be shaped to be like heaven (*syurga*). However, Hamka retorted, it was ironic that there were more suicides in his time and more large-scale conflicts than at any other period in history.[71]

Hamka also discussed the role of desires (*hawa nafsu*) that could lead to unguided reasoning. Left unchecked, desires could cloud human reasoning to such an extent that individuals might not be able to differentiate between what was beneficial and what could lead to harm. Desires could even cause human beings to lose their basic senses, which would then affect their reasoning processes. They would become people who "have eyes but cannot see, have ears but cannot hear and have minds as well as hearts but cannot think; all of which have been clouded by filth. That is the spiritual filth. This is because they follow their desires, instead of following reason."[72]

What, then, was guided reason? For Hamka it was, first, a form of reason guided by revelation taught to humankind by God's prophets. The prophets addressed humans' queries about the secrets of divine creation through the medium of sacred texts inspired through revelation. The prophets not only explained revelation; they enforced it by way of laws and manifested it in their lives for their followers to emulate. Hamka demolished the Mu'tazilite stand that the philosophers were similar to the prophets, or even superior to them. The prophets were chosen by God and endowed with spiritual and worldly skills. Their hearts were pure, and their minds were inspired to differentiate between good and evil. "This is why the prophets were never afflicted by the sickness that often befell the [Muslim] philosophers, who were able to promulgate new philosophies but were unable to patch their own pants without the help of others."[73] Again, one detects some embellishment on Hamka's part in regard to the frailties of the Muslim philosophers. The reality was actually radically different from Hamka's take on these philosophers, many of whom were scientists and inventors. Like the prophets, the Muslim philosophers were also embroiled in many trivialities of life, just as they were active in politics and power brokering.[74]

Still, for Hamka, Muhammad was the greatest prophet who provided guidance as to how humans should use their reason. The Qur'an was revealed to humankind

---

[68] Hamka, *Pelajaran Agama Islam*, iv.

[69] Hamka, *Tafsir Al-Azhar*, 21:369.

[70] Hamka, *Pandangan Hidup Muslim*, 13.

[71] Ibid., 16.

[72] Hamka, *Tafsir Al-Azhar*, 11:3401.

[73] Hamka, *Pelajaran Agama Islam*, 265.

[74] George Saliba, *Islamic Science and the Making of the European Renaissance* (Cambridge, MA: MIT Press, 2007).

through Muhammad as the final messenger of God. It calls on humans to recognize the divine and the unity of all creation. Through the light of revelation, people are guided to recognize that while they have the power to create, invent, and discover new things, such inspiration comes from the one True God.[75] The Qur'an also teaches people to think rationally about issues pertaining to politics, economics, social life, laws, education, and social psychology in ways that not only are specific to one community but apply to humankind in general. The Qur'an calls on its readers to reflect, rethink, research, and rediscover using the instrument of reason. This explains why Muslim intellectuals were once admired thinkers in the world. They used their ability to reason, guided by revelation, and were open-minded. Whenever they found that their reason contradicted revelation, they gave priority to revelation and sought ways to reconcile it with their ideas.[76] Hamka's belief that there could be no true reason without revelation, and his view that reason and revelation must always be in harmony, brought him close to the medieval Syrian scholar Ibn Taymiyya, whom he cited frequently. Ibn Taymiyya asserted, "[I]t is inconceivable that an unrevealed proof should oppose a revealed proof and be preferable to it."[77] Sophia Vaselou cements this point by stating that "Ibn Taymiyya signals that revelation does not merely appeal to our reason, but indeed *constitutes* reason, and is vested with the power to arbitrate what rationality—what *true* or *sound* rationality—consists in."[78]

Hamka endorsed this line of reasoning and expressed his viewpoints in a manner that was somewhat similar to Ibn Taymiyya's—methodical and often combative against groups that advocated the supremacy of reason over revelation.

Guided reason, in Hamka's mind, also meant a form of reasoning guided by fine character. Hamka used the expression *akhlaqul karimah* (refined character) to describe someone whose behavior and manners are set aright and who uses his reason to accomplish goodness. A person's character structures how she thinks about herself and the things surrounding her. Whether that person is a scholar, a student, or a layperson, a strong intellect may not necessarily ensure that she will direct her intellectual powers to good ends. Hamka gave the example of the many scholars in his day who knew much about atomic energy but used their discoveries toward destructive ends, unconcerned about the harmful effects of their work.[79] By contrast, if an intelligent person's reason is guided by fine character, then he will devise only those innovations that will benefit humankind as a whole. Hamka believed that one does not need to be a Muslim in order to have a fine character. Even non-Muslims may manifest fine character and let their character structure the ways in which they think. Muslims, however, are endowed with revelation that serves to shape their character to become good human beings and faithful servants of God. Through the combination of fine character and reason, a human being may "know what is good and what is bad, what is ugly and what is beautiful."[80]

---

[75] Hamka, *Revolusi Agama* (Djakarta: Pustaka Antara, 1949), 73.

[76] Hamka, *Pelajaran Agama Islam*, 285–86.

[77] Quoted in Binyamin Abrahamov, "Ibn Taymiyya on the Agreement of Reason with Revelation," *Muslim World* 82, nos. 3–4 (1992): 267.

[78] Sophia Vaselou, *Ibn Taymiyya's Theological Ethics* (New York: Oxford University Press, 2016), 236.

[79] Hamka, *Pandangan Hidup Muslim*, 20.

[80] Hamka, *Pelajaran Agama Islam*, 222.

In addition, Hamka saw guided reason as a form of reason that is directed by the exigencies of changing contexts and constant encounters with new knowledge. He believed that people with sound minds must be sensitive to all the changes in the world around them. A person with guided reason will not be mentally stagnant or allow his or her mind to be enslaved by old habits, customs, and traditions that have lost their relevance in an ever-changing world. This is why the Qur'an describes human beings as the vicegerents of God on earth. Guided by their reasoning ability and their sensitivity to their shifting surroundings, human beings can gain mastery over nature and society.[81]

To be sensitive to the changes around them, people have to embrace what Hamka called "the freedom to practice independent reasoning [*kebebasan ijtihad*]."[82] While some scholars of Islamic jurisprudence define *ijtihad* "as an activity, a struggle, a process to discover the law from the texts and to apply it to the set of facts awaiting decision,"[83] Hamka viewed ijtihad as more than just a tool for deriving laws. He regarded it as the ability to reason based on a comprehensive understanding of texts and contexts encountered by individual Muslims in their struggles to deal with the problems they faced in their lives. It was therefore a "personal ijtihad" meant to resolve the challenges of daily life. Hamka used himself as an example, pointing to a time when he had faced difficulties in finding *halal* (permissible) food during his visit to America in the late 1950s. He decided to dine at any restaurant that did not serve pork. This was, in Hamka's observation, a form of ijtihad, or a guided form of reasoning that was based on the demands of the context yet did not transgress the precepts of Islam.[84]

Hamka acknowledged, however, that there is another form of ijtihad that is practiced by scholars. It is based on an intensive study of the sacred sources of Islam, the latest findings in various areas of secular knowledge, and also new developments in society. Scholars practicing such ijtihad must be aware of the effects their pronouncements have on the rest of the Muslim community. Hamka claimed that the ulama of his era were opposed to the use of ijtihad. They argued that it ought to be restricted to those who had a deep knowledge of many branches of Islamic knowledge. Unfortunately, there were not many ulama in the twentieth-century Malay world with such qualifications. The new generation of Muslim thinkers hence was not obligated to subscribe to such a rationale. Hamka argued that they should deepen their knowledge of the Qur'an, Hadith, languages, Islamic jurisprudence, and all other sciences "so that they could practice ijtihad. . . . And if we practice ijtihad, that does not mean we can resolve all problems.'[85] Hamka cemented his point: 'No *mujtahid* [scholar who does ijtihad] can dictate that his ijtihad is absolute and binding."[86] But the process of ijtihad could move society closer to resolving issues in a more creative, adaptive, and dynamic way.

---

[81] Hamka, *Tafsir Al-Azhar*, 1:71.

[82] Hamka, *Falsafah Hidup*, 258–59.

[83] Imran Ahsan Nyazee, *Theories of Islamic Law: The Methodologies of Ijtihad* (Kuala Lumpur: The Other Press, 2002), 287.

[84] Hamka, *Empat Bulan di Amerika, Djilid 2*, 56–57.

[85] Hamka, *Teguran Suci dan Jujur Terhadap Mufti Johor*, 64.

[86] Hamka, *Tafsir Al-Azhar*, 8:2360.

Hamka argued that with guided reasoning, humans would eventually attain *hik-mah* (or *hikma*), which means wisdom, and come to the recognition that everything comes from God.[87] He borrowed from Muhammad Abduh, who described hikmah as the epitome of all knowledge and reasoning. Hikmah would also dissuade people from following their stray imaginations (*khayal*), which could lead them down the path of error. Hamka also interpreted hikmah as the ability to understand the meanings of the Qur'an. Someone with a degree from a university may not be able to attain hikmah since it cannot be gained from reading books or attending lectures given by renowned professors. Hikmah is given by God to those who use their reason to arrive at a comprehensive understanding of life and of sacred texts.[88] The intellect "is the repository of ideas and the source of hikmah, hence the ordinances of religion are formulated through the intellect. Religious ordinances are binding only on the person of sound mind. Thus, insane persons and children are not duty-bound by religious observances."[89] This comment on hikmah clearly shows the influence of Al-Ghazali on Hamka's thought, even though he was very critical of some aspects of Ghazalian thought and his impact on later generations of Muslims. Ebrahim Moosa, one of the foremost contemporary experts on Al-Ghazali, observed that "The refinement of the contemplative faculty results in wisdom [*hika*], says Ghazali, as promised in the Qur'an: 'He gives wisdom to whom he pleases; and the one to whom wisdom has been given, has received much good.' One endowed with a refined contemplative faculty can easily make a judgment between truth and falsehood in doctrinal matters."[90]

The Iranian thinker Abdolkarim Soroush has succinctly divided the concept of reason into two types. The first is reason as a destination. It is a conception of reason as the ultimate cradle and repository for all truths. The second type sees reason as a path, "as a critical, dynamic, yet forbearing force that meticulously *seeks* the truth by negotiating tortuous paths of trial and error."[91] Hamka saw reason as a path toward uncovering the truths of life and of divine creation but also as a path that was strewn with obstacles. Conservatives and colonizing forces had blocked the path and stifled the Muslim mind. Living up to his vocation as a cosmopolitan reformer, Hamka took it upon himself to write against the practice of taqlid and sought to salvage the use of reason in the minds of Muslims in the Malay world by making it clear that critical thinking and reflection were encouraged rather than forbidden in Islam.

Hamka was, however, acutely aware that liberating reason could lead to other perils. Among these were extremism and the uninhibited use of the intellect to the extent of doubting the divine and the moral codes defined by Islam. From Hamka's perspective, such perils could be overcome by guiding reason with the light of revelation, with fine character and sensitivity to changing contexts. Armed with guided reason, Muslims could reach a balance between exercising their freedom to think and adhering to

---

[87] Hamka, *Dari Lembah Chita-Chita*, 19.

[88] Hamka, *Tafsir Al-Azhar*, 3:655–58.

[89] Hamka, *Falsafah Hidup*, 47.

[90] Ebrahim Moosa, *Ghazali and the Poetics of Imagination* (Chapel Hill: University of North Carolina Press, 2005), 243.

[91] Abdolkarim Soroush, *Reason, Freedom, and Democracy in Islam* (Oxford: Oxford University Press, 2000), 89–90.

the demands of the divine. They would also be able to continuously reconstruct their ideas and practices of Islam and adapt effectively to a modernizing world.

In view of Hamka's extensive borrowing from other thinkers, one may ask, Was there any originality in Hamka's attempt to reclaim guided reason in Muslim thought? The answer to this question is contingent on how we define originality. If originality is defined as the first instance in which a given set of ideas is conceived, then Hamka was not an original thinker. To develop his points he drew on and synthesized the works of Muslim thinkers ranging from the medieval period right up to the modern period. But if originality is understood in the manner to which the Palestinian-American scholar Edward Said has it, as "not for first instances of a phenomenon, but rather to see duplication, parallelism, symmetry, parody, repetition—echoes of it,"[92] then Hamka's detailed expositions on guided reason and its place in Muslim life can be regarded as novel and innovative, and sometimes even radically distinct. Hamka not only duplicated and echoed the discourses of intellectuals who belonged to the millennium-old rational tradition of Islam. He developed their ideas further and explained these ideas in ways that appealed to his readers. It is no coincidence that, thanks largely to his extensive list of works touching on the theme of reason coupled with his expressive and provocative writing style, Hamka's popularity remains stronger among Muslims in the Malay world today than does that of any scholar of his generation. In reclaiming the concept of guided reason for Malay-Islamic thought, Hamka inspired Muslims in that part of the world to stretch their minds and exercise their imaginations at a time when irrationality and the tendency to blindly follow tradition had yet to lose their charm.

---

[92] Edward Said, *The World, the Text and the Critic* (Cambridge, MA: Harvard University Press, 1983), 135.

CHAPTER TWO

IN PRAISE OF MODERATION

Can Muslims be moderate? Although the answer to this question seems straight-forward enough, media portrayals and academic analyses have tended to obscure the reality that most Muslims uphold the ideal of moderation. Themes such as extremism and radicalism dominate the headlines of major newspapers and magazines across the globe, emphasizing the bouts of Muslim intolerance arising from their ardent commitment to Islam. The roots of Muslim rage in the twentieth century, as an influential Orientalist explored it an oft-cited essay, were to be found in the feelings of being left behind and engulfed by civilizations that were once inferior to Islam. Had Muslims fully embraced secularism in their lives, they would have become less prone to the allure of "Islamic fundamentalism."[1] The Palestinian scholar Edward Said summed up such long-standing stereotypical and negative images of Islam and Muslims well when he wrote that there has been

> a strange revival of canonical, though previously discredited, Orientalist ideas about Muslim, generally non-white, people—ideas which have achieved a star-tling prominence at a time when racial or religious misrepresentation of every other culture are no longer circulated with such impunity. Malicious generaliza-tions about Islam have become the last acceptable form of denigration of foreign culture in the West; what is said about the Muslim mind, or character, or religion, or culture as a whole cannot now be said in mainstream discussion about Afri-cans, Jews, other Orientals, or Asians.[2]

Having lived through the decolonizing and globalizing era as described by Said, Hamka observed that Muslims and moderation are two concepts that have become polar opposites as a result of a crisis of ignorance caused by Orientalism and the media. Global events such as the Algerian war for independence (1954), the Arab-Israeli war (1967), and the war in Afghanistan (1979–89), as well as the Islamic revolution in Iran (1979), coupled with Malay-Muslim support of such rebellions and revolutions against oppressive regimes in the Middle East, added to perception that the Malay world was but another hub for the spread of religious radicalism.[3] "In this regard," Hamka wrote in the same spirit as Said, "the second line of attack by the colonizers has succeded, after the first attempt to kill Islam has outright failed.

---

[1] Bernard Lewis, "The Roots of Muslim Rage," *Atlantic*, September 1990, 47–60.

[2] Edward W. Said, *Covering Islam: How Media Experts Determine How We See the World* (New York: Vintage, 1997), xi–xii.

[3] Fred R. Von der Mehden, *Two Worlds of Islam: Interaction between Southeast Asia and the Middle East* (Gainesville: University Press of Florida, 1993), 64–101, and Howard M. Federspiel, *Sultans, Shamans, and Saints: Islam and Muslims in Southeast Asia* (Honolulu: University of Hawai'i Press, 2007), 159–62.

Today, Islam is heckled and ridiculed not only by the Dutch. The Dutch have left, Islam is now looked down on by those who descended from Islam itself."[4] What was most worrying for Hamka was the growing acceptance among Muslims of the view that their religion promoted immoderation and extremism. Muslims, Hamka wrote emotively, felt ashamed of saying that they were committed to the fundamentals of their religion for fear of being labeled "fanatic."[5] Some Muslims, he observed, had even accused their own coreligionists of being extremists for observing the basic injunctions of Islam.[6]

Hamka saw the need to address such intellectual confusion by stating in clear terms what moderation and its antithesis entailed. This chapter pursues Hamka's concept of *kesederhanaan di dalam segala perkara* (moderation in all things) by examining first his elaborate definition of it and his expositions of the different forms of moderation as well as ways to achieve it. Hamka's idea of moderation in all things exhibits a creative blend of Greek and Islamic scholarly insights. This links up to the second section of this chapter, which delves into the opposite of moderation—extremism. Hamka provided a detailed explanation of why some Muslims departed from being moderate and the implications of this aberration. He held that the forms of extremism that had bedeviled Muslims in Southeast Asia and globally in the twentieth century were born out of the ruptures caused by modernity. The last part of this chapter will discuss Hamka's decentering of the dominant image that Muslims were prone to extremism. Extremism was, to Hamka, a malady that affected human beings in general and not Muslims per se. But specific groups had cast Muslims in the Malay world as fanatics as a means to serve their exploitative agendas.

MODERATION IN ALL THINGS

Since the mid-twentieth century, modern Muslim thinkers have written extensively on the topic of moderation in Islam in response to the challenges of sectarianism. Moderation was analyzed primarily through the lens of the Qur'an and other sacred sources of Islam. For example, Badawi Abdel Latif Awad, the president of the Al-Azhar University in Egypt from 1969 to 1974, asserted that moderation is an essential core of Islam. Muslims are commanded by God to be a moderate community, and this commandment is enshrined in the chapter "Al-Baqarah" (The Cow), verse 143, in the Qur'an, which reads, "We have made you [true Muslims] a moderate nation so that you could be an example for all people and the Prophet an example for you." "This moderation and reasonableness," Badawi concluded, "extends itself to all aspects of Islam—the ruling for fasting, the rite of washing, a husband's duty to his wife, provision for one's children, prohibited items of food. All these have definite rules, but all such rules can be modified if special circumstances warrant it—the basic principles are clemency, reasonableness, and moderation."[7] Badawi's view on moderation paralleled that of other influential scholars of the time—namely, Mahmud Shaltut and Abul Kalam Azad, both of whom Hamka admired and whose works he frequently cited.

---

[4] Hamka, *Pelajaran Agama Islam*, 432.

[5] Hamka, *Pandangan Hidup Muslim*, 170.

[6] Hamka, *Ghirah dan Tantangan Terhadap Islam* (Djakarta: Pustaka Panjimas, 1982), 15.

[7] Badawi Abdel Latif Awad, "The Moderation of Islam," *Islamic Quarterly* 7, nos. 3–4 (1963): 89.

Departing from these perspectives, which relied largely on Islamic sources, Hamka took as his starting point Greek philosophy. He attributed the idea of *kesederhanaan di dalam segala perkara* to Plato.[8] Plato and the ancient Greeks understood the idea of a balance between the spiritual (*rohani*) and the physical (*jasmani*) in human life. They believed that good human beings would naturally strive toward achieving moderation in everything that they did. This is congruent with Islam's message of the just balance in all aspects of human activities. In Hamka's estimation, many of the teachings of Plato and the ancient philosophers were so similar to Islamic ethical teachings that they had inspired medieval Muslim scholars such as Ibn Sina, Ibn Farabi, and Ibn Rushd to translate Greek texts and develop new sciences from their study of Greek philosophy. There was nothing wrong, he said, in drawing on Platonian insights following the lead of past scholars. But, ever cautious of being misunderstood, Hamka added a caveat: "Religion is not philosophical speculation! However, critical philosophy can help improve a man's faith in his religion."[9]

Hamka did not, however, clearly indicate the source of his ideas. Nor did he reference any of Plato's writings to support the idea of moderation in all things. A survey of Plato's works indicates that the concept of moderation was explained in his books *The Republic* and *Charmides*. Plato wrote about the virtue of *sophrosyne* (moderation)—along with courage, justice, and wisdom—in the path to achieving happiness. These virtues are the essential building blocks in the creation of an ideal society. For Plato, moderation is a form of self-discipline or "a mastery of pleasures and desires, and a person is described as being in some way or other master of himself."[10] Hamka read Plato through Arabic translations of the latter's works.[11] Unlike some Muslim reformists who opined that Greek philosophy was alien to Islamic thought, Hamka thought otherwise. He viewed Plato along with Socrates, Aristotle, and other Western philosophers as troves of wisdom, to be read, studied, and drawn on in any discussion of noteworthy virtues that Muslims should embody. Such an inclusive approach to Western philosophy was indicative of Hamka's cosmopolitan intellectual predisposition.[12]

For Hamka, Islam not only cemented the Platonian concept of moderation in all things but brought the concept into sharp focus and actualized it. At the core of Islam's teachings was moderation to be practiced daily by the community of believers.[13] Here, Hamka leaned closer to the mainstream Muslim scholars' ideas on moderation. He brought to the fore the concepts *wasat* and *i'tidal* found in the Qur'an and Hadith, both of which indicate temperance, equilibrium, and moderation. Referencing the medieval scholar Al-Tabari (839–923), Hamka explained that moderation is the position in between *berlebih-lebihan* (excessiveness) and *terlalu berkekurangan*

---

[8] Hamka, *Falsafah Hidup*, 82.

[9] Ibid., 79.

[10] Plato, *The Republic*, trans. Tom Griffith (Cambridge: Cambridge University Press, 2003), 124. See also Thomas M. Tuozzo, *Plato's Charmides: Positive Elenchus in a Socratic Dialogue* (New York: Cambridge University Press, 2011).

[11] Rush, *Hamka's Great Story*, 14–15.

[12] Rosnani Hashim, "Hamka," 199, and Rush, *Hamka's Great Story*, 197.

[13] Hamka, *Doktrin Islam yang Menimbulkan Kemerdekaan dan Keberanian* (Jakarta: Idayu Press, 1977), 11.

(falling short).[14] To be moderate as a Muslim is "to put things in its rightful place, and to choose whatever deeds would lead to goodness. Goodness lies in the middle way."[15] Ahmad Burhani, in his study of Indonesian Muslim scholars' interpretations of the verses on moderation in Qur'an, showed the salient commonalities Hamka shared with the Iranian thinker Ali Shariati (1933–77). Both argued that "Islam lies between Christian esoteric-extremism and Jewish exoteric-extremism."[16]

Islam was, to Hamka, not only a religion of moderation but a moderate religion that addresses all aspects of human life. Islam attends to the question of the bonds among human beings and between human beings and God. It is a religion that touches on the issues of ethics, politics, economics, and the environment; in fact, it "addresses all aspects of the activities of human beings in this world, the ways to undergo life, be it as an individual or as a collective."[17] In Hamka's eyes, Prophet Muhammad was an embodiment of the Platonian ideal of moderation in all things. By making this point, Hamka was implicitly informing his readers that Greek and other philosophies were useful tools of thinking and heuristic devices that could enable one to appreciate the comprehensiveness of Islam. These ideas were not absolute frames of reference for Muslims, who were endowed with a religion that is all-encompassing and perfect. Hamka stressed that Prophet Muhammad was not a philosopher but that his philosophy of moderation grounded what the Greeks philosophized. He wrote at length,

> The Prophet Muhammad (peace be upon him) emerged in the desert of Arabia to bring the teachings of constructing the *Ummatan Wasatan* [Moderate Community], a community that threads the middle way, that dealt with the vagaries of life. They believed in the hereafter and do good deeds on this earth. They sought fortune to uphold justice, placing importance on the well-being of the soul and the body, because the two are interconnected. They were concerned with the adroitness of the intellect, but were also strong in their worship in order to soothe their emotions. They pursued wealth profusely, because wealth was a tool for doing good. They fulfilled the task of being the vicegerents of Allah on earth, as their deeds will be provisions in the road to the hereafter when they meet and are questioned by God. So long as this community [the Muslims] traverses along the *Shiratal-Mustaqim*, [the Straight Path], they will remain as the moderate community.[18]

There are many facets of moderation that all Muslims should take note of in their endeavor to gain happiness in worldly life and the hereafter. In his book *The Philosophy of Life* (*Falsafah Hidup*), Hamka listed these facets in a manner that made the book read more like a self-help book than a strictly religious text. This was a style that

---

[14] Mahmoud Ayoub, *The Qur'an and Its Interpreters*, vol. 1 (Albany: State University of New York Press, 1984), 171.

[15] Hamka, *Falsafah Hidup*, 148.

[16] Ahmad Burhani, "Liberal and Conservative Discourses in the Muhammadiyah: The Struggle for the Face of Reformist Islam in Indonesia," in *Contemporary Developments in Indonesian Islam: Explaining the "Conservative Turn,"* ed. Martin van Bruinessen (Singapore: ISEAS, 2013), 137.

[17] Hamka, *Hak Asasi Manusia dalam Islam dan Deklarasi PBB* (Selangor, Malaysia: Pustaka Dini, 2010), 7.

[18] Hamka, *Tafsir Al-Azhar*, 2:333.

Hamka maintained throughout his life, which made his tomes "perennial favourites" among many Southeast Asians from different Islam persuasions.[19] The most important element for achieving happiness, he contended, was being moderate in intention and objectives. He urged Muslims to avoid having lofty dreams of becoming rulers and famous people but to instead focus on having pure intentions of contributing to humankind. Hamka placed into sharp relief the postrevolution period of Indonesia when everyone was chasing power and glory through titles and positions. He pointed out that left unmanaged, the love for power could lead to the emptiness of the soul and a culture of narcissism, as well as to a dog-eat-dog environment. A moderate Muslim would logically work hard to rise in the ranks of any profession, but that person would not do it at the expense of people around him because he or she would know that status and position are but ways to serve humanity. Pure intentions, if they became prominent, would eventually become the compass for Muslims. Hamka's points contradicted his own personal and sometimes grand ambitions. In his autobiography, he explicitly mentioned his dreams to be like Tagore of India and Iqbal of Pakistan. "I hope to be the 'Hamka of Indonesia.'"[20]

The second element in moderation, according to Hamka, was moderation in thought—that is, to think positively about life, to give due importance to material things but at the same time to have faith in the unseen and the nonrational. The Muslim mind must also be trained to be strong-willed and to avoid being dispirited in the face of challenges.

The third facet was moderation in expression. Hamka urged Muslims to be truthful in their speech and writings. Muslims must steer clear of dishonesty, exaggeration, and propaganda that would lead mankind astray. The media, especially the newspapers, were avenues where moderation in expression was often compromised, leading to chaos in society.[21] Hamka raised the issue of media effects probably as a way to remind Muslims that they were constantly under the surveillance of the colonial rulers. In 1940, the year when the first edition of *The Philosophy of Life* was published, Hamka was called in by the Dutch authorities for writing controversial pieces in the *Society's Compass* magazine.[22]

Hamka brought to light living within one's means as yet another facet of moderation. Muslims should avoid excessiveness and pompousness while combating the idea that living life in abject poverty could lead one to heaven. To be prudent was difficult for Muslims in Hamka's milieu because they were captivated by their own desires and the illusion that they could own anything they wanted simply by borrowing from banks and credit firms. Hamka's jab at the institutions that supported the capitalist system, which he believed had led to the rise of false consciousness among Muslims, will elaborated in greater detail in chapter 4. Hamka's reproach was directed primarily at the Muslims who made themselves willing victims of an exploitative economic system. In this, he shared the same line of thought as the Algerian writer Malek Bennabi. Bennabi wrote about how modern Muslims had made themselves vulnerable to

---

[19] Julia Day Howell, "Revitalised Sufism and the New Piety Movements in Islamic Southeast Asia," in *Routledge Handbook of Religions in Asia*, ed. Bryan S. Turner and Oscar Salemnik (New York: Routledge, 2015), 282.

[20] Hamka, *Kenang-kenangan Hidup*, 215.

[21] Hamka, *Falsafah Hidup*, 161.

[22] Hamka, *Kenang-kenangan Hidup*, 290.

capitalism, thereby falling into the condition of "coloniability," that is, the tendency of some societies to be susceptible to colonial rule and subjugation.[23] On the other side of the coin, Hamka highlighted the allure of being poor that was also equally strong because of the influence of wayward Sufism. All these tendencies had resulted in the breakdown of families and Muslim society.

In another book, *Pandangan Hidup Muslim* (The Muslim Worldview), Hamka again urged striking a balance in life:

> We need material things just as we are in need of spirituality. We must be rich in order to provide *zakah* [religious tax] to the destitute and the poor. We must establish ourselves in this world in order to climb the stairs to heaven. We will be burdened by suffering if we do not hold on to two ropes, that is, "the rope of Allah" and "the rope of earthly life." Let not our bodies be obese, but our souls thin. Let not our bodies be magnificent, but our souls meager. Let not our bodies be fully fed, but our souls dying of hunger. Give sustenance to both.[24]

Hamka's discussion on aspects of moderation drew to a close with the subject of fame. He laid bare the craze of seeking fame that was so obvious in the twentieth-century Malay world. Everyone was craving popularity to a point of engaging in corrupt practices to accomplish it. Muslims, in particular, had become childish (*keanak-anakan*) because they sought fame for its own sake.[25] A moderate person did not seek fame but embraced it with humility when it was bestowed on her. When faced with setbacks in life, moderation would be a guide for a person to temper her sadness. There was no need to celebrate fame beyond what was necessary or to be depressed when things failed. Plato's traces are noticeable in Hamka's elaborations on moderation in seeking fame. Hamka took from Plato an outright disdain toward those who are in search of fame to satiate their personal desires. Fame is not all bad. Plato opined that the search for fame must not supersede the higher goals of attaining wisdom, upholding justice, and leading a virtuous life.[26]

How does one achieve moderation in all things? Hamka put on his hat as a movement activist—namely, of the modernist Muhammadiyah mold—in answering this question. He believed that moderation is not a product of chance or coincidence; it has to be learned and nurtured at all stages of the human lifespan. Moderation has to be systematically taught for it to be fully realized. Shamsul Nizar, in his study of Hamka's ideas about education, explained that Hamka had used the Arabic terms *tarbiyah* and *ta'lim* to refer to nurturing, cultivating, expanding, guarding, enriching, and developing the full potential of a human being. It is a lifelong process that requires patience, love, and commitment. The persons responsible for this protracted process of education are parents, teachers, friends, and families, as well as oneself.[27] Shamsul Nizar is silent, however, about Hamka's stress on "teaching oneself" (*ajar diri*) to be moderate, on top on learning from and being nurtured by others. As an autodidact and an avid

---

[23] Malek Bennabi, *Islam in History and Society*, trans. Asma Rashid (New Delhi: Kitab Bhavan, 1999), 46–52.

[24] Hamka, *Pandangan Hidup Muslim*, 152.

[25] Hamka, *Falsafah Hidup*, 63.

[26] Plato, *Dialogues of Plato*, trans. Benjamin Jowett (New York: Simon & Schuster, 2001), 195.

[27] Shamsul Nizar, *Memperbincangkan Dinamika Intelektual*, 106–7.

Figure 3 Young Hamka (*right*) in the 1930s, standing with Yunus Anis, one of the leaders of Muhammadiyah. Courtesy of Suara Muhammadiyah.

reader of Ibn Tufayl's *Hayy Ibn Yaqzan,* a twelfth-century Arab philosophical tale about a man who discovered the ultimate truth through his own faculties, Hamka was convinced that self-education toward achieving moderation was possible.[28]

Whether through self-education or discipleship, developing and educating a moderate Muslim necessitates paying attention to four interrelated aspects that form part of human nature (*fitrah*): the soul (*al-ruh*), the heart (*al-qalb*), the body (*al-jism*), and the intellect (*al-aql*). Following Al-Ghazali, Hamka comprehended the soul as the seat of emotions, intellect, and actions.[29] Human beings are endowed by God with souls that are superior to those lower creatures and are therefore able to discern all aspects of life in a manner that those creatures cannot. The soul is predisposed to goodness. It is able to recognize evil and good. But it is also often swayed by desires that upset its balance and ability to guide the heart, body, and intellect to do good. The soul must be properly fostered because it is a gift from God to the best of his creations. In order for the soul to realize its fullest potential, Muslims must avoid excessiveness and engage in acts that bring the soul closer to God and the rest of human society. Hamka explained all of these in his exegesis of the chapter "Al-Isra'" (Night Journey), verse 85.[30]

The most effective method to discipline the soul is engaging in obligatory and supererogatory acts of worship. Hamka gave added prominence to fasting as a way to discipline the soul toward achieving moderation. "Fasting in the month of Ramadan guides us to lead a moderate life and the ways to manage desires that have no limits."[31] Among the desires that Hamka felt could destroy the soul were *nafsu shahwat* (carnal desires) and *nafsu perut* (gluttony or overeating). Carnal desires had led to rampant premarital sex and the mushrooming of the pornographic industry. Both had resulted in people's behaving like animals in their approach to sexual relations. They brought about the growth of prostitution, so much so that in the Malay world during Hamka's time, it grew to become a *penyakit masyarakat* (ailment of society) that could not be easily eradicated by governments.[32] Gluttony in turn had led to the struggle for power, positions, economic exploitation, and greed, which had bred injustice in society.[33]

Much like the soul, the heart, the body, and the intellect too had to be trained and restrained because these three facets of human life were all vulnerable to laxity and extremism. The best means to nurture them was to engage in meditation, contemplation, proper diet, reading works of beneficial knowledge, and regular exercises. Drawing again from Plato, Hamka recommended that Muslims consider gymnastics their sport and that they listen to soothing music.[34] More attention, Hamka proposed, should be paid to the development of the intellect because the intellect keeps the

---

[28] Hamka, *Falsafah Hidup,* 125 and 314. See also Ibn Tufayl, *Hayy Ibn Yaqzan: A Philosophical Tale,* trans. Lenn Evan Goodman (Chicago: Chicago University Press, 2009).

[29] Al-Ghazali, *On Disciplining the Soul,* trans T. J. Winter (Cambridge: The Islamic Texts Society, 1995).

[30] Hamka, *Tafsir Al-Azhar,* 15:4110–11.

[31] Hamka, *Tuntutan Puasa, Tarawih dan Salat Aidilfitri* (Selangor: Pustaka Dini, 2009), 6.

[32] Hamka, *Terusir* (Selangor: Pustaka Dini, 2007), 66.

[33] Hamka, *Tuntutan Puasa,* 26–27.

[34] Hamka, *Lembaga Hidup: Perhiasan Hidup Cemerlang* (Shah Alam, Malaysia: Pustaka Dini, 2007), 40–41.

heart from being impulsive. The intellect guides the body to nourish itself with permissible and healthy things.[35]

If the soul is the engine of human life and action, the intellect steers it. Hamka enjoined Muslims to immerse themselves in the path of seeking knowledge about their religion and if possible, about other faiths as well. Through this, they would recognize that all religions promote good values and respect for others. This is a hallmark of Hamka's cosmopolitan reform and outlook. He called on Muslims to use their intellect and thereby rethink Islam in a manner that would transcend racial, cultural, and other differences and divisions. Islam's key emphasis is *ukhuwwah* (brotherhood of man), among Muslims and also non-Muslims.[36] Hamka encouraged Muslims, once they had learned about their faith and were practicing it moderately, to write and participate in dialogues to sharpen their minds further. "Be moderate and write; be moderate and engage in discourses. And once that is done, your writings and discourses will impact society, may guide it towards righteousness. They [writings and discourses] may also mislead if society is ignorant and unrepentant. As long as we are moderate, as long as our intentions are noble, we are no longer accountable for the waywardness of society."[37]

VARIETIES OF EXTREMISM AND FANATICISM

Moderation as a fundamental concept in Islam cannot be fully understood without comprehending its opposite. Indeed, among the trademarks of the Islamic scholarly tradition is the practice of delving deeply into the definition of a given concept and explaining the opposite of it.[38] Hamka is a product of this tradition. He used the Arabic term *ghulat* (extreme) as well as the Malay terms *berlebih-lebihan* (excessiveness), *extrim* (extremism), and *fanatik* (fanatic) to explain various forms and implications of fanaticism in the Muslim world. For Hamka, all these concepts pointed to one thing: indulging in specific types of thinking and practice that were contrary to the Islamic ideal of moderation and, most important, to human nature. He argued that excessiveness, extremism, and fanaticism had no place in Islam. In fact, Muslims who were extreme or fanatic could end up nullifying or ruining their faith should they believe or practice things that were forbidden or transgressed the boundaries of *tawheed* (oneness of Allah). Hamka termed this problem *shirk di zaman moderen* (polytheism in the modern age), which had fueled the many forms of extremism and fanaticism among Malay-Muslims.[39]

The legal scholar Hashim Kamali has called our attention to a long-standing form of extremism among Muslims: the "fanatic advocacy of one view or opinion to the exclusion of all others, despite knowledge of additional existing views."[40] Hamka shared this view in that he saw fanaticism toward a particular religious

---

[35] Hamka, *Falsafah Hidup*, 43–48.

[36] Hamka, *Pribadi* (Kuala Lumpur: Pustaka Antara, 1965), 98.

[37] Hamka, *Falsafah Hidup*, 159.

[38] Franz Rosenthal, *Knowledge Triumphant: The Concept of Knowledge in Medieval Islam* (Leiden: Brill, 2007), 59.

[39] Hamka, *Filsafat Ketuhanan*, 80–83.

[40] Hashim Kamali, *The Middle Path of Moderation in Islam* (Oxford: Oxford University Press, 2015), 38.

view or opinion as an endemic problem in the Malay world for many centuries. He called it *fanatik mazhab* (doctrinal fanaticism).[41] Such extremism and fanaticism had divided the Malay-Muslims into several antagonistic camps, especially between Muslims who studied in secular institutions and those from Islamic schools. Muslim groups who were averse to Western knowledge condemned other Muslims who were influenced by those ideas. Some went so far as to label all Western-educated Muslims as enemies.[42]

Muslims who studied in secular institutions, on the other hand, were against Muslims who studied in Islam schools because the latter promoted the expansion of religion in society and politics. These secularly educated Muslims argued that religion ought not to interfere in public affairs. Religion should be limited to addressing issues pertaining to faith and devotion. Hamka gives the examples of Syaikh Ali Abdulraziq (1888–1966), Khalid Muhammad Khalid (1920–96) from Egypt, Sir Sayyid Ahmad Khan (1817–99) from India, and Kamal Attaturk (1881–1938) in Turkey as propagators of the idea that Islam and politics should be kept separated. Some young intellectuals in Indonesia also embraced such ideas.[43] These Muslims were so mesmerized by all that came from Europe that they interpreted their own faith through a European lens. They looked at pious Muslims with disdain and regarded their strong attachment to Islam as a sign of backwardness. In a twist of irony, Hamka notes, when these secular Muslims died, their families would call on the Islamic-educated Muslims to conduct the funeral rites because they did not have any inkling of the proper ways to conduct such rites.[44]

In building his case, Hamka runs the risk of setting up false dichotomies and oversimplifying different groups of Muslims in the Malay world. The sharp distinction made between secular Muslims and those who studied in religious schools did not align well with the realities on the ground. Granted, there were Muslims from secular institutions who were hostile toward those who were religiously trained and vice versa. But the majority of Muslims in the Malay world from all educational backgrounds coexisted easily for most of history even if they differed in terms of commitment and approaches to Islam.[45] We may surmise that what Hamka sought to achieve in highlighting these divisions was to bring into sharp relief the need for all Muslims to take the moderate and cosmopolitan path of accepting one another as brothers even though their approaches and understanding of Islam might differ.

Another manifestation of fanaticism toward a particular religious view or opinion found among Muslims in the Malay world pertained to religious rituals and has been termed "ritual purism."[46] Hamka chastised those Muslims who argued vehemently about fine details regarding the reading aloud of the *niyyah* (intentions) in prayers and about whether activities such the *Maulid* (celebration of the birthday of the Prophet) and the *talkin* (reading of prayers for the deceased) were allowed in Islam. Both groups

---

[41] Hamka, *Sejarah Umat Islam* (Singapore: Pustaka Nasional, 1994), 441.

[42] Hamka, *Tafsir Al-Azhar*, 1:206.

[43] Hamka, *Hak Asasi Manusia dalam Islam dan Deklarasi PBB*, 26.

[44] Hamka, *Pelajaran Agama Islam*, 432.

[45] I explore this fact in my book *Muslim Cosmopolitanism: Southeast Asian Islam in Comparative Perspective* (Edinburgh: Edinburgh University Press, 2017).

[46] Adeeb Khalid, *Islam after Communism: Religion and Politics in Central Asia* (Berkeley: University of California Press, 2007), 145.

had grown to be malicious until they lost sight of larger problems in society such as poverty, apostasy, and social exclusion. "These debates," Hamka contended, "intense as they are, have caused a segment of such groups to prefer working with Communists who are godless rather than Muslims because their opponents did not read intentions in prayers or may have read them!"[47]

Finally, Hamka highlighted fanaticism that came in the shape of religious sectarianism in the Malay world. Some Muslims claimed that only their version Islam was the true and authoritative sort. All other groups that did not subscribe to their thinking were not part of *Ahlus Sunnah wal Jemaah* (People of the Sunnah and the Community). The traditionalists during Hamka's time accused the modernists of being deviants and a sect seeking to change Islam.[48] These differences between Sunnis and Shi'ites, between Salafis and Sufis, and between different schools of jurisprudence had wasted the energies of Muslims for generations. Hamka argued that all Muslims should move beyond such debates and learn to accept that "we are Ummatan Wahidatan, one ummah."[49] Muslims would be united when they were moderate.

If fanaticism toward religious opinions and views has divided Muslims within specific localities, nationalist extremism has created fault lines between Muslims from different countries in the Malay world. Many Islamic thinkers before Hamka have highlighted the problem of nationalist fanaticism among Muslims. Influential Muslim intellectuals such as Amir Shakib Arslan (1869–1946), Muhammad Abduh, and Jamaluddin Al-Afghani urged Muslims to unite under the banner of a Pan-Islamic coalition in the face of colonialism. These Muslim intellectuals were critical of all forms of local and nationalist parochialisms. They saw the nation as a mere medium rather than an end in itself.[50] Intellectually, Hamka placed himself in the genealogy of thinkers who were critical of nationalist extremism.

To him, some Muslims in the Malay world had become so extreme with their nationalist feelings that the nation was placed above and beyond Islam. Nationalism became such an obsession that they thought of everything within that overarching framework. In the end, nationalism was the root cause of destruction. Such extreme love for one's nation, Hamka stressed, had led to bloodshed as Muslims waged wars against one another. Not only the Muslims but the whole twentieth-century world was afflicted with "a major crisis, crisis without end, especially because human beings have been enslaved by narrow nationalist feelings."[51] Hamka advocated that Muslims lead the rest of the world in transcending nationalist feelings and embracing the ideals of universal brotherhood. Muslims must be the first to acknowledge and promote the fact that all people originated from Adam and Eve and that human beings should not be treated differently because of their color, race, status, or class but should be judged by their deeds and devotion to God.[52]

Still, it is important to acknowledge that Hamka was not totally against nationalism. He himself endorsed the idea of Indonesia and called on Muslims to work together

---

[47] Hamka, *Pelajaran Agama Islam*, 501–2.

[48] Hamka, *Iman dan Amal Saleh* (Jakarta: Pustaka Panjimas, 1982), 11.

[49] Hamka, *Membahas Kemusykilan Agama* (Selangor: Pustaka Dini, 2010), 60–61.

[50] Nikki R. Keddie, "Pan-Islamism as Proto-Nationalism," *Journal of Modern History* 41, no. 1 (1969): 17–28.

[51] Hamka, *Pandangan Hidup Muslim*, 228.

[52] Ibid.

with other communities in the making of an Indonesian nation. But his understanding of nationalism was colored by Islamic ideals in that the nation must never supersede the notion of the ummah and the universal needs of humanity. In this sense, Hamka was an "Islamic nationalist" who was not in favor of extreme "fatherland nationalism." This was the stance taken by many Islamic movements in the Malay world at the time in which he was writing, the most prominent being the Sarekat Islam, of which he was a keen supporter.[53]

Hamka cites a Hadith from Prophet Muhammad to support his stance. The Hadith states, "None of you will believe until you love for your brother what you love for yourself." Cementing this injunction, according to Hamka, is verse 213 in the chapter "Al-Baqarah" from the Qur'an: "All people are a single nation." Hamka added that if Muslims actually abide by the universal ideals of Islam, then unity and cooperation among mankind beyond the trappings of nationalism can be achieved:

> Mankind is in essence, united; their God is one and the same, their ancestors come from one source. Everyone believes in justice and is willing to sacrifice for it. They help one another, and work together toward goodness and faith, not assist one another and cooperate in sin and enmity. The ways of the world are such that even if human beings come in different races, tribes with different names, from different climates, from a variety of colors, hatred is not embedded in their hearts as they see the need to have relations with one another. [They go] through difficult times together and celebrate good times together. Even if religions differ, the objective is the same, that is, to pray to The One. For that is the essence of Islam: liberation, freedom and moderation![54]

Another extremist tendency among Muslims was the renunciation of worldly pleasures and possessions. In chapter 5, I will discuss in detail Hamka's critique of the concept of *zuhud* (asceticism) used by Sufis in the Malay world to justify poverty and seclusion from the larger society. Hamka believed that the Sufis were predisposed to be extreme in renouncing all that was worldly and vain. Non-Sufis were also culpable of this reasoning, which in effect lent credence to the idea that to be a good Muslim was to be poor. These extremist Muslims often used a Hadith of Muhammad to justify their stance: "The world is a prison house for a believer and Paradise for a non-believer."[55]

The understanding of this Hadith by world-renouncing Muslims, according to Ismail R. Al-Faruqi, "runs diametrically counter to the Qur'an."[56] Hamka agreed with Al-Faruqi and disputed such thinking by giving a new interpretation of the Hadith. In his view, the Prophet did not use the analogy of the world as a prison for believers to dissuade Muslims from obtaining wealth and comfort. Rather, the prison was a metaphorical device used to remind Muslims that they should be cognizant of the

---

[53] Arskal Salim, *Challenging the Secular State: The Islamization of Law in Modern Indonesia* (Honolulu: University of Hawai'i Press, 2008), 51–54.

[54] Hamka, *Pandangan Hidup Muslim*, 242–43.

[55] Muslim Ibn al-Hajjaj al-Qusayri, *Sahih Muslim: Being Traditions of the Sayings and Doings of the Prophet Muhammad as Narrated by His Companions and Compiled under the Title al-Jāmi' al-ṣaḥīḥ*, vol. 4, trans. Abdul Hamid Siddiqui (Lahore, Pakis.: Sh. Muhammad Ashraf, 1976), 1529.

[56] Ismail R. Al-Faruqi, "On the Raison D'Etre of the Ummah," *Islamic Studies* 2, no. 2 (1963): 187.

limits that are placed on them by the divine in everything they do. There is no such thing as absolute freedom in Islam. The laws and injunctions in Islam act as barriers and measures for Muslims to lead a moderate life—a life free from debauched acts and guided by reason and revelation.[57]

Hamka posited that Muslims would be neither world-renouncing nor overly indulgent in worldly pleasures if they internalized the spirit of moderation in all things. He drew from the ideas of Al-Ghazali. Al-Ghazali asserted that Muslims must seek a balance between seeking happiness in this world and the hereafter and not neglect either of the two. Al-Ghazali placed heavy importance on doing good deeds, being devoted to God, accumulating wealth, establishing a family, having status in life, maintaining one's well-being, and being proud of one's lineage in order to gain the best from this world. These were the factors that would prepare a person for eternal happiness in heaven.[58] In Hamka's own words,

> Worldly wealth is a gift from Allah. But do not be heedless with such wealth because you will encounter death after this life. The wealth of this world, whether little or plenty will surely be left behind on earth. When we die, not a single thing will be brought to the hereafter. Hence do good, give the sustenance endowed by Allah for the path of social welfare. Perchance, when you pass on some day, the impact of your deeds for the hereafter will be multiplied many times by Allah. And do not forget what is due for this world. Live in a good house, drive a good vehicle and may all of these along with a loyal wife lead to the epitome of happiness.[59]

Hamka was optimistic that Muslims in the Malay world would continue to be moderate in their approach to Islam. The various types of extremism and fanaticism that had arisen were caused by modern life, upsetting the balance that Muslims used to have. Hamka regarded modernity as a new form of idolatry (*penyembahan berhala*), in which the totems were material things gained at the expense of human feelings and sensibilities as well as spirituality. As a result, mankind had forgotten the notion of moderation and had become one-sided in their approaches to life. They had become egoistic and selfish, concerned mainly with filling up their bellies and pockets. They had forgotten the people around them and their duties to God.[60] For Malay-Muslims to be moderate, they must free themselves from negative ideologies. One of these ideologies was the image propagated by Western scholars and the media that Muslims could never be moderate.

DECONSTRUCTING THE MYTH OF MUSLIM EXTREMISM

If Muslims in the Malay world have been by and large moderate in their practices and discourse on Islam, why then has Islam in the region been associated with violence and bigotry? Hamka blamed Western colonizers, Christian missionaries, and Orientalists, finding them responsible for the growth of negative images of

---

[57] Hamka, *Membahas Kemusykilan Agama*, 55–59.

[58] Hamka, *Tasauf Modern* (Medan, Indonesia: Tokobuku Islamijah, 1939), 29–30.

[59] Hamka, *Tafsir Al-Azhar*, 20:5376.

[60] Hamka, *Lembaga Hidup*, 385–94, and Hamka, *Membahas Kemusykilan Agama*, 58.

Muslims to justify their policies and programs. These images scarcely represented realities. They were, in Hamka's eyes, myths and embellishments of the state of Muslim societies.[61]

Reading Hamka's account of Western agendas against Muslims may give one the impression that he was overly discriminatory and propounded an Occidentalist view of the West.[62] And yet, when placed against the wider context of the decolonizing age and the determination of former colonized peoples to question all previous presumptions and suppositions about their communities, Hamka's diagnoses were but representative of a wider body of the "decolonizing the mind" scholarship that was gaining ground from the 1920s onward. Writers from Asia, Africa, Latin America, and even the heart of Europe itself were questioning long-standing pejorative depictions of colonized societies while providing alternative interpretations of their past and present situations.[63]

What were the programs and policies that fostered these negative images of Muslims in the Malay world? Hamka highlighted the establishment of educational institutions in the region where studies of Islam and Muslims were removed or downplayed from the syllabi.[64] By removing or downplaying religious subjects, the colonial powers encouraged those Muslims who were secular in outlook and disapproved of other Muslims who exhibited any forms of close attachment to Islam. These secularized Muslims positioned themselves as moderates in society. They portrayed Muslims who did not embrace their nominal approach to Islam as extremists and fundamentalists. Hamka felt that they were mere cogs in the colonial administrative machinery, assisting the colonial powers to exploit the Muslims at large for their own well-being.[65]

The other manner in which the Europeans framed Muslims as fanatics and extremists was through the writings of scholars known as "Orientalists" because of their interest in Asian subjects. Hamka singled out Thomas Stamford Raffles (1781–1826), Christiaan Snouck Hurgronje (1859–1936), and Bertram Johannes Schrieke (1890–1945) as the key Orientalists who were under the service of the British and Dutch colonial governments. They influenced the public mind through their own reinterpretations of Islam and local Muslim societies. The Orientalists accused Islam of encouraging polygamy, implying that it was an uncivilized religion.[66] They also churned out a large corpus of works promoting the idea that Islam was suited only for the Arabs. Underlining this supposition was the argument that Malays had a higher civilization before Islam came to the Malay world from the Arab world. Having adopted Islam from the Arabs, the Orientalists maintained that the Malays spread it by the sword through the agency of fanatical Muslim kings. Among

---

[61] Hamka, *Membahas Kemusykilan Agama*, 167–85.

[62] Ian Buruma and Avishai Margalit, *Occidentalism: The West in the Eyes of Its Enemies* (New York: Penguin, 2004).

[63] Robert J. C. Young, *Postcolonialism: A Historical Introduction* (Oxford: Blackwell, 2001).

[64] Contemporary studies of Dutch and British schooling systems confirm Hamka's position. See Jean Gelman Taylor, *Global Indonesia* (London: Routledge, 2013), 97, and Rosnani Hashim, *Educational Dualism in Malaysia: Implications for Theory and Practice* (Kuala Lumpur: Oxford University Press, 1996), 6.

[65] Hamka, *Dari Lembah Cita-Cita*, 51.

[66] Hamka, *Renungan Tasauf* (Jakarta: Pustaka Panjimas, 1985), 56–57.

the Orientalists who held such a view were John Crawfurd (1783–1868), Pieter Johannes Veth (1814–95), and Pieter Brooshooft (1845–1921).[67]

European Orientalists with support from the colonial states represented nominal Muslims as moderates in their endeavor to paint the majority of Malay-Muslims as fanatics and extremists. These nominal Muslims were provided with much publicity in order to structure public perception of what moderate Muslims ought to be—that is, secular and slipshod in their piety and faith. Furthermore, moderate Muslims were given high positions in the colonial administrative bodies. Through the use of propaganda tools, they were differentiated from those Muslims who were religious. The colonial states defined fanatics "as those people who are dogged in defending their stance, hateful of people with differing views, with the most evident form of fanaticism developing from religious faith."[68] By depicting the large bulk of Muslims as such, the colonial powers justified the crushing of all forms of resistance against them. Hamka highlighted the cases of Imam Bonjol in Sumatra, Cik Tiro in Aceh, and many other rebellions against the Dutch colonizers until the eve of the Indonesian revolution in 1949. All these freedom fighters were deemed fanatics when their true objectives were to defend their own homeland from invaders.[69]

Recent scholarship has validated Hamka's representation of the European Orientalists. Karel Steenbrink, for example, maintained that during colonial times, the "idea of fanaticism" was promoted chiefly by Hurgronje. As an adviser to the colonial government, he disagreed with his older colleague, K. F. Holle, who considered the "religious brotherhood (*tarekat*) to be the most threatening aspect of Islam. Snouck Hurgronje held the opinion that both legalistic and mystical Islam may occur in political and apolitical garb."[70] Following Snouck Hurgronje's lead, other Orientalists highlighted the adverse impact of pilgrimage to Mecca on Southeast Asian Muslims. The returned pilgrims (*hajjis*) tended to become more "Arabized" upon their return, and many became involved in violent protests against the colonial powers. Such a view was on the whole an exaggeration of the reality of the day, but it served a colonizing function just as well. Pilgrimage to Makkah had little bearing on the outbreak of rebellions in the Malay world.[71]

Hamka deconstructed these negative images of anticolonial movements and reformist activists in the Malay world by contending that they were not extremists and fanatics. Rather, they were Muslims who manifested the ideal of *ghirah* (justifiable jealousy), which prompted them protect their homes, families, and country from oppression and exploitation by people whom they regarded as their enemies. For Hamka, ghirah was necessary in mobilizing Muslims against colonialism. When used effectively, it could actually bring back moderation in Muslim societies that had been effectively destabilized by European colonizers. The colonizers had brought with

---

[67] Hamka, *Dari Lembah Cita-Cita*, 51. See also Khairudin Aljunied, "Edward Said and Southeast Asian Islam," *Journal of Commonwealth and Postcolonial Studies* 11, nos. 1–2 (2004): 159–75.

[68] Hamka, *Dari Hati ke Hati* (Selangor: Pustaka Dini, 2009), 174.

[69] Hamka, *Ghirah dan Tantangan Terhadap Islam*, 15.

[70] Karel Steenbrink, "Hamka (1908–1981) and the Integration of the Islamic *Ummah* of Indonesia," *Studia Islamika* 1, no. 3 (1994): 126.

[71] Aljunied, "Edward Said and Southeast Asian Islam," 159–75.

them colonial modernity and godless secularism, which impacted balance and harmony in society, politics, and the economy of the Malay world.[72]

Hamka brought to light *al-ghazwul fikr* (the war of ideas) directed against Islam and Muslims globally. He characterized it "as a potent propaganda, through many channels, be it overt or subtle, be it through cultural or intellectual means, in order to change the thought patterns of the Muslims away from the fundamentals of their religion and without Muslims realizing that they have internalized the belief that the path towards progress is to leave Islam."[73] Hamka's trepidation about the problem of al-ghazwul fikri differed, however, from the thinking of ideologues of the Muslim Brotherhood in the 1970s, which also highlighted the influence of foreign ideas on Muslims. While the Muslim Brotherhood called for a total rejection of all that came from non-Muslims in the study and teaching of Islam, Hamka called for broad-mindedness and intellectual rather than emotional responses toward all forms of propaganda against Islam. As a cosmopolitan reformer, he enjoined Muslims to respond to ideas with the use of more powerful ideas. This could be achieved when they studied all sorts of ideas rather than simply brushing them off as irrelevant or frivolous. Negative ideas should be confronted in a respectable manner. Erroneous thought about Islam by Muslims themselves ought to be addressed peacefully and with an open heart, which is a key principle of Hamka's cosmopolitan reform.[74]

Hamka's espousal of the ideal and practice of moderation in Islam and his critique of extremism and fanaticism were spurred on by his desire to be a teacher of society.[75] Like a teacher who sought to gain the attention of his students, Hamka used a persuasive rhetorical style to drive home his messages. To Hamka, the reform and the reconstruction of Islam in the Malay world could be made possible only by bringing Muslims back to embracing a balance between the world and the hereafter. No wide-ranging reforms could come into effect if Muslims could not find a mean between the material and the spiritual. And very little change could be imagined if Malay-Muslims, whom Hamka saw as his attentive students, were unable to find the equilibrium between passion and reason as well as between the love of one's nation and society and the love of mankind and the religion of God. Cosmopolitan reform would begin with moderation and end with the dismantling of extremism, fanaticism, and the forces that fueled these vices.

Indeed, as Hamka intimated, "True religion broadens empathy and consideration between human beings. There would not be fanaticism and racial animosities would end. What will persist is brotherhood. Mutual cooperation and assistance."[76] In calling for moderation and railing against fanaticism and extremism, Hamka hoped that his fellow Muslims would develop sensitivity (*halus perasaan*) for others. When one is

---

[72] Hamka, *Ghirah dan Tantangan Terhadap Islam*, 51.

[73] Hamka, *Beberapa Tantangan terhadap Ummat Islam Dimasa Kini: Secularisme, Syncritisme dan Ma'shiat* (Djakarta: Penerbit Bulan Bintang, 1970), 5.

[74] Hamka, *Pelajaran Agama Islam*, 429. On Indonesian Muslim conceptions of ghazwul fikri during and after Hamka's times as well as the influence of the Muslim Brotherhood and other Islamic movements, see Martin van Bruinessen, "Ghazwul Fikri or Arabization? Indonesian Muslim Responses to Globalization," in *Southeast Asian Muslims in the Era of Globalization*, ed. Ken Miichi and Omar Farouk (Basingstoke, UK: Palgrave Macmillan, 2014), 61–85.

[75] K. S. Yudiono, *Pengantar Sejarah Sastra Indonesia* (Jakarta: Grasindo, 2010), 100.

[76] Hamka, *Pandangan Hidup Muslim*, 174.

sensitive toward other people's feelings, that person will avoid behaving in ways that would upset the people around him or her. A sensitive person will not get angry too easily and will not be too pushy over his beliefs. A sensitive person will be in control of base desires that might lead him to excessiveness, striving continuously to find moderation even under extreme circumstances.[77] Sensitivity is a key to moderation, and moderation is the path to eternal happiness.

---

[77] Hamka, *Pribadi*, 152, and Hamka, *Falsafah Hidup*, 163.

CHAPTER THREE

MUSLIMS AND SOCIAL JUSTICE

Upholding justice in society was, to Hamka, a core obligation of all Muslims and a key component of his cosmopolitan reform. Justice is such a fundamental obligation in Islam that its importance is often repeated during weekly Friday congregational prayers that are made mandatory for Muslim men. To be sure, it has been a millennium-old practice of *khatibs* (those who deliver religious sermons) to recite verses of the Qur'an that remind Muslims of their duties to uphold justice. Among these verses is the one found in the chapter "An-Nahl" (The Bees), verse 90, which reads, "Surely Allah enjoins the doing of justice and the doing of good [to others] and the giving to kindred, and He forbids indecency and evil and rebellion; He admonishes you that you may be mindful." Malise Ruthven, a noted analyst of Muslim societies, underlines this point well when he writes, "If one could sum up in a phrase the essential difference between the two great Western monotheisms, one might say that whereas Christianity is primarily the religion of love, Islam is above all the religion of justice."[1]

Hamka would have agreed with Lawrence Rosen that justice is "the term that suffuses every element of Islamic thought and culture, from the Qur'an to the most commonsensical of aphorisms."[2] But he held that social justice as Muslims in the Malay world have conceived it ought to be rethought, redefined, and communicated clearly to help his coreligionists navigate through the manifold challenges in the age of decolonization, nation building and Islamic resurgence.[3] From Hamka's perspective, the Great Depression, the Indonesian revolution in 1949, and the subsequent founding of new independent states across Southeast Asia brought about significant social and political transformations that impacted Muslims and non-Muslims alike. Autocratic regimes and political violence loomed large. Added to this was the rise of militancy among radical Muslim groups and communists that saw violence as the best means to address the unjust practices of colonial and secular nation-states. These problems were compounded by underdevelopment, unemployment, inequality, and deprivation that characterized Muslim societies all over the Malay world.[4]

It would not be excessive to suggest that the Malay world was divided sharply along class lines from the 1930s onward, with the majority of the population belonging to the bottom end of society. The global economic meltdown in 1929 left among its ruins a growing Muslim underclass that lived in abject poverty. These poor Muslims, to put it figuratively, were wretched in their own homeland, caught in between the

---

[1] Malise Ruthven, *Islam in the World* (New York: Oxford University Press, 2006), 219.

[2] Lawrence Rosen, *Varieties of Muslim Experience: Encounters with Arab Political and Cultural Life* (Chicago: University of Chicago Press, 2008), 60.

[3] Hamka, *Keadilan Sosial Dalam Islam* (Kuala Lumpur: Pustaka Antara, 1966).

[4] Mark T. Berger, "Decolonisation, Modernisation and Nation-Building: Political Development Theory and the Appeal of Communism in Southeast Asia, 1945–1975," *Journal of Southeast Asian Studies* 34, no. 3 (2003): 421–48.

heavy hand of the state, the ruling elites, and the exploitative schemes of transnational corporations. Fictionalizing this predicament in his most successful novel, *Di Bawah Lindungan Ka'bah* (Under the Protection of Ka'bah), published in 1938, Hamka imagined conversations between a commoner and his mother about his dream to marry a higher-class Muslim only to be told that although love is just and God created love with justice, society was tainted by class divisions such that love between persons of different classes was impractical if not impossible.[5] These and many attendant challenges could explain the widespread appeal of socialism among Muslim intellectuals and writers who were calling for the restoration of social justice in the Malay world.[6] Muslims were becoming increasingly divided between many camps—religious, secular, socialist, capitalist, anticolonial, and elitist. The divisions between them were defined by how they understood and espoused the notion of social justice.

As a cosmopolitan reformer who had gained fame from the many books he had written prior to the Second World War, Hamka sought to deconstruct these conflicting conceptions. He was devoted to upholding the Islamic conception of social justice above all others. He achieved this through a few argumentative steps. The first was to deconstruct partial conceptions of social justice. Hamka took issue with materialist rendering of social justice, which he believed had failed to ensure equality in global societies. At the same time, he also critiqued problematic Islamic conceptions of social justice, highlighting the weaknesses of these partial ideas. Hamka was particularly critical of Muslim thinkers who viewed the world in Manichaean terms, that is, a split and unending conflict between two opposing groups—those who were in state of ignorance (*jahiliyyah*) and those who held fast to the *shari'a* (Islamic legal and ethical code) and were therefore on the path of righteousness. Among the thinkers contemporaneous with Hamka who presented the world in a binary fashion were Sayyid Qutb (1906–66) and Abul A'la Maududi.

Having questioned these conceptions and exposed their weaknesses, Hamka propounded his own unique ideas of social justice. In his view the Islamic conception was guided by the practical concepts of khalifatullah fil'ard (vicegerents of God on earth), amanah (sacred trust), shura (mutual consultation), and maslahah (general welfare). Hamka underscored the Qur'anic view that human beings are the khalifatullah fil'ard, whose principal task is to preserve and protect the rights of humankind. Social justice therefore is an amanah bestowed by God. The sacred trust of upholding social justice by vicegerents of God can be fully realized only when human beings learn how to communicate well with one another and agree on the best means to reform an unequal society. It is here that the concept of shura is crucial to guarantee the common good of all. Hamka saw modern-day ideas of democracy as compatible with shura. What was urgently needed was to infuse religious ethics into the practice of democracy along the path to achieving justice.

Hamka's intellectual third step was to foreground the various enablers that could facilitate the actualization of social justice. These included good leaders and institutions such as the state, the judiciary, and political parties as regulating bodies in ensuring that social justice prevailed. Hamka also stressed the critical role writers and grassroots movements could play in advocating for social justice. He was equally

---

[5] Hamka, *Di Bawah Lindungan Ka'bah*, 21–22.

[6] Tiong Vu, "Socialism and Underdevelopment in Southeast Asia," in *Routledge Handbook of Southeast Asian History*, ed. Norman G. Owen (London: Routledge, 2014), 188–98.

mindful that social justice required the participation of the common people. For him, zakah (compulsory tax) in Islam and charitable works driven by a sense of humanity and universal responsibility were effective mediums that could be used by the common people to ensure that the weakest in society were being cared for.

CRITIQUING PARTIAL CONCEPTIONS OF SOCIAL JUSTICE

John Rawls, in his classic *Theory of Justice*, outlines the differences between the concepts and conceptions of justice. There exists, according to Rawls, only one concept of justice but a wide variety of conceptions of social justice. All these different conceptions "are the outgrowth of different notions of society against the background of opposing views of the natural necessities and opportunities of human life. Fully to understand a conception of justice we must make explicit the conception of social cooperation from which it derives. But in doing this we should not lose sight of the special role of the principles of justice or of the primary subject to which they apply."[7] Hamka was cognizant of the many conceptions of justice that dominated the minds of Muslims in post–World War II Southeast Asia. The materialist conceptions came under Hamka's sharp analytical knife.

By the materialist conception of social justice, Hamka was referring first to the capitalist idea that free-market forces can bring about social justice. Such a belief, according to Hamka, was born out of the capitalists' conviction that men are rational beings and their material pursuits would not necessarily dissuade them from becoming responsible members of society. From this line of reasoning, the capitalists contend that states and other governing institutions should not play a direct role in regulating society. Rather, these institutions should act as facilitators for market forces to run smoothly and to structure society so as to achieve equilibrium and harmony, which capitalists recognize as essential to the growth of the economy.[8]

Hamka believed the capitalist conception of social justice was illusory and dishonest. Capitalism had resulted in the exploitation of men by other men through the agency of profit-driven establishments such as banks and multinational companies as well as corporations. History bore testimony to the reality that these establishments had fueled the colonizing goals of the European powers, which led to the domination over and abuse of non-European peoples to serve the economic interests of the West. Colonial capitalism widened the gaps between the haves and the have-nots in colonized societies. Colonial capitalism laid the foundations for the creation of the *masyarakat riba* (society of usury), which encouraged the poor to believe that they too could be like the rich by living on borrowed cash, without realizing that they had been enslaved by banks and credit firms.[9] Colonial capitalism also led to the manipulation of droves of Muslim women—particularly in Sumatra, where Hamka grew up—who entered the workforce with the promise of riches, only to realize soon enough that they were objects of male pleasure.[10]

These points were reinforced by a Malaysian scholar's study of the impact of colonial capitalism on the Malay world. In *The Myth of the Lazy Native*, published in 1977

---

[7] John Rawls, *A Theory of Justice* (Cambridge, MA: Harvard University Press, 1999), 9.

[8] Hamka, *Keadilan Sosial Dalam Islam*, 85.

[9] Hamka, *Tafsir Al-Azhar*, 1:672.

[10] Hamka, *Merantau Ka-Deli* (Kuala Lumpur: Pustaka Antara, 1966), 16–18.

during the same period when Hamka was actively writing about social justice, Hussein Alatas stated that colonial capitalism had ravaged almost all aspects of Malay life, from the moral to the economic to the spatial, and had even affected health. Colonial capitalism had led to the growth of many diseases such as malaria, tuberculosis, venereal disease, and dysentery. "The hasty development of settlements, the crowding of people, bad sanitation and sewage, prostitution, injurious habits such as opium smoking and drinking amongst those of modest means, had resulted from the opening of the mines and estates with its attendant urbanization."[11]

Workers were subjected to capitalism during and even after the colonial phase in history. They remained unjustly treated because the economic system was driven more by profits than by ethics and human rights. Hamka pointed out that workers' salaries were barely commensurate with the number of hours they worked, and yet they had been made to believe that they would someday be able to live a luxurious life like the people in Europe and America if they worked hard enough. This illusion was made more persuasive through aggressive advertising in the media. The capitalist conception of justice, Hamka wrote, would inevitably bring about injustice. In Indonesia, it had ruined the *kehalusan budi* (refined ethics) of the locals.[12] The United States of America, which was the heart of the capitalist conception, had become a "society of laborers-employers." Capitalism, Hamka concluded, was therefore "poisonous to our sense of priority in life. Life becomes overly focused upon externalities, with an empty soul. 'Kuntsmatig.'[13] Falsity!"[14]

Hamka's trenchant critique of capitalism as a negating force on social justice gives us the impression that he was leaning toward the Marxist, communist, and socialist conceptions of justice that were making a comeback during the 1950s when Hamka was penning his book *Social Justice in Islam* (first published in 1951).[15] But this was not the case. He was equally critical of the writings of Muslim socialists who preceded him, such as Abdul Rahman al-Kawakabi. Charles Tripp argues that al-Kawakibi "portrayed Islamic principles of social justice and ethical economic organisation as identical with those of modern socialism. By his account, therefore, Islamic law and principles called for economic equality for all, for the public ownership of the means of production and for the right and indeed duty to work for the good of all."[16] Hamka did find some affinities between Islam and socialist ideas but he emphasized that stark differences also exist between them.

For him, the Marxists, communists, and socialists had all committed the error of conceiving of social justice narrowly from the perspective of material factors. They believed that social justice could be delivered when capitalism was thoroughly dismantled and when all people were rewarded equally regardless of their position in society. From Hamka's perspective, such visions were utopian, as seen in case of

---

[11] Hussein Alatas, *The Myth of the Lazy Native* (London: Frank Cass, 1977), 225.

[12] Hamka, *Tuan Direktur* (Kuala Lumpur: Pustaka Antara, 1966), 122.

[13] Dutch word for "artificial,"

[14] Hamka, *Keadilan Sosial Dalam Islam*, 90.

[15] For a comprehensive history of Indonesian Marxism and communism in the 1950s and their ideas, see Rex Mortimer, *Indonesian Communism under Sukarno: Ideology and Politics* (Ithaca: Cornell University Press, 1974).

[16] Charles Tripp, *Islam and the Moral Economy: The Challenge of Capitalism* (Cambridge: Cambridge University Press, 2006), 36.

Stalin's Russia, where justice was nowhere to be found.[17] In many ways, they were un-Islamic because Marx's theory of historical materialism and other related postulations downplayed the importance of religion in the reformation of society. Marx "viewed religion as an invention of the economy, and in some instances [maintained that] religion is an enemy that would obstruct the emergence of the dictatorship of the proletariat and the Global Revolution!"[18]

Hamka's disapproving views of Marxism must be read against developments in the Masyumi (Partai Majelis Syuro Muslim Indonesia, or the Council of Indonesia Muslim Associations) that he was a part of. A number of the Masyumi's leaders were becoming increasingly influenced by Marxist ideas. This trend reflected the rapid growth of Marxism and communism among a segment of Muslim elites in Indonesia and the wider Malay world in the postwar period, much to the consternation of the ulama and other Muslim activists.[19]

But unlike the conservative Muslims who saw that there was nothing to be gained from Marxist and communist ideas, Hamka conceded that some of Marx's ideas were congruent with the Islamic conception of social equality and that communism had brought some good to many societies. But the overall thrust of Marxist and communist theories, in Hamka's estimation, was problematic because these ideas were regressive and obstacles to social justice. Hamka caricatured Marxist and communist conceptions of social justice as ideologies that regarded human beings "as things, that happen to have the intelligence to breathe . . . as if they are creatures that gravitate around the economy only."[20]

It is obvious that Hamka was as censorious of Marxist and communist conceptions of justice as he was of the capitalist variant. If capitalism had brought about stark inequalities in society and never fulfilled its aims of achieving social justice through market forces, Marxism and communism had resulted in the making of dictatorships. These dictators justified autocratic rule by reasoning that communism could be realized only when human beings were conditioned and coerced to act justly toward one another. Railing against the materialist conceptions and practice of social justice, Hamka wrote,

> Before the collapse of capitalism, people felt the painful pressures of capitalists [who were] scattered everywhere, divided among themselves. But after the establishment of communism, the capitalists were gathered under one power, that is, the power of a dictatorial regime. The regime has unrestricted powers, exercising so wide an authority that it determined the lives of every individual. There is no freedom. If under capitalist rule, the laboring classes are forced to work only six hours a day, when he [the communist] is in power, there is nothing to stop him from forcing people to work 14 hours a day.[21]

---

[17] Hamka, *Revolusi Agama*, 75.

[18] Hamka, *Keadilan Sosial Dalam Islam*, 24.

[19] Rémy Madinier, *Islam and Politics in Indonesia: The Masyumi Party between Democracy and Integralism*, trans. Jeremy Desmond (Singapore: NUS Press, 2015), 31–34.

[20] Hamka, *Keadilan Sosial Dalam Islam*, 131.

[21] Ibid. Hamka was perhaps more harsh toward communism than capitalism. He wrote, "Dictatorships—which history has shown to be oft-recurring—are dependent on powerful men or men who are perceived as powerful. If Stalin dies, will there be anyone more powerful than

Hamka did not reserve his critiques for materialist conceptions of social justice alone. He rebuked Muslims who comprehended social justice in a narrow and parochial way and who maintained there was nothing to be learned from non-Muslims. This was a position taken by renowned writers such as Abul A'la Maududi. Maududi, for example, confidently asserted that "justice is the only objective of Islam," and that "there is justice in Islam only."[22] Hamka admired Muslim writers such as Maududi but saw their stances towards Western and non-Muslim thought as too contemptuous. He came closer to the Egyptian thinker Sayyid Qutb during his early years as a writer prior to joining the Islamic movement. Qutb forcefully argued that rather than rejecting, Muslims must be selective in adopting all ideas that came from the West, especially during the period of decolonization when Muslims were rebuilding their societies from the ashes of foreign rule.[23]

From Hamka's perspective and in line with his cosmopolitan reform, Western and other non-Muslim thinkers, intellectuals, organizations, and movements offered conceptions and practices of social justice that Muslims could benefit from as long as they were in keeping with the ethical guidelines provided by the Qur'an and Sunnah (words and acts of Prophet Muhammad). He gave the example of the Universal Declaration of Human Rights (UDHR), adopted in 1948 by the United Nations. Although the declaration was largely drafted by Europeans at a time when many countries were still subjected to Western colonialism and although the Europeans had not lived up to the articles in the UDHR, Hamka contended that all except articles 16 and 18 were in line with the spirit of Islam and could aid in the process of enforcing social justice in Muslim societies.[24] Hamka urged Muslims to adopt what was best from Europe and reject anything that contradicted Islam.[25]

THE ISLAMIC CONCEPTION OF JUSTICE

Hamka sought to provide an alternative between materialist and spiritualist as well as between Asian and European conceptions of social justice. To achieve this, he offered a clear definition of social justice as "doing good to others with commitment and sincerity, defending humanity, loving the homeland, upholding morality, [encouraging] charity and ensuring equal rights."[26] He added that in its most elementary form social justice involves "avoiding doing evil towards others, with the exception of protecting oneself from being harmed. Doing what is necessary to uphold the rights of other human beings, and doing what is appropriate to ensure the protection of one's

---

Stalin? Will history that repeats itself ever change, in that when powerful men are gone, their henchmen will split among themselves and become disunited, because they all vie to fill positions that their leaders have left behind? Will there be a struggle for influence? And the need for brutality and mass murder?" See Hamka, *Keadilan Sosial*, 37.

[22] Syed Abul A'Ala Maududi, *Economic System of Islam* (Lahore, Pakis.: Islamic Publications, 1984), 103.

[23] William Shepard, *Sayyid Qutb and Islamic Activism: A Translation and Critical Analysis of Social Justice in Islam* (Leiden, Neth.: Brill, 1996), 329.

[24] Hamka, *Hak Asasi Manusia dalam Islam dan Deklarasi PBB*, 281–95.

[25] Hamka, *Keadilan Sosial*, 23, and Hamka, *Ghirah dan Tantangan Terhadap Islam*, 29–32.

[26] Hamka, *Falsafah Hidup*, 256.

own rights."[27] The opposite of justice, Hamka added, is *zulm* (injustice). According to Fazlur Rahman, "All Arab philologists assure us that *zulm* in Arabic originally meant "to put something out of its proper place," so that all wrong of any kind is injustice."[28] Hamka's idea of zulm was congruent with Fazlur Rahman's. He extended this rendering of zulm to explain that the word implies darkness in the soul of human beings, which leads to a few consequences: individualism and selfishness, defending what is morally wrong, exploiting other human beings to serve one's greed, and causing disharmony and destruction to society.[29]

From this definition, Hamka argued that social justice must rest on four key concepts: khalifatullah fil'ard, amanah, shura, and maslahah. These concepts are not mere abstractions or figments. They are what could be described as practical concepts, which Hamka used to explain the pillars which social justice in Islam rests on so as "to achieve the objectives of Islam and to give the Ummah, or the Muslim community, an enlightened vision capable of eliminating uncertainty, impotence and hesitation."[30]

All expositions on social justice are defective without acknowledging that human beings are khalifatullah fil'ard, which, according to Hamka, has a scriptural basis in the Qur'an. It is found in the chapter "The Cow," verse 30, which reads, "And, when your Lord said to the angels, 'Indeed, I will make upon the earth a vicegerent,' they said, 'Will You place upon it one who causes corruption therein and sheds blood, while we declare Your praise and sanctify You?' Allah said, 'Indeed, I know that which you do not know.'" Hamka interpreted this verse as indicating that human beings are chosen as vicegerents of God on earth because they are endowed with the necessary intelligence and intellect that are not found in the rest of creation.[31] Human beings are therefore obligated to fulfill two main responsibilities: to live in accordance with divine ordinance as enshrined in the sacred sources and to devise ways to uphold human dignity and freedom in society.

The reality of life on earth, however, is that not all human beings will feel obliged to accomplish the functions of the vicegerent of God, even if they are Muslims. Human beings are often swayed by their *nafs* (desires), which inhibit their innate realization of the need to uphold justice. The task of reminding human beings of this duty lay squarely on the shoulders of the *mu'minun* (true believers of Islam). These were select group of deeply devoted Muslims who were cognizant that social justice was an amanah. When amanah was neglected, corruption in society would soon follow.[32]

Hamka's ideal types of persons who upheld social justice were the prophets. On this score, his ideas are in line with those of Ibn Qayyim, who wrote, "Justice is the supreme goal and objective of Islam. God has sent scriptures and messengers to establish justice among people . . . any path that leads to justice is an integral part

---

[27] Ibid., 289.

[28] Fazlur Rahman, *Major Themes in the Qur'an* (Chicago: University of Chicago Press, 2009), 25.

[29] Hamka, *Falsafah Hidup*, 284.

[30] Taha Jabir Al-Alwani, introduction to *Imam Al-Shatibi's Theory of the Higher Objectives and Intents of Islamic Law*, by Ahmad Raysuni (Herndon, VA: International Institute of Islamic Thought, 2006), xiii.

[31] Hamka, *Tafsir Al-Azhar*, 1:163.

[32] Hamka, *Keadilan Sosial Dalam Islam*, 10.

of the religion and can never be against it."[33] According to Hamka, devoted Muslims such as the prophets were aware of the "sacred trust, and the consciousness of gravity of the sacred trust becomes the stimulus to reform society into becoming just and prosperous. There are the teachings of Social Justice!"[34] They fulfilled the sacred trust of social justice because it was one of the means by which human beings could live together harmoniously and was a factor that would allow the message of God to be disseminated more effectively. Little wonder then that all prophets were unjustly persecuted. Their call for the restoration of justice threatened the rule of despotic rulers from the time of the pharaohs right up to the time of the prophethood of Muhammad, when the monopolistic trade practices of the Jews and Arab tribes bred injustice in society.[35]

The practical concepts of social justice did not end there. Hamka posited that shura was a linchpin in the process of creating a just society. According to Ilyas Ba-Yunus, no "sociological approach to the understanding of Islam can afford to ignore the meanings and implications of *shura,* which seems to be a dynamic process of seeking solutions to the problems of living in a plural society."[36] Hamka shared this position and felt that shura must exist at many levels for social justice to be in full operation. At the basic level, shura refers to open and respectful discussions between common people of diverse views and backgrounds—siblings, spouses, friends, and neighbors—regarding matters affecting everyday life. This is a form of shura that has minimal impact on the larger society. More decisive than that is shura in the arena of politics. Hamka expressed his contempt for all forms of autocratic, authoritarian, and tyrannical tendencies in political leadership that stifled mutual consultation among elites and between elites and the masses. Muslims should not be quietists, therefore allowing despots and tyrants to reign at the expense of the masses. Hamka termed such Muslims as people who were besieged by *jilatisme,* that is, the ailment of always wanting to lick the boots of their oppressors.[37]

Hamka encouraged Muslims to be dynamic in actualizing shura. Shura ought to be put in practice in accordance with "the developments of thought, space, and time." This is in line with the Prophetic tradition: "You know best the affairs of your worldly life."[38] One of the political systems that could enable shura to take root was democracy. Hamka encouraged Muslim scholars to embrace democracy and respect political leaders as and when they abided by democratic principles.[39] Political leaders, in turn, must consult the scholars and the masses in matters of governance and allow freedom of expression. Still, for Hamka, democracy as the West understood it was

---

[33] Ibn Qayyim al-Jawziya, *Al-Turuq al-Hukmiyya fi'l-Siyasa al-Shari'yya* (Cairo: Mua'assa al-'Arabiyya li'l-Taba'a, 1961), 16.

[34] Hamka, *Keadilan Sosial Dalam Islam,* 11.

[35] Hamka, *Khutbah Pilihan Buya HAMKA: Juma'at, Idul Fitri & Idul Adha* (Jakarta: Pustaka Panjimas, 2005), 78.

[36] Ilyas Ba-Yunus, "Ideological Dimensions of Islam: A Critical Paradigm," in *Interpreting Islam,* ed. Hastings Donnan (London: Sage, 2002), 106.

[37] Hamka, *Dari Hati Ke Hati,* 361, and Hamka, *Berkisah Nabi dan Rasul* (Kuala Lumpur: Pustaka Melayu Baru, 1982).

[38] Hamka, *Tafsir Al-Azhar,* 25:6521.

[39] Hamka, *Khutbah Iftitah Ketua Umum Majelis Ulama Indonesia* (Jakarta: Sekretariat Majelis Ulama Indonesia, 1978), 9.

Figure 4 Hamka (left) in 1931, wearing traditional Surakartan costume. Courtesy of Suara Muhammadiyah.

not shura because, in the European countries, divine laws were made subservient to secular laws. The type of democracy that came close to shura was one that acknowledged God as the supreme arbiter of human affairs and that utilized the Qur'an and the Hadith as its sources of policymaking. Hamka called it "God-conscious democracy" (*demokrasi taqwa*).[40]

Hamka's notion of a God-conscious democracy was in part a reaction against the *Demokrasi Terpimpin* (Guided Democracy) enforced by President Sukarno from 1959 till 1966. He viewed guided democracy as but a veiled form of totalitarianism. The idea of God-conscious democracy was also emblematic of the discourses of Muslim reformist thinkers during his time that theorized alternatives to Western ideas of democracy. These thinkers called for a comprehensive evaluation of the ideas of democracy as against the Islamic understanding of shura. They were divided into three camps: the rejectionists, who saw democracy as alien to the Islamic political system; the accommodationists, who viewed aspects of democracy as compatible with Islam and looked for means to marry democratic ideals with shura; and the secularists, who wholeheartedly embraced Western democracy and saw that there was no need to return to the concept of shura, or to use divine laws as the basis of the legal and political order.[41] Hamka belonged to the second group. He was optimistic about infusing the practical concept of shura into modern ideas of democracy to deliver social justice in Muslim societies. He was forthright that his idea of *demokrasi taqwa* was akin to that of a thinker in Pakistan—indirectly referring to Maududi—who had coined the term "theo-democracy" to describe a political system that was neither a theocracy nor a democracy in the Western sense but a middle way between both systems.[42] Democracy with the divine left out, Hamka wrote, would lead to greed, oppressiveness, and the chasing of positions and status among elites. The masses would be rendered helpless and exploited. For Hamka, this was the sickness that had affected Muslim societies in the modern world.[43]

The culmination of shura is the achievement of maslahah (general welfare). Hamka emphasized that not only Muslims but all human beings stood to benefit from shura. He departed from many traditional thinkers by interpreting maslahah, a concept derived from the *usul fiqh* (principles of Islamic jurisprudence), in a universalist sense. For him, the "objective of Islam is not to bring good to the lives of one group only. The objective of Islam is to bring good to the life of everyone. . . . Islam is not the property of Muslims. It is born out of God's Revelation for the goodness of all mankind."[44] Individualism is not tolerated in Islam, for all individuals must see themselves as part of the larger society and must work toward the fulfillment of public good.

The practical concept of maslahah is also important because it guides Muslims to be context-driven in their implementation of social justice. Some punishments, programs, and policies may lead to the general welfare at a given time but not in others.

---

[40] Hamka, *Keadilan Sosial Dalam Islam*, 26.

[41] Yvonne Y. Haddad and John L. Esposito, *The Islamic Revival Since 1988: A Critical Survey and Bibliography* (Westport, CT: Greenwood Press, 1997), xiii.

[42] Asma Asfaruddin, "Mawdudi's 'Theo-Democracy': How Islamic Is It Really?," *Oriente Moderno* 87, no. 2 (2007): 306, and Hamka, *Keadilan Sosial Dalam Islam*, 26.

[43] Hamka, *Pelajaran Agama Islam*, 94.

[44] Hamka, *Keadilan Sosial Dalam Islam*, 26.

Hamka gives the example of the punishment of cutting off the hands of robbers and thieves. Although prescribed in the Qur'an and a medium that could uphold social justice, such a punishment must take into consideration the general welfare of the community before it can be implemented. In times when a country is experiencing economic difficulties and when the person who is prosecuted for theft is known to be in poverty, such a ruling can be suspended in view of the wider problems affecting the community in general. Maslahah is a useful thinking and analytical tool to determine whether a stated punishment, policy, or program can indeed bring about the common good or run contrary to it.[45] Clearly, Hamka's ideas on maslahah were built on Mahmud Shaltut's discussions of maslahah in his classic *Al-Islam: Aqidah wa Syariah*. Shaltut maintained that maslahah is a useful tool for deriving, and in fact revising, age-old laws and scholarly consensus (*ijma'*) to meet the changing contexts and circumstances faced by Muslims in the modern world.[46]

THE ENABLERS OF SOCIAL JUSTICE

Taken together, the practical concepts of justice provide the ideological framework for Muslims in their pursuit of social justice. But this is barely enough, in Hamka's approximation, because conceptual discussions without action are *khayal* (stray imagination) and *angan-angan* (wishful thinking) lapsing into pointless philosophizing.[47] All theorizations and postulations about social justice must lead to some form of implementation. To implement and enforce social justice, Hamka underlined the significance of a few enablers. The first were the leaders in society and in politics. Hamka highlighted that it is natural for animals and also human beings to take on leadership when a group is formed. Drawing on the theories of Al-Farabi, who wrote the influential treatise *Al-Madinah Al-Fadilah* (The Perfect City), Hamka suggested that the end goal of all leaders should be the achievement of happiness and the regulation of uncontrolled passions among people under their care.[48]

Whether heads of families, organizations, religious collectives, political parties, or states, leaders are the determining factors for social justice to take hold. Hamka's own study of history and of Muslim societies informed him that leaders are instrumental in safeguarding social justice. Such leaders should exhibit a few key characteristics: health, knowledge, rationality, courage, forgiveness, charity, inclusiveness, patience, openness to criticisms, and honesty. "A leader," Hamka wrote in a realist mode, "is not an angel who is endowed with perfect attributes."[49] He faulted those Muslims who concentrated so hard on finding minor weaknesses in their leaders that eventually they were left with no leaders at all. These Muslims had caused backwardness in their societies. In developed societies, enlightened leaders were upheld and supported in order for social justice to reign supreme. Hamka gave some examples of outstanding leaders who had fought for the benefit of the masses, including Prophet Moses,

---

[45] Ibid., 52–60.

[46] Mahmud Shaltut, *Al-Islam: 'Aqidah wa Shari'ah* (Cairo: Dar al-Syuruq, 2001), 546.

[47] Hamka, *1001 Soal-Soal Hidup* (Djakarta: Penerbit Bulan Bintang, 1961), 83–87.

[48] Hamka, *Pandangan Hidup Muslim*, 25–26. See Muhsin Mahdi, *Alfarabi and the Foundation of Islamic Political Philosophy* (Chicago: Chicago University Press, 2001), 84.

[49] Hamka, *Pemimpin dan Pimpinan*, 10.

Iskandar Dzulkarnain, Prophet Muhammad, and Caliph Omar Abdul Aziz.[50] He contrasted them with tyrants such as Hitler, Mussolini, and Stalin.[51]

Leaders from different sectors of society form the state. Hamka saw the state as the most powerful institution that could bring about social justice because it had at its disposal the necessary resources and expertise. Hamka was not entirely clear or consistent about which state system he preferred. My own reading of his writings suggests that he was open to any state system that defended social justice. Whether a sultanate, a constitutional monarchy, or the modern state that separates the executive, legislative, and judiciary, all these states have the capacity to maintain social justice as long as the spirit of shura prevails and divine values are imbued in the state's management of its citizens. An ideal state is one that protects the sovereignty of the masses. Hamka called such states that protect the sovereignty of the masses "just states."[52]

Just states have the greatest capacity to ensure social justice because they allow citizens the freedom to think and express their concerns. Just states allow political parties to be formed, giving enough room for these parties to function and gain the support of the people. Just states ensure a proper distribution of resources while combating corruption, cronyism, and clientelism, all of which were, in Hamka's perspective, analogous to infectious diseases. Just states also put emphasis on the development of morally upright individuals.[53]

Having laid out the characteristics of just states, Hamka pointed out that colonial states embodied injustice. They were unjust states that created fissures in the Malay world by introducing new hierarchies in line with the policy of divide and rule. Colonial states aided Christian missionary activities and treated the Christian converts as the *anak mas* (golden child) while neglecting and abusing the rest of the indigenous populations. Such injustice "destabilized the relationships among the people who belong to our common ethnicity, the adherents of Christianity, Catholics and Protestants, who have been living together harmoniously."[54]

In addition to leaders, writers were also enablers of social justice. This group had the propensity to defend society and expose the excesses of states as well as other powerful institutions. Hamka rested his hopes on the intellectuals, scholars, and journalists to correct all forms of injustice through the force of their writings. He likened them to the doctors of society. The responsibility of a writer is to use one's pen "to awaken the community toward progress and civilization, defending urbanity, and vindicating purity, to the extent that one's community will be seen as equal to other communities."[55] Many states had devised schemes to silence the media and co-opt the best writers, understanding the crucial roles that these writers could play in society. The ulama and intellectuals had been the most vulnerable group of writers. They suffered under tyrannical regimes for their refusal to accept and endorse the states' unjust policies. In Indonesia, Hamka brought to the light the complicity of the ulama

---

[50] Hamka, *Lembaga Hikmat* (Kuala Lumpur: Pustaka Antara, 1967), 26–29.

[51] Hamka, *Pemimpin dan Pimpinan*, 13.

[52] Hamka, *Lembaga Hidup*, 28.

[53] Hamka, *Tafsir Al-Azhar*, 2:399.

[54] Hamka, *Cara Zending dan Missi Menyerang 'Aqidah Kita* (Kuala Lumpur: Pustaka Melayu Baru, 1979), 40.

[55] Hamka, *Lembaga Budi: Perhiasan Insan Cemerlang* (Shah Alam, Malaysia: Pustaka Dini, 2008), 137.

in supporting the exploitative policies of the Dutch colonial state and the brutality of the Sukarno regime (1945–67).[56] He held that the reason writers had succumbed to the co-option of states and eventually failed to speak on behalf of society was that they wanted to reap worldly benefits. They hid the truth to save themselves and the powers that had given them status and positions.[57] Viewed from another angle, Hamka was somewhat self-indulgent, considering that he was one of those writers who did challenge the order of things and was eventually imprisoned.

The third enabler of social justice was social movements. Hamka maintained that social movements stood midway between the powerful elites and the masses. The Muslim world, in particular, was in need of social movements because these movements could serve different purposes in the realm of social justice. Social movements could address suffering by setting up various institutions that states might not be willing to establish. They could also influence the minds of the public through their educational programs to combat propaganda. Moreover, social movements could pressure governments and also co-opt scholars and intellectuals to work hand in hand with them to realize social justice rather than to stifle it. Wherever necessary, social movements could also engage in impactful activities, or what Charles Tilly and Sidney Tarrow termed "contentious politics," to thwart oppression.[58]

Hamka gave examples of global social movements, highlighting their effectiveness in compelling states to be just and attentive to problems of discrimination and abuse. He encouraged Muslims to be cosmopolitan and learn from other non-Muslim activist such as Gandhi and his civil disobedience movement in India to reclaim social justice for Muslims and non-Muslims alike. Gandhi was, according to Hamka, but one out of many social movement leaders who represented the colonized peoples against the colonizing power of the West. Gandhi's strength lay in his composure and nonviolent approach to agitating for the restoration of human dignity. He was willing to sacrifice everything he had for the sake of other repressed human beings. However, Hamka reminded his Muslim leaders to be judicious when taking non-Muslims as their role models in issues other than achieving social justice. He cited Gandhi once again as a personality who, although worthy of praise as a mobilizer of social movements, was also someone who had deep reservations about Hindus converting to Islam.[59]

Another social movement advocating for social justice that had a prominent place in Hamka's writings was the Muslim reformist movement in Indonesia. Hamka dedicated many pages to describing the contributions of the Muhammadiyah in the struggle for equality and justice in Indonesia. A branch of Muhammadiyah that he believed necessitated a full-length study was at Minangkabau in Sumatra, Indonesia. This is understandable given that Hamka had been one of the leaders of Muhammadiyah in Sumatra since the 1930s. It was a social movement that delved into missionary work, education for all, and welfare activities, as well as social advocacy campaigns. One of the issues that it fought for was gender justice. Muhammadiyah members permitted women to take center stage in Islamic movements and allowed them to make public speeches in

---

[56] Hamka, *Tafsir Al-Azhar*, 5:1258.

[57] Hamka, *Revolusi Agama*, 45–48.

[58] Hamka, *Beberapa Tantangan terhadap Ummat Islam Dimasa Kini*, 3. See also Charles Tilly and Sidney Tarrow, *Contentious Politics* (Boulder: Paradigm Publishers, 2006).

[59] Hamka, *Ghirah dan Tantangan Terhadap Islam*, 30.

the presence of men. This was something that was considered a taboo then, even within reformist circles. After much debate and resistance, Muslim women had their way. This marked a revolutionary change in the Muslim approach toward women's involvement in public forums throughout Indonesia and in the Malay world as a whole.[60]

Finally, Hamka wrote, the common people were the most important enabler of social justice. The duty of ensuring that poverty was eradicated and that everyone was treated equally regardless of gender, status, class, or age rested on the shoulders of every human being. For Muslims in particular, social justice was an obligation (*kewajiban*) demanded of them by Islam. Hamka assigned this obligation to a few key areas of life. The first was the obligation toward oneself. After considering the ideas of European philosophers such as Jean Jacques Rousseau, Immanuel Kant, and John Stuart Mill, Hamka surmised that every human being is obligated to seek knowledge and learn ethics.[61] These were the two elements that would spur the person to contribute and be conscious of the environment around him or her without the need of laws and incentives. That being said, Hamka was nevertheless against the discourse which states that people are poor simply because they "lack personal responsibility."[62] He acknowledged that structural factors such as unjust states or abusive elites might have been the actual causes. He enjoined the people to rebel and rise against such states and elites to bring back equality and justice.[63]

After the self, Hamka argued that the next area of life that Muslims were obligated to preserve was the family because it is the smallest unit in society where social justice is put into practice. From this angle of vision, Hamka seemed to take into account what David Miller calls "modes of human relationships"—that is, how different actors in society interact and share resources and how this affects social justice.[64] Hamka saw the family as a microcosm of the state. Families that manifested social justice would inevitably shape the character of the state. In point of fact, influential families determined the fates of Muslim empires and regimes throughout Islamic history, a topic that Hamka dealt with extensively in *Sejarah Umat Islam*.[65] He held that the general texture of social justice at large was shaped by the mercy and compassion shown in families. The family is where justice begins and ends.[66]

The obligation to society comes after the family. Hamka explained that for Muslims to fulfill their obligations to society, they must begin with recognizing that Islam is a religion for humanity (*agama kemanusiaan*): "The impact and benefits [of Islam] must be felt not only by Muslims but also by mankind as a whole. The advent of Islam brought benefits and mercy to the whole world. Regardless of race or community. Muslims must respect everyone wholeheartedly, even if they are of a different faith than Islam, for religion is a matter of relationship between human beings and God."[67] The Qur'an, Hamka added, made it obligatory for Muslims to contribute to society

---

[60] Hamka, *Muhammadiyah di Minangkabau* (Jakarta: Yayasan Nurul Islam, 1974), 48–52.

[61] Hamka, *Akhlaqul Karimah* (Jakarta: Pustaka Panjimas, 1992), 99.

[62] Iris Marion Young, *Responsibility for Justice* (New York: Oxford University Press, 2011), 23.

[63] Hamka, *Keadilan Sosial Dalam Islam*, 7.

[64] David Miller, *Principles of Social Justice* (Cambridge, MA: Harvard University Press, 1999), 25–26.

[65] Hamka, *Sejarah Umat Islam*.

[66] Hamka, *Pemimpin dan Pimpinan*, 3.

[67] Hamka, *Lembaga Hidup*, 165.

in the interest of social justice as evidenced in verses on zakah and charity. Hamka rationalized that only states that were built on the foundations of the shari'a were obligated to collect the zakah. In the event that such states did not exist, then the duty was placed on ordinary Muslims to fulfill their zakah obligations. This is not the place to elaborate at length about the groups of people that are deserving of the zakah as stipulated in Islamic laws. Suffice is it to state here that Hamka viewed the zakah as a means to alleviate poverty, to level off differences in society, and as a mechanism to foster a sense of social responsibility between the haves and the have-nots.[68] Hamka's observations on zakah and charity were echoed by the doyen of Islamic studies, John Esposito, who noted,

> One of the most striking and controversial elements of the Qur'an at the time when it was revealed was its firm commitment to social justice, a significant threat to the tribal power structures in place. Rather than accepting the principle that the strongest are the most powerful, the Qur'an emphasized the responsibility of Muslims to care for and protect one another, regardless of socioeconomic status. In fact, the Qur'an repeatedly emphasizes the need to care especially for those who were outcasts under the tribal system—widows, orphans, and the poor. One way of doing this was through zakat (alms-giving), which is one of the Five Pillars of Islam. Zakat consists of giving 2.5 percent of one's total wealth annually to support the less fortunate. In addition, usury, or the collection of interest, was forbidden because it served as a means of exploiting the poor. False contracts were also denounced. The Qur'an and Sunnah (example of the Prophet) further give Muslims permission to engage in armed defense of downtrodden men, women, and children (Qur'an 4:74–76) and those who have been wronged, particularly those who have been driven out of their homes unjustly (22:39–40).[69]

True to his cosmopolitan outlook, Hamka pushed the interpretation of the Qur'an much further: zakah could be given to needy Jews and Christians after Muslims had been provided with the necessary assistance. The same applied to charity. Hamka admonished Muslims to use charity to help others in need, regardless of whether they were Muslims or non-Muslims. Such a view was radically out of the mainstream of Islamic thought in the Malay world in his time, with the exception of a select group of Muslim reformists. Hamka openly admitted that he was inspired by H. O. S. Chokroaminoto, the leader of the Sarekat Islam, who promulgated the idea of a *Bank Sedekah* (Charitable Bank).[70] Such banks were also opened in colonial Malaya in the late 1940s, providing loans and assistance to Muslims and non-Muslims.[71]

Hamka's conception of social justice bears evidence of his sensitivity toward the ideals, beliefs, and contextual realities of his time. Critical of the capitalist notions of

---

[68] Hamka, *Tafsir Al-Azhar*, 10:3000–3013.

[69] John L. Esposito, *What Everyone Needs to Know about Islam* (New York: Oxford University Press, 2002), 163.

[70] Hamka, *Keadilan Sosial Dalam Islam*, 86.

[71] Khairudin Aljunied, *Radicals: Resistance and Protest in Colonial Malaya* (Dekalb: Northern Illinois University Press, 2015), 134–35.

social justice and equally disapproving of the Marxist, communist, and socialist alternatives, Hamka utilized the sacred sources of Islam—the Qur'an and the Hadith—and ideas from Muslim and non-Muslim thinkers as bedrocks of his new rendering of social justice. For him, the Islamic conception of social justice could not be comprehensively understood without a proper explication of the practical concepts that governed how every Muslim should think. These practical concepts had been made real by Muslims of the past but neglected by the later generations, thereby accounting for their eventual decline during the modern period. The return of Islam as a force in the Malay world, in Hamka's eyes, must therefore begin with the reinstatement of social justice in the minds of Muslims.

Majid Khadduri, in a pioneering study of the Islamic conceptions of justice, argues that modern-day Muslim theorists of social justice could be divided into two opposing camps. The first was the modernist camp. They argue that social justice should be conceptualized by way of reason and through a deep understanding of the contextual needs of the people. For the modernists, there is no need to draw upon the sources of Islam for guidance and inspiration. On the contrasting side are the revivalists. They in turn underline the importance of revelation in the rethinking of social justice in the modern world. Until the 1980s, when Khadduri wrote his classic text, no synthesis between the two groups had emerged.[72]

Where did Hamka fit in between these two camps? At first glance, he seemed to be closer to the revivalists in that revelation was the starting point of his conception of social justice. But he did not reject the use of reason in the reformulation of social justice, nor did he ignore the actualities on the ground. In that sense, he shared some common ideas with the modernists. Indeed, if Khadduri had looked beyond the Arab world in his study of justice and analyzed what Malay world scholars such as Hamka had written, he would have found the amalgamation of revivalist and modernist ideas of social justice through the eyes of a local Muslim intellectual. Hamka, unlike many Arab thinkers, was able to bring together opposing conceptions of social justice because his views were not stifled by the divisions that characterized Islamic discourses of his time. He employed his pen in the cause of bridging different ideas and reinterpreting them for one purpose: cosmopolitan reform.

---

[72] Majid Khadduri, *Islamic Conception of Justice* (Baltimore: Johns Hopkins University Press, 1984), 218–19.

CHAPTER FOUR

WOMEN IN THE MALAY WORLD

The state of Muslim women was one leitmotif that pervaded Hamka's cosmopolitan reform. This does not come as a surprise given that Hamka was a child of polygamy and divorced parents. In his memoirs, he documented the painful experience of growing up deprived of the presence of a father figure who stayed with the family. The men in Hamka's society took pride in having multiple wives at different stages of their lives and divorcing them whenever they deemed it necessary or when the circumstances were not favorable for their own well-being. Hamka described himself as an outcast, disliked by his father's family and ostracized by his maternal family. The suffering that he underwent in his early life was among the chief factors that prompted him to write about the relations between men and women in the Malay world.[1]

The seismic transformations within Muslim societies across the Malay world in Hamka's time provided him with another impetus to think deeply about the struggles of women. The advent of Islamic reformism, which called for a breaking away from traditional attitudes and ways of thinking that had denied women access to formal education and schooling, yielded antithetical outcomes. On the one hand, Muslims in the Malay world slowly became receptive to allowing girls to be sent to schools established by the colonial and postcolonial governments. The flip side of this was the defensive reaction of traditionalist Muslims (also known as *kaum tua*) toward modern understandings of women's roles at home and in society. For many decades after the 1920s, they opposed Western-style schooling for girls. Women, according to them, should be nurtured to become good wives and mothers. In colonial Malaya, the British had to devise a system of fines for Malay parents who refused to send their children to school.[2] The countercurrent against allowing women to play more roles in public life was exacerbated, ironically, by some reformists. Hamka's father, for example, refused to accept women's leadership in any organizations. He and the many who followed his path were against women's delivering public speeches in the presence of men. Hamka's cosmopolitan outlook informed him that both strands of thought needed correction.[3]

Resistance against women's public participation did little to stunt the growth of Muslim women's movements and organizations in the Malay world. The first such movement, Poetri Mardika (Liberated Women), was established in Batavia in 1912. Its founder was (Mrs.) Abdoel Rahman, who received support from a male reformist organization, the Boedi Oetomo (Noble Endeavour). Members of this movement

---

[1] Hamka, *Kenang-kenangan Hidup*, 63–64.

[2] Susan Blackburn, *Women and the State in Modern Indonesia* (New York: Cambridge University Press, 2004), 47, and Aljunied, *Radicals*, 32.

[3] Hamka, *Ayahku: Riwayat Hidup Dr. H. Abdul Karim Amrullah dan Perjuangan Agama di Sumatera* (Djakarta: Djajamurni, 1967), 164.

agitated for the provision of scholarships for local girls. The organization inspired many other bodies of its kind throughout Indonesia and also Malaya; the first women's congress attended by over a thousand participants was held in December 1928 at the city of Yogyakarta.[4] Hamka was impressed by such boldness and tenacity on the part of Muslim women. He wrote a booklet titled *Religion and Women* (published in 1929), calling for the reform of women's status and questioning long-standing ideas about male dominance in Muslim societies. The book was an instant success, with several editions reprinted well beyond Hamka's lifetime.

More than a dozen other congresses were held in the decades that followed Hamka's book on the plight of women, the most prominent being in Jakarta (in 1935) and in Semarang (in 1941). Among the recurrent issues discussed were the "status and progress of women, marriage and divorce laws, child marriage, women and Islam, social work, child care, education, health, economic, and labor issues, nationalism, suffrage, and the responsibilities of women."[5] Women's activism remained uninterrupted during the Japanese Occupation (1942–45). The Indonesian revolution (1945–49) and the achievement of Indonesian independence further broadened the scope of women's involvement in public life, notably in the areas of nation building. By the late 1950s, women's organizations in Indonesia had attracted international attention for their efforts and were aggressively challenging many laws pertaining to marriage and the family that were enacted by the state.[6]

Hamka witnessed the growth of what has become known as "Islamic feminist activism" in Indonesia from the 1960s until his death in 1981. Led by the Muslimat NU and Aisyiyah, the women's wings of the Nahdatul Ulama (NU) and the Muhammadiyah, respectively, Islamic feminist activists advocated for women's rights within the framework of the shari'a. These activists employed the terms "feminism" and "activism" to refer to "activities that work to improve the condition of women and men of all classes, strive for equality between sexes and classes, and engage in Islamic discourse with the goal of empowering women, men, and the suppressed."[7]

Islamic feminist activism grew alongside various intellectual currents that were flowing into the Malay world through Europe and the Arab world, which also informed Hamka's thinking about the plight of Muslim women and the crucial roles of men in rectifying gender injustice. One of the books on gender issues that impressed him most was a novel, *La Dame aux Camélias* (*The Lady of the Camellias*), by Alexandre Dumas *fils*. Hamka translated it from Arabic into Malay with a new title, *Margaretta Gauthier*.[8] The book tells the story of a French courtesan, Margaretta, whose love for a man was hindered by the morals of society in the late nineteenth century.

---

[4] The papers and resolutions presented during this iconic congress have been published in Susan Blackburn, ed. and trans., *The First Indonesian Women's Congress of 1928* (Clayton, Aus.: Monash University Publishing, 2008).

[5] Elizabeth Martyn, *The Women's Movement in Post-colonial Indonesia: Gender and Nation in a New Democracy* (London: Routledge, 2005), 41.

[6] Nani Soewondo, "Organisasi2 Wanita dan Pekerdjaanja," *Madjalah Kedudukan Wanita Indonesia* 1, no. 1 (1959): 39–41.

[7] Pieternall van Doorn-Harder, *Women Shaping Islam: Reading the Qur'an in Indonesia* (Urbana: University of Illinois Press, 2006), 37.

[8] Alexandre Dumas *fils*, *Margaretta Gauthier*, trans. Hamka (Bukit Tinggi, Malaysia: Nusantara, 1940).

Aside from translating this book, which places the travails and tribulations of women at the center of the plot, Hamka also disseminated ideas about female emancipation that developed in Egypt. He discussed the works of thinkers such as Muhammad 'Abduh, Rashid Rida, Taha Hussayn (1889–1973), Muhammad Husayn Haikal (1888–1956), Ahmad Amin (1886–1954), and 'Abbas Mahmud 'Aqqad (1889–1964) in many of his essays and books. These Egyptian thinkers were part of the liberal Arabic movement that called for the emancipation of Muslim women in the modern age.[9] Hamka introduced them to local readers along with the ideas of Qasim Amin, whose seminal text *Taḥrir al-mar'a* (The Liberation of Women) was published in 1899. This book was read by a small group of Malays who were plugged into the Egyptian scholarly scene. It gained a wider audience within the Muslim community when Hamka began to write extensively about the importance of Qasim's proposed reforms in the remaking of Malay Islam.[10]

These overlapping contexts shaped Hamka's preoccupation with the position of Muslim women in the Malay world. This chapter examines the new intellectual pathways that Hamka crafted to address this issue. His writings on Muslim women are best described as attempts at recasting gendered paradigms that were current and prevalent during his prodigious writing career. This process involved interrogating, critiquing, reinterpreting, reenvisioning, and reconfiguring various discourses and ideas about Muslim women. By paradigms, I refer to what Thomas Kuhn has defined as "the entire constellation of beliefs, values, techniques, and so on shared by the members of a given community."[11] Gendered paradigms are thus beliefs, values, and techniques that have served to represent women's issues in partial ways. Gendered paradigms may be masculinist or feminist in orientation. The promoters of such paradigms may come from different backgrounds, including traditionalist, modernist, liberal, or fundamentalist. Hamka subjected each of these points of view to his scholarly scrutiny.

First, he questioned the inflexibility of classical and literalist Islam, the limitations of the modernist paradigm, and the approaches of proponents of an emerging group of liberal thinkers toward gender issues. Toward that end, Hamka reinterpreted Qur'anic verses as an avenue to redefine the place of Muslim women in Islam and society. Women, according to Hamka, should be honored, protected and respected as the equals of men in society. He confronted the misconceived notions of those who argued that women should not be given opportunities and rights. He also upheld the idea that the Qur'an is still relevant as a guide for modern Muslims in addressing women's issues, and this could be achieved only by embracing exegetical methods in keeping with contemporary developments in society. Hamka's exegesis of the Qur'an was therefore not only a mirror of society in his day and age, as Wan Sabri posits. It was also a lever for the cosmopolitan reform of Muslim women in the Malay world.[12]

---

[9] Albert Hourani, *Arabic Thought in a Liberal Age* (Cambridge: Cambridge University Press, 1983).

[10] Hairus Salim HS, "Indonesian Muslims and Cultural Networks," in *Heirs to World Culture*, ed. Jennifer Lindsay and Maya H. T. Liem (Leiden, Neth.: KITLV Press, 2012), 76–89.

[11] Thomas S. Kuhn, *The Structure of Scientific Revolutions* (Chicago: University of Chicago Press, 2012), 454.

[12] Wan Sabri, "Hamka's 'Tafsir al-Azhar,'" 1.

Second, Hamka reconfigured the understanding and importance of traditional Malay adat. Although he stressed that adat should still be upheld and respected and, to some extent, promoted, Hamka maintained that its preservation should not lead to the marginalization of Islamic laws and values, particularly on contentious issues such as inheritance and marriage. Adat should thus be in harmony with Islam and, at the same time, be dynamic and fluid enough to keep up with the demands of the modernizing world. To buttress his arguments, Hamka drew on *usul fiqh*, while providing sociological evidence as to why adat should be reformed for the benefit of men and women in society.

Hamka's arguments about adat were linked to the way he conceptualized the paradigm of empowerment to argue for the opening up of more spaces for women in the Malay world. He urged Malay-Muslims to permit more roles for women and allow them to participate in public affairs without threatening the fabric of the family.[13] Hamka was a strong advocate for the right of women to hold leadership positions in social movements and political parties. He supported his stand by giving historical examples of prominent women in Islam. Even though men must continue to fulfill some crucial roles in society such as serving as ritual leaders and forming the core part of the religious as well as social establishments, he held that women must also be accorded places within these frameworks so that their views and concerns were heard before the passing of any judgments and policies. However, he cautioned against mimicking hedonistic lifestyles and pursuing freedom without any moral and religious constraints, which Hamka saw as inherent in modern-day Western notions of women's empowerment.

Reinterpreting the Qur'an

Hamka's approach to women's rights was eclectic, and he sought a moderate balance between the divergent interpretations of the Qur'an. Barbara Stowasser observes that there are multiple contemporary approaches to Qur'anic exegeses on issues relating to women.[14] Such classifications could well be applied to the interpretations of Hadith (the Prophetic sayings and traditions), as argued by Jonathan Brown in his masterly survey of Hadith literature since the time of Prophet Muhammad.[15] The first was the classical and literalist approach, by which gender issues were addressed in ways that echoed medieval interpretations of the roles of women as enshrined in the shari'a. In this approach, women were regarded as the equals of men in the eyes of God but were expected to be obedient and submissive. The classical and literalist approach asserted that men had precedence over women in intellectual and leadership matters and other public duties.

Stowasser calls the second approach a "modernist" approach, a contemporary form of interpretation, which emphasizes a clear division of roles between men and women in the family and society. Modernist exegetes also highlighted the need to

---

[13] Hamka, *Ghirah dan Tantangan Terhadap Islam*, 3.

[14] Barbara Stowasser, "Gender Issues and Contemporary Qur'an Interpretation," in *Islam, Gender and Social Change*, ed. Yvonne Yazbeck Haddad and John L. Esposito (New York: Oxford University Press, 1998), 32–42.

[15] Jonathan A. C. Brown, *Hadith: Muhammad's Legacy in the Medieval and Modern World* (Oxford: Oneworld Publications, 2009).

ensure the personal protection and fair treatment of women and their access to education. The modernist approach was developed further by scholars who stresses the Qur'anic principles of equity, harmony, and social justice in laying down the rights and responsibilities of Muslim women and women in general. Mahmud Shaltut was among such scholars who, as I have discussed earlier, played a defining role in shaping Hamka's cosmopolitan thought. Egyptian by origin and internationally respected as a distinguished rector of the Al-Azhar University in Cairo, Mahmud Shaltut was at the forefront of the reformist movement in the Arab world in the early twentieth century. His writings on the modernization of Muslim societies globally influenced an emerging generation of Muslim thinkers in the Malay world.[16]

The third approach to Qur'anic exegesis radically departs from the above. Stowasser (1998) calls it the "new epistemology," promulgated by the late Fazlur Rahman (1919–88) and developed by Amina-Wadud Muhsin and Abdullah An-Na'im, among others, who argue that past interpretations of the Qur'an were obsolete because they did not adequately address the complexities of modern times. Proponents of the new epistemology thus interpret the subject of Muslim women anew and draw on the sciences of linguistics and semiotics as well as discourses of human rights to argue against the idea of male guardianship and the authority of men over women. In Indonesia, a prominent Muslim thinker who shared the same paradigm as the new epistemology group was Nurcholish Madjid, who wrote and gained prominence in the 1970s. More crucially, these approaches to the Qur'an reflect the various paradigms regarding women adhered to by different segments of the Muslim population.

Hamka criticized, first of all, the classical and literalist interpretation of the origins of women. The first woman (Eve) was regarded as an inferior derivative of the first man (Adam); thus women were by nature "crooked." This presumption was based on the overreliance of classical and literalist exegetes on the Jewish rendition of the story of Adam and Eve, which teaches that God created Eve from one of Adam's ribs. In the words of one Hadith, "Treat women kindly. Women have been created from a rib and the most bent part of the rib is the uppermost. If you try to turn it straight, you will break it. And if you leave it alone, it will remain bent as it is. So treat women kindly."[17] Hamka said that classical and literalist exegetes had misinterpreted this to support their theory of female crookedness and had for too long embraced the fallacious theory that the first woman was created from the rib of the first man to validate their societal and cultural suppositions about women.[18] This forceful assertion in a context in which creation theories about the inferiority of women in the Qur'an were predominant corresponds with more recent feminist scholarship on the subject. For example, Etin Anwar notes,

> Muslim feminists have taken the issue of the creation of humans and its implication for the making of gender inequality seriously. Hassan, who has pioneered the reinterpretation of the creation theory in Islam, considers the issue of equality in creation as "more basic and important, philosophically and theologically . . .

---

[16] Kate Zebiri, *Mahmud Shaltut and Islamic Modernism* (Oxford: Clarendon Press, 1993).

[17] M. Nashiruddin Al-Albani, *Ringkasan Shaiḥ al-Bukhari*, vol. 3, trans. Abdul Hayyie al-Kattani dan A. Ikhwani (Jakarta: Gema Insani, 2008), 442.

[18] Hamka, *Tafsir Al-Azhar*, 1:166–70.

because if men and women have been created equal by Allah who is the ultimate arbiter of value, then they cannot be unequal, essentially, at a subsequent time."[19]

Similarly, Hamka argued that there is no mention in the Qur'an of the creation of Eve from the rib of Adam and that the Hadith about creation from a rib is meant to be an analogy and not to be accepted as a literal representation. It was the Prophet's way of urging his followers to treat women with delicate care, gentleness, and kindness so as to avoid fractures, splits, and conflicts in the family.[20]

In essence, Hamka emphasized that men and women share common origins (*nafs wāḥida*). They were created as equals and are given similar acknowledgments by God as evidenced in Qur'an 4.1: "O mankind, fear your Lord, who created you from one soul and created from it its mate and dispersed from both of them many men and women." Hamka explained,

> This verse shows that the origins of human beings are but one. . . . It follows then that even though there are two kinds [of creation], male and female, the crux of the matter is that they are essentially one and the same, that is, they are human. Both men and women are similar human beings. And because of their shared origins, which are divided into two, both will naturally feel that they are in need of one another. Life will not be complete if both men and women are not reunited.[21]

Hamka registered his disagreement with classical exegetes who regarded women as intellectually inferior and prone to follow their desires rather than their intellect. He took issue with the idea pervasive among many classical exegetes that Eve was responsible for the fall of Adam, more commonly referred to as "original sin" in Judeo-Christian theology. The Qur'an, Hamka added, clearly states that both Adam and Eve were responsible for transgressing the rules set by God.[22]

Hamka's departure from the gendered approaches of classical exegetes does not necessarily imply that he was totally against that paradigm. His thirty-volume *Tafsir al-Azhar* exhibits a judicious utilization of the classical method of exegesis and new methods of interpreting the Qur'an drawn from modernist thinkers. Hamka analyzed Qur'anic verses about women through *tafsīr bi-al-ma'thur* (exegesis by way of using the Qur'an itself, the Hadith, and the sayings of the Companions) and *tafsīr bi-al-ra'y* (exegesis by way of reason).[23] He went a step further by providing his own contextualized readings of the Qur'an in order to make it congruent with the demands of the present moment. This aspect of his approach brought him closer to the modernist paradigm and the new epistemology paradigm.

Hamka's deployment of the modernist paradigm was manifested in his frequent references to Egyptian scholars such as Muhammad 'Abduh and Rashid Rida in his *Tafsir al-Azhar* and his discussions of both the prospects and the problems of modern

---

[19] Etin Anwar, *Gender and Self in Islam* (London: Routledge, 2006), 47, quoting Riffat Hassan, "Feminism and Islam," in *Feminism and World Religions*, ed. Arvind Sharma and Katherine K. Young (Albany: State University of New York Press, 1999), 258.

[20] Hamka, *Tafsir Al-Azhar*, 1:166–70.

[21] Hamka, *Kedudukan Wanita dalam Islam*, 4.

[22] Hamka, *Tafsir Al-Azhar*, 8:2333–35.

[23] Milhan Yusuf, "Hamka's Method in Interpreting Legal Verses," in *Approaches to the Qur'an in Contemporary Indonesia*, ed. Abdullah Saeed (Oxford: Oxford University Press, 2005), 42–44.

life. For instance, he cited Rashid Rida's *Tafsir al-Manar* and his interpretation of the verses about the treatment of wives. Hamka's reading of Rida's works led him to conclude that Rida gave much weight to the importance of husbands' fidelity to their wives. A good Muslim must also look beyond the weaknesses of his wife to unceasingly acknowledge her strengths and sacrifices and ensure that her needs are attended to.[24]

Rashid Rida also provided Hamka with the intellectual basis to reinterpret the roles that women can play in public life. Hamka explained that the Qur'an and the Hadiths provide many examples of women who participated in political life, social reform, and war. Many classical and contemporary Muslim thinkers have, however, suppressed this aspect of Islam to propound the idea that women should be confined to domestic roles. Scholars in the Arab world were guilty of such flawed reasoning about the roles of women. In Hamka's own assessment, some Indonesian ulama who took Rashid Rida's exegesis seriously had permitted women to participate in many social, religious, and political movements in the twentieth century, but a majority were still resistant to these ideas because of the burden of traditional interpretations of the Qur'an and their personal biases.[25]

Hamka did not speak in the language of Fazlur Rahman and his protégés but rather foreshadowed many of the exegetical approaches of the new epistemology. This accounts for the currency of his writing even now, though he died in 1981. He interlaced his interpretations with the research and findings of social scientists, which parallels the approach taken by Fazlur Rahman. His approach to selected Qur'anic verses shows some striking parallels with that of Amina Wadud, who wrote, "It was not the text [of the Qur'an] which restricted women, but the interpretations of that text which have come to be held in greater importance than the text itself."[26]

This is seen in his discussion of the chapter "Al-Isra'" (The Night Journey), verse 32, which reads, "And do not approach unlawful sexual intercourse. Indeed, it is immoral and an evil way." Instead of interpreting this verse from the perspective of laws per se and from the idea that women are the main reason why men commit illicit acts—an interpretation that is common among many classical and even modernist Qur'an interpreters—Hamka (like Fazlur Rahman) explicated the Qur'anic verses in a manner that "takes into account the conditions of the times of the revelation and those of the modern period, and thus relates the text to the needs of the community."[27] The notion that mankind should not come close to unlawful sexual intercourse, Hamka explained, is as relevant now as it was during the time of Prophet Muhammad if one takes a sociological view of modern society. Among the problems that Hamka vividly highlighted were fornication and adultery.

Hamka cited research conducted by medical practitioners such as Dr. Marion Hilliard (1902–58) of Toronto, Canada, who showed in an influential study that the modern world is rife with elements that promote fornication and adultery. Renowned for her specialization in gynecology and women's health, Hilliard advocated for the total well-being of women. She researched and wrote some informative, commonsense

---

[24] Hamka, *Tafsir Al-Azhar*, 4:1141–42.

[25] Ibid., 3:794–95.

[26] Amina Wadud, *Qur'an and Woman: Rereading the Sacred Text from a Woman's Perspective* (New York: Oxford University Press, 1999), xxi–xxii.

[27] Abdullah Saeed, *Interpreting the Qur'an: Towards a Contemporary Approach* (London: Routledge, 2006), 128.

Figure 5 Hamka with his family of eight children. Courtesy of Pusat Studi Uhamka.

articles for popular, mainstream magazines that touched on the causes of chronic diseases and mental problems among women in the 1950s. In 1957, she compiled and expanded on the articles' topics in her first book.[28] According to Hamka, Dr. Hilliard found that unmarried women who were exposed to pornographic films and intimate relationships with men were most vulnerable to becoming pregnant outside marriage. It was for this reason that the Qur'anic injunction "Do not approach unlawful sexual intercourse" was germane. Avoidance as enjoined in the Qur'an was the key to overcoming fornication and adultery and the social problems that came with them. The problem of fornication and adultery, Hamka stressed, should not be seen as a malaise rampant only in the West. It was a problem that affected Muslims and non-Muslims alike globally:

> Thinking about life in the modern world makes us shiver. The elements that encourage fornication and adultery are made available everywhere. Uncensored films, pornographic magazines and books, and, more recently, free mixing has become more noticeable. In this land of ours, we used to say that the West is decadent, but of late, marrying off girls who became pregnant out of wedlock in

---

[28] Marion Hilliard, *A Woman Doctor Looks at Love and Life* (New York: Doubleday, 1957), and Marion Hilliard, *Women and Fatigue: A Woman Doctor's Answer* (New York: Doubleday, 1960). For more information on Hilliard, see *The Canadian Encyclopedia*, accessed August 1, 2015, http://www.thecanadianencyclopedia.ca/en/article/anna-marion-hilliard.

order to conceal the shame that comes with it has become commonplace in our society. Anyone brave enough to highlight such issues [in our society] for fear of the effects on future generations will be laughed at. But the truth is that the European and American societies no longer conceal such matters. They look at the issue from the perspective of societal effects and the destructive implications as evidenced in the work of the lady doctor from Toronto, Canada.[29]

In sum, Hamka's approach to the Qur'an was a creative melding and filtering of the different approaches that had become paradigmatic in his context. In dealing with the question of Muslim women from the vantage point of sacred scriptures in Islam, he demonstrated the dire need for Muslims to incorporate and appreciate varying interpretations, or as Abdullah Saeed has put it, to adopt an inclusive, sociological, and up-to-date approach to the Qur'an without compromising the basic precepts and values of Islam.[30] Hamka adopted such an approach because he wanted Muslims to arrive at a more nuanced understanding of the high status that women occupy in God's word, and, more important, the various functions that women can play in both the private and public spheres.

Reconfiguring Adat and Its Relationship with Islam

The tensions between adat and Islam lay at the center of the debate about the role of Muslim women in the Malay world. Wazir Jahan Karim observed that adat and Islam are the two main components of Malay culture that "serve to provide contradictory and conflicting statements of gender relations, particularly in areas of ritual, economic and political activity."[31] Hamka was confronted with these contradictions and conflicts. He was situated in a context in which adat and Islam had become reified and rigidified. This was the upshot of the many decades of colonialism and the colonial policy of systematizing and codifying Malay social systems. The wars between adat chiefs and Islamic reformers coupled with the forces of Islamic reformism and secularization in the Malay world in general and in Minangkabau in particular all contributed to the dichotomization and dilution of adat and Islamic practices.[32]

Hamka criticized those who placed adat above Islam. Although he himself was regarded by Muslims in the Malay world as an expert on matters pertaining to adat, as is evidenced in the illustrious title conferred on him by members of his village community—Datuk Indomo—he took to task the defenders of a regressive form of adat in his home region of Minangkabau and also in Negri Sembilan, where the same adat practices were enforced.[33] Hamka would probably have agreed with the conclusions of the Minangkabau anthropologist Peggy Sanday that adat had grown to be "a hegemonic ideology . . . which legitimizes and structures political and ceremonial

---

[29] Hamka, *Tafsir Al-Azhar*, 15:4049.

[30] Saeed, *Interpreting the Qur'an*, 63.

[31] Wazir Jahan Karim, *Women and Culture: Between Malay Adat and Islam* (Boulder: Westview Press 1992), 7.

[32] Hadler, *Muslims and Matriarchs*, 117–80.

[33] Hamka, *Adat Minangkabau Menghadapi Revolusi* (Djakarta: Firma Tekad, 1963), 73.

life in the villages."[34] He was thus scathingly critical of uncontrolled polygamy, the high frequency of divorce, and the lack of responsibilities given to men in that society. These prevailing practices, which were upheld and sustained by both men and women, had, in Hamka's analysis, proven to be detrimental to Muslim women. He used the character Shamsiar in his short story "Angkatan Baru" (New Generation) to highlight how polygamy in Minangkabau became a sort of hobby for the rich. "If there were already three, it has to be perfected by four" (wives in total).[35] In another place, Hamka wrote,

> It is clear then that polygamy as it is practiced in Minangkabau is not as Islam has outlined, because in Islam, men are supposed to be the heads of their families, as husbands and fathers, but the practice of polygamy in Minangkabau has it that the father is from a different tribe than his own son. Divorce happens easily, because even though there are children aplenty, these children are usually closer to their mothers than their fathers. When Islam came, the people of Minangkabau selected aspects of Islam to strengthen their adat. In the event that it is stipulated that property should be handed down to the children, the *ahli adat* [experts of adat] will insist that the child has no rights whatsoever according to *adat Perpatih* [customary laws of Minangkabau].[36]

At the other end of the debates about the place of Muslim women within adat and Islam were the Muslim puritans. This group agitated for a radical transformation of adat to give way to the enforcement of the shari'a. The Muslim puritans called for an end to matrilineal and matrilocal customs, which, to them, were residues of pre-Islamic practices in Malay society. They were concerned, as Hamka acutely observed, "with the rediscovery of the Islamic spirit" rather than with blind obedience to customs and traditional laws.[37] There were a select few among these puritans who were impatient with the slow rate of change in society and therefore migrated away from Minangkabau. Hamka cited the cases of Syeikh Ahmad Khatib and Syeikh Tahir Jalaluddin, who left their homes and died in self-imposed exile because they could not accept the culture of pre-Islamic ignorance (*adat jahiliyyah*) that had plagued Minangkabau for too long.[38]

Hamka began his writing career on the side of the Muslim puritans but changed his own viewpoints as he encountered fierce resistance from the adat groups and as he delved more deeply into writings on Islam and its relationship to local customs.[39] From the early 1940s onward, Hamka occupies a third space between adat and Islamic groups on the path to recast both paradigms. On the road to reconcile adat and Islam, he reconceptualized the term *adat*, defining it as habitual practices (*kebiasaan*) developed

---

[34] Peggy Reeves Sanday, "Androcentric and Matrifocal Gender Representations in Minangkabau Ideology," in *Beyond the Second Sex: New Directions in the Anthropology of Gender*, ed. P. R. Sanday and R. G. Goodenough (Philadelphia: University of Pennsylvania Press, 1990), 146.

[35] Hamka, *Angkatan Baru* (Selangor, Malaysia: Pustaka Dini, 2007), 67.

[36] Hamka, *Adat Minangkabau menghadapi Revolusi*, 35.

[37] Taufik Abdullah, "Adat and Islam: An Examination of Conflict in Minangkabau," *Indonesia* 2 (1966): 22.

[38] Hamka, *Adat Minangkabau menghadapi Revolusi*, 37.

[39] Wan Sabri, "Hamka's 'Tafsir Al-Azhar,'" 157.

through the passage of time. Adat shaped the codes of conduct, mannerisms, values, rights, and responsibilities of those who adhered to it, but it was not fixed or cast in stone. It was dynamic, adaptive, and responsive to changing times. Hamka maintained that there was no such thing as a pure form of adat. The Malay adat, which included the Minangkabau adat, was a hybrid product of the synthesis between local practices and customs that came from other societies. It was the outcome of interactions between the indigenous ways of life and the processes of religious conversion, as well as of encounters with modernity.[40]

Some aspects of adat should therefore be recast, while others should be carefully preserved in order to strengthen the Malay-Islamic identity. Hamka insisted that uncontrolled polygamy and divorce should be stopped and that men should fulfill their responsibilities to their families. He was strongly opposed to the practice of polygamy except in rare circumstances. Islam, Hamka contended, allowed polygamy only when a man was able to uphold justice and equality for all his wives in terms of love, respect, and basic necessities. This requirement in itself was difficult, if not impossible, to fulfill, and so most men should be monogamous. In one instance, Hamka stressed, "And we can surmise that monogamy is the best and most ideal practice. Indeed that is our ultimate goal."[41]

Hamka also expressed his disapproval of the rules of inheritance as specified by the Minangkabau adat, and he subscribed to the view that men's share should be twice that of women when it came to the disbursement of wealth. He explained that this provision had little to do with men's being intellectually superior to women, as most classical and literalist Muslim scholars would argue. In Hamka's view, both men and women shared the same intellectual capacities, and they should complement each other to bring about harmonious family life and proper management of wealth and other affairs. As to why Islam stipulated that men's share should be twice that of women, he clarified that this clearly showed that men were responsible for their women, including their mothers, sisters, and wives. The greater amount of inheritance given to men must be utilized not for themselves but for the welfare of those under their care.[42] The traditionalists who disagreed with Hamka's stance contended it was not the rules of inheritance or, for that matter, adat that needed to be changed. What needed to be changed was the manner in which Islamic laws were understood vis-à-vis the adat. For them, the local customs and cultures were important primary sources to be taken into consideration in any scholar's attempt to derive Islamic laws. In some instances, as Taufik Abdullah has shown, some traditionalists argued that local customs could override the codified Islamic law to meet the exigencies of the Minangkabau context.[43]

It is obvious that Hamka's main preoccupation was to ensure that adat was congruent with the codified Islamic law. In the event of conflict between the two, he encouraged scholars and adat chiefs to engage in dialogue so as to guarantee the continued protection of both aspects of Minangkabau society. The process of reforming adat and the preponderant paradigms linked to it, Hamka contended, should be carried out as quickly as possible. For him, many aspects of adat were akin to what

---

[40] Hamka, *1001 Soal-soal Hidup*, 52–58, and Hamka, *Pribadi*, 112.

[41] Hamka, *Tafsir Al-Azhar*, 4:1072.

[42] Ibid., 1116–17.

[43] Taufik Abdullah, "Adat and Islam," 22.

he termed *batu sudah berlumut* (stones covered with moss), which should be kept in museums to inform people of what the society was like before. If these practices were not stopped and changed, many youths would leave Minangkabau in search of new places where they would find a just balance between Islam and adat.[44]

Hamka's nuanced approach toward polygamy was extended to adat in that he did not call for a total obliteration of local customs and cultures. As he put it, "Taking this standpoint does not necessitate the complete removal of adat, and adat cannot possibly be removed, but it will undergo change and transformations. If adat does not follow this course, then we cannot term it as such."[45] To hasten the process of transforming adat and harmonizing it with Islam without doing away with either one of these elements in Malay society, Hamka opined that the government should flex its legislative muscle. It was the duty of the Indonesian government, Hamka argued, to bring order and restrict the practice of polygamy and customary practices. It is here that we see the legalist element in Hamka's thinking. This was partly a byproduct of his upbringing within a family of reformist scholars and his position as a government official from the 1950s onward. Hamka saw the use of laws as effective tools to change the conditions of Muslim societies.

ON THE EMPOWERMENT OF MUSLIM WOMEN

One of the major transformations that Muslims in the Malay world were confronted with in the early twentieth century was the coming into prominence of new discourses regarding women's empowerment. The spread of ideas from Egypt and Europe into Southeast Asia and the publication of novels such as *Ḥikāyat Farīdah Hānum* (the Story of Faridah Hanum, 1925) by the reformist thinker Syed Shaikh al-Hadi brought to public attention the notion of women's empowerment during the pre–World War II period, when Hamka become a public figure.[46] By the eve of Hamka's demise in 1981, Malaysian women were already collaborating with other Muslim and non-Muslim female activists in the Malay world to address problems of domestic violence and unfair treatment at home and in the workplace by setting up crisis centers and help lines.[47]

Hamka reacted to these emerging paradigms about women's empowerment in three ways. First, he argued that such calls were already embedded in the Islamic tradition. Hamka also sought to contextualize the ideas of empowering Muslim women by urging men not to trivialize women's choices in life. Above all, he questioned Western notions of women's empowerment, which he believed could prove to be detrimental to Muslims if such ideas and practices were not filtered to fit in with the cultures and beliefs of Muslims in the Malay world.

Hamka stressed that the empowerment of women was one of the cornerstones of the Islamic tradition. It was embedded in the Qur'an, the Hadith, and many other classical texts through narratives about the contributions of women in the making of

---

[44] Hamka, *Adat Minangkabau menghadapi Revolusi*, 62.

[45] Ibid., 96.

[46] Virginia Hooker, *Writing a New Society: Social Change through the Novel in Malay* (Honolulu: University of Hawai'i Press, 2000), 26.

[47] Maila Stivens, "(Re)framing Women's Rights Claims in Malaysia," in *Malaysia: Islam, Society and Politics*, ed. Virginia Hooker and Noraini Othman (Singapore: ISEAS Press, 2003), 126–47.

human civilization and the shaping of Islam. The stories of the Queen of Sheba, the pharaoh's wife, Mary the mother of Jesus, and the noble women during the time of the prophet Joseph that had been read and studied by Muslims for over a millennium were proofs of Islam's acknowledgment of the critical roles that women had played in politics and in many areas of social life. In fact, the first converts and martyrs in Islam were women. In Islam, Hamka asserted, women are akin to "the pillars of the nation. If the women are good, the nation will be good, and if they are decadent, so shall be the nation. . . . This is a clear guidance from the al-Qur'an."[48]

By arguing in this way, Hamka was setting the perimeters of any discussions about women's empowerment within the framework of Islam. He urged his readers to think through the notion of women's empowerment in the light of the sacred Islamic scriptures first, before consulting other sources. Hamka therefore obliquely undercut a dominant idea in his time that the idea of women's empowerment was a modern phenomenon in Islamic societies. This was a mistaken view, according to Hamka. Islam had acknowledged women's rights to inheritance and property long before the coming of modernity.[49] The implication of such an argument was that Muslim women did not necessarily need modern values in order to be empowered. Rather, Muslim societies as a whole must return to the spirit of the Qur'an, the Hadith, and the best practices of the early generations of Muslims in order to realize the fair and just treatment of Muslim women.

Hamka readily admitted that modernity posed many challenges to Muslim women in the Malay world. It dictated a rethinking of standard views about the noble place that women occupy in the sacred sources of Islam. It was for this reason that Hamka sought to provide a more contextualized view of what women's empowerment was all about, aside from citing idealized examples found in Islam. He stressed the need to respect women's personal choices and preferences. No woman should be stopped from pursuing formal education. No woman should be coerced into marrying someone she did not approve of or consider appropriate. No woman should be forced to obey her husband in situations where her rights were transgressed.[50] Hamka advocated women's involvement in civil society and encouraged them to take up leadership positions in public institutions, social movements, and political parties in order to safeguard their rights. On this score, he differed significantly from other influential thinkers in his time, including the late Sayyid Qutb, an Egyptian intellectual whom Hamka personally admired. Qutb promoted the opinion that the modern world was unkind to women and that women should therefore focus on their roles as wives and mothers and not as social activists and public figures in order to reform society.[51]

The issue of women's taking up leadership roles has probably been one of the most contentious questions in the Malay world, especially in the 1930s. Even Muslim reformers such as Hamka's own father, Haji Abdul Karim, had reservations about women's leadership in the public sphere.[52] Hamka differed from his own father on

---

[48] Hamka, *Kedudukan Wanita Dalam Islam*, 15.

[49] Ibid., 111.

[50] Ibid., 23.

[51] Lamia Rustum Shehadeh, *The Idea of Women under Fundamentalist Islam* (Gainesville: University of Florida Press, 2003), 74.

[52] Hamka, *Ayahku*, 164.

this issue. He provided examples of women in Islamic history who had become rulers in the medieval Arab world and the Malay world. The Queens of Aceh, whose reigns were supported by the ulama, buttressed this point.[53] These examples clearly showed that Islam did not prohibit women from becoming leaders, even at the highest levels. What was more crucial was for women to demonstrate the ability to uphold justice and equality. They should also exhibit the necessary intelligence to govern and the wisdom to lead and should be advised and backed by experts "who are willing to provide useful and constructive ideas to the women leading them."[54]

While Hamka was adamant in his outspoken advocacy for the empowerment of Muslim women, he was careful about giving his all-out intellectual endorsement to the feminist movement of his own day and age. Feminism should be supported only because it was one of the avenues by which women's issues could be aired and advocated. The problem, in Hamka's appreciation, lay in selected strands within modern-day secular feminism, which propagated the secularization of Muslim societies and gender relations.[55] This brand of feminism assumed that men and women were in constant tension with one another and that the empowerment of women began and ended with the liberation of women from local customs that were regarded as unjust. Hamka's views on secular feminism parallel the later view of Ahmed Souaiaia, who noted that "some self-proclaimed feminists see their success in promoting women's rights to be contingent on framing the movement in the secular and liberal discourses. It is argued that only in the secular framework could Muslim women achieve their goals. Clearly, this is a direct response to some Muslim women who are working within the Islamic system to reform it."[56] In contrast, Hamka posited that any form of feminism should be grounded in the experiences and traditions of Muslims in the Malay world. Muslim men and women were equal partners in relationships and complemented each other. The individuality of Muslim women was clearly seen in that they used their own surnames rather than their husbands' surnames and asserted their rights when necessary. "The modern women," Hamka wrote, "should not be overly worried. Islam does not enjoin anyone to prostrate to other than God."[57] In other words, the problem, in his view, did not lie in feminism or in feminist aspirations per se but rather, in the sort of feminism that was imperialistic and imposed its ideals on Muslim women.

Moreover, respecting feminist aspirations did not mean that all codes of Muslim conduct must also be thoroughly changed. Hamka highlighted the issue of free interaction between men and women as a consequence of modernity and ultraliberal feminism. Traditionally, men and women in Malay society were always careful about how they conversed with each other. Women were, of course, allowed to speak to men but usually in public areas or in the presence of their family members. The coming of

---

[53] Hamka, *Tafsir Al-Azhar*, 4:1041. An excellent study of the prominent roles that women played in shaping Southeast Asian Muslim societies is found in Barbara Andaya, *The Flaming Womb: Repositioning Women in Early Modern Southeast Asia* (Honolulu: University of Hawai'i Press, 2006).

[54] Hamka, *Pemimpin dan Pimpinan*, 3–4.

[55] Hamka, *Umat Islam menghadapi tantangan Kristenisasi dan Sekularisasi* (Jakarta: Pustaka Panjimas, 2003), 76.

[56] Ahmed Souaiaia, *Contesting Justice: Women, Islam, Law and Society* (Albany: State University of New York Press, 2008), 90.

[57] Hamka, *Kedudukan Wanita Dalam Islam*, 23.

modernity had changed all this. Hamka lamented: *"Pergaulan sopan* [decent socializa-tion] is slowly fading away. The influence of Western norms and their impact on old ways of interacting are most felt by the young women."[58]

The Westernization of Malay society, especially of Malay women during the 1960s, occupied a substantial part of Hamka's thinking and writing. As mentioned above, he did not regard everything Western as bad and decadent. He actually admired the intel-lectual and scientific culture that was visible in Western society.[59] He was, however, critical of the capitalist project and the unbridled materialism that it had fostered among Muslims. These developments contributed to the dilution of Islamic norms and moral codes, which in turn resulted in the breakdown of families, the loss of a sense of honor and shame, and the loss of the sense of respect toward one's own body.

> How can women ever be attentive in protecting their honor and harmony in their families when the modes of women's clothing [*mode pakaian wanita*] are deter-mined by the textile capitalists, who are always seeking to introduce new and updated styles and that which is always strange, changing each and every time, to the point that clothes have to change even before they are frequently used because the fashions have changed?[60]

Hamka's recasting of the paradigm about women's empowerment was therefore nei-ther a total acceptance nor a total rejection of secular modernity and feminism. It was reflective of his cosmopolitan reform in that he drew from what was best from the different cultural traditions and intellectual currents. To be empowered as a Muslim woman was to be deeply aware of the Islamic notions of empowerment, to use moder-nity as a tool to realize such notions, and to appropriate feminism within the ambit of local traditions on the road to overcoming the gendered paradigms advocated by various groups in society.

Hamka's writings about Muslim women in the Malay world have gained so much traction in the region that he has been described as providing the germ of inspiration for many studies of women's rights and gender justice.[61] I would go even further to argue that Hamka was a male Islamic feminist who sought to probe the question of Muslim women in the Malay world by interrogating the various gendered paradigms. I use the term "male Islamic feminist" to describe him because he was indeed *doing* Islamic feminism in the manner that Margot Badran has explained as the articulation of "socially just Islam rooted in a Qur'anic ethos." Badran elaborates further that Islamic feminism "aims to recuperate the idea of the *ummah* as shared space—shared by women and men equally—and as a pluralistic global community. Islamic feminism transcends dichotomies of East-West, public-private, and secular-religious. It is in opposition to divide and rule, divide and contain, or divide and discipline, which are

---

[58] Hamka, *Ghirah dan Tantangan Terhadap Islam*, 3.

[59] Hamka, *Empat Bulan di Amerika*, 1:39–40.

[60] Hamka, *Iman dan Amal Soleh*, 84.

[61] Nina Nurmila, "Feminist Interpretation of the Qur'an," *Journal of Qur'an and Hadith Studies* 2, no. 2 (2013): 155–66.

hegemonic tactics and not an expression of the Qur'anic message."[62] Hamka's critique of gendered paradigms and his offering of alternative views about women are clearly reflected in Badran's definition of Islamic feminism.

As an Islamic feminist rooted within the reformist tradition of Islam, Hamka questioned and recast various exegetical approaches to verses in the Qur'an that depicted women as inferior and second to man. In contrast, he showed that the Qur'an and other sacred scriptures of Islam endorsed the equality of men and women and their shared functions and roles in the making and reconstructing of Islamic societies. Hamka also sought to make the adat pertaining to women in his society more congruent with Islamic ideals while arguing for women's empowerment in the light of an Islamic worldview. This multifaceted project of recasting gendered paradigms and reconstructing the understanding of the place of Muslim women in society places Hamka on the same plane as renowned Islamic thinkers in Egypt, to whom he owed intellectual debts and whose spirit of advocacy for the reformation of the state of Muslim women expanded their fame in their country. In using his erudite pen to expose the effects of masculinist religiosity, highlight the problems that came with local cultures, and air the disenfranchisement of Muslim women as they encountered modernity, Hamka provided Malay-Muslims with tools to reflect on and rethink the issues relating to gender relations, and more specifically, to the empowerment of women. Indeed, he was a prominent male advocate of women's rights and gender equality in the Malay world.

---

[62] Margot Badran, *Feminism in Islam: Secular and Religious Convergences* (Oxford: Oneworld Publications, 2009), 323.

CHAPTER FIVE

RESTORING SUFISM IN THE MODERN AGE

No discussion of Hamka's cosmopolitan reform is complete without considering his deep engagement with the mystical dimensions of Islam—Sufism. As a cosmopolitan thinker, Hamka was firmly opposed to hard-line approaches to Sufi thought, doctrines, and followers. He saw how his contemporaries' harshness and severity toward Sufism had earned them a long list of epithets from traditionalists, including *kafirun* (disbelievers), *sesat lagi menyesatkan* (led astray and leading others astray), *mu'tazilah* (extreme rationalist), and *zindiq* (heretic). Hamka regarded these bitter attacks on Sufism as an exercise in futility because they had placed the very people whom they were seeking to reform on a defensive path of resistance.[1] At the same time, Hamka was aware that corrupted versions of Sufism could do much harm to Islam and Muslims. Rather than siding with the anti-Sufi reformists and modernists on one side of the religious divide or with the Sufis and traditioalists on the opposing side, Hamka sought to reconcile them. He wanted to build a conduit between the Sufis and the anti-Sufis, one based on what he termed "restoring Sufism" (*mengembalikan tasauf ke pangkalnya*). He believed that this could be accomplished by questioning the inherited understandings of Islamic mysticism and the ways in which it had been practiced for many centuries.

There were several distinct but closely interrelated aspects of Hamka's effort to restore Sufism. First, he sought to clarify the origins of Sufism, emphasizing its historical role as a fundamental aspect of Islam by linking it to the time of the Prophet Muhammad. Sufism, from such a perspective, was not an innovation of later generations. It began with the Prophet himself and ought to be conceptualized as part of the Prophetic tradition (instead of being treated as a posterior development). Linked to this historical perspective was his delineation, in clear terms, of what Sufism was and was not. He outlined the actual objectives of Sufism and explained, via philosophical and cultural currents, those un-Islamic or "foreign" elements that had been accepted into the tradition. At the same time, Hamka documented the positive contributions of Sufism. He showed the multifarious achievements of Sufis in the global venture of Islam and the multiple roles that they played in Muslim societies. Hamka's third approach in restoring Sufism was to encourage Sufis to regain their historical dynamism by reinterpreting some key concepts in Sufi cosmology and ridding Sufism of superstition and irrationality. He urged Sufis and, by implication, ordinary Muslims in the Malay world to adapt to the demands of the modern world, admonishing them and their interlocutors to focus on and emphasize the positive aspects of spirituality in the lives of Muslims. "Indeed," Hamka emphasized, "true Sufism does not enjoin the fleeing of man from the realities of life. True Sufism serves as a guide for one to confront

---

[1] Hamka, *Ayahku*, 106.

the challenges of life. True Sufism does not encourage the flight to forests other than to immerse in the heart of society. Because the society needs spiritual guidance."[2]

Hamka's intellectual position, straddling and balancing between opposing views and proclivities, has earned him hybrid descriptions, such as a "pioneer of neo-Sufism in Indonesia," "a mystical teacher," "a Sufi without tariqah," "a cryptic Sufi," "Salafist Sufi," "*Sufi sederhana*" (moderate Sufi) and "*Sufi berakal*" (rational Sufi), and a contributor "to the process of rehabilitation for the mystical path in Indonesian Islam."[3] These descriptions confirm the place that Hamka has carved for himself in popularizing modernized notions of Sufism. And yet previous studies on Hamka and Sufism suffer from one weakness—that is, they limit the reach of Hamka's visions of Sufism to the Indonesian context per se and exclude the modern Malay world (which includes Singapore, Malaysia, Brunei, Indonesia, South Thailand, and South Philippines).

A close reading of Hamka's works shows that not only was he concerned with the well-being of Indonesians or Indonesian Sufism, but he was seeking to restore Sufism as it was practiced by Malays in general—a group that constitutes one of the largest Muslim populations in the world.[4] In *Sejarah Umat Islam*, part of which was first published in Singapore in 1950, Hamka registered the dialogues among local Muslim scholars in the Malay world regarding *hal ilmu tasawwuf* (developments in the knowledge of Sufism) and pointed to the need for Sufism to be analyzed from the perspective of connections and interactions within the region and the Muslim world in general.[5] As a result of his broad approach to issues affecting the Malays, Islam, and Sufism, as early as the 1930s Hamka's writings had begun circulating outside Indonesia into various parts of the Malay world, particularly in the Malay Peninsula and Singapore. *Pedoman Masyarakat*, a magazine that Hamka edited and contributed actively to in the years between 1936 and 1942 (on the eve of the Second World War in Asia), was read by students at the Sultan Idris Training College (SITC) in Perak.[6]

More crucially, Hamka sought to transcend ideological boundaries between reformists and modernists on the one hand and Sufis on the other. He achieved this in a few ways. First, he defined Sufism differently than did other Muslim scholars. Second, he outlined the parameters of Sufism in ways that unsettled the conceptions of dissenters and defenders of Sufism and reasserted the place of Sufism in modern society. Above all, Hamka showed that Sufism had been and could still be a constructive force in the remaking of Muslim societies in the Malay world. In developing these ideas, Hamka positioned himself between Sufi and anti-Sufi thoughts of his time,

---

[2] Hamka, *Pandangan Hidup Muslim*, 56.

[3] See Karel Steenbrink, "Hamka (1908–1981): A Mystical Teacher as Political Leader of Islam in Indonesia" (unpublished paper presented at IAIN [Institut Agama Islam Negeri], Syarif Hidayatullah, Indonesia, 1982); Nurcholish Madjid, *Dialog Keterbukaan: Artikulasi Nilai Islam dalam Wacana Sosial Politik Kontemporer* (Jakarta: Paramadina, 1998), 320; Azyumardi Azra, *Menuju Masyarakat Madani: Gagasan, Fakta dan Tantangan* (Bandung, Indonesia: Remaja Rosadakarya, 1999), 103; Peter Riddell, *Islam and the Malay-Indonesian World: Transmission and Responses* (Honolulu: University of Hawai'i Press, 2001), 264; and Julia D. Howell, "Indonesia's Salafist Sufis," *Modern Asian Studies* 44, no. 5 (2010): 1032.

[4] "Mapping the Global Muslim Population," Pew Research Center, accessed February 17, 2015, http://www.pewforum.org/2009/10/07/mapping-the-global-muslim-population.

[5] Hamka, *Sejarah Umat Islam*, 729.

[6] Byungkuk Soh, "Ideals without Heat: Indonesia Raya and the Struggle for Independence in Malaya, 1920–1948," *Wacana: Jurnal Ilmu Pengetahuan Budaya* 7, no. 1 (2005): 5.

problematizing both positions and articulating his own visions of what Sufism was and ought to be. It is for this reason that Hamka's cosmopolitan approach to Sufism demands our attention and may be compared to attempts by Muslim thinkers around the world who sought to close the ideological gulf between Sufis and anti-Sufis.

ON THE ORIGINS OF SUFISM

When did Sufism begin? There have been protracted debates among scholars over this question. Hamka was well acquainted with various interpretations when he began writing about Sufism in the 1930s. His method of establishing the true origins of Sufism was to use what Emile Durkheim has termed "the argument by elimination."[7] Hamka systematically rejected all possible alternative explanations to establish his own rendering of how, when, and why Sufism had come into being. He directed his initial criticisms against the European Orientalists and, in consequence, also against the Muslim reformists and modernists who claimed that Sufism was a byproduct of the Persian, Hindu, Christian, and Greek philosophical traditions rather than a product of Islam itself. Hamka regarded Max Horten (1874–1945), Edgard Blochet (1870–1937), Louis Massignon (1883–1962), Ignac Goldziher (1850–1921), De Lacy O'Leary (1872–1957), Theodor Noldeke (1836–1930), R. A. Nicholson (1868–1945), and Edward Browne (1862–1926) as some of the scholars who had popularized this interpretation to the point that Muslims themselves had accepted it as authoritative.[8]

Hamka eliminated the Orientalists' postulations systematically. The Orientalists had committed a few fallacies that led to spurious conclusions about Sufism. They were overly reliant on the writings of selected Muslim scholars who drew connections between Sufism and other spiritual and philosophical traditions. Hamka gave the example of the theory of the Hindu origins of Sufism. Proponents of this theory were influenced by the writings of Al-Biruni, who compared Indian and Islamic spiritual practices in his ethnographic work. From this, the Orientalists concluded that Sufism must have originated from Hinduism. But, Hamka pointed out, Al-Biruni was writing in the eleventh century, while Sufism existed many hundreds of years prior to that era. Moreover, there was no clear-cut evidence pointing to the use of Sanskrit or any Indian loanwords whatsoever within many early Sufistic writings and sayings.[9] Arguing in the same vein as Hamka, Francesco Alfonso Leccese states that the Orientalists' tracing of the origins of Sufism back to Hindu monasticism and asceticism was born out of their perception of Sufism as a "universal spiritual doctrine." That is to say, they negated the predominant assumption among many Muslim scholars that Sufism was a distinct form of spirituality that originated from the Islamic tradition and not elsewhere.[10]

The second fallacious theory assumed that Sufism emerged out of a creative borrowing from earlier beliefs. This strand of reasoning was premised on the assumption

---

[7] Émile Durkheim, *Rules of Sociological Method* (New York: Free Press, 1982), 78.

[8] Hamka, *Tasauf: Perkembangan dan Pemurniannya*, 48.

[9] Ibid., 56.

[10] Francesco Alfonso Leccese, "Islam, Sufism, and the Postmodern in the Religious Melting Pot," in *Routledge Handbook of Islam in the West*, ed. Roberto Tottoli (London: Routledge, 2015), 441.

that Muslims were too "primitive" to be able to devise their own spiritual philoso-phies.[11] Hamka faulted the Orientalists for asserting that Sufism must have drawn its inspiration from the mystical beliefs that were already present in Christianity, a religion that was popular among a large segment of the Arabs before the coming of Prophet Muhammad. To counter this, he explained that early Muslims had acknowl-edged both Christians and Jews as "People of the Book" who were given revelations by the One True God. However, spiritual practices within Islam differed from the practices of these religions, and Sufis relied on the Qur'an and the Hadith rather than Christian or Jewish texts. Hamka further problematized the Orientalists' hypothesis that the wearing of wool by Sufis provided clear evidence of Sufism's Christian alle-giances. This supposition was untenable to him because woolen clothes were worn by most desert Arabs in the classical period. Wearing such clothes had little to do with Sufis' treading the paths of the Christian mystics.[12] Hamka's reasoning predated Nile Green's assertion that "even if Muslim ascetics did copy the style of Christian ascet-ics, this does not necessarily point toward a Christian 'origin' for the Sufis, because far from being the direct heirs of the ascetics, the Sufis may be better understood as their rivals and critics."[13]

Finally, Hamka criticized the Orientalist theory that Sufism developed from the fusion of Muslim and Greek thought. He conceded that Greek thinkers such as Socrates (470–399 BC), Plato, and Aristotle (384–322 BC) did have a defining impact on Muslim thinkers during the Umayyad period and thereafter. But the influence of Hellenism on Muslim thinkers was not evident during the time of the Prophet, nor could the origins of Sufism be attributed to encounters between early Muslims and Greek thought because the influence of Greece on the Arabs was minimal during the time of the Prophet. Even though Muslim thinkers after the time of the Prophet incor-porated Greek ideas into their writings, they used these ideas "merely as tools [*bahan*] and not as ends in themselves. They [the Muslim thinkers] stood within their own philosophical tradition under the ambit of Islam."[14]

Hamka felt that the problem of bias undergirded all these Orientalist fallacies. Ori-entalists had allowed their prejudices against Islam to color their analyses of Islamic history, making it seem that the origin of Sufism was not to be found within Islam but rather was attributable to factors that were external to the religion itself.[15] This strong contention that Hamka made about the Orientalists' misrepresentations of Sufism has been partially validated by more recent studies on the topic. As Linda Sijbrand points out, even the most ardent admirers of the Sufis, such as Louis Massignon, "understood Sufism through the lens of Christianity."[16]

Then again, the problem of bias could well be applied to Hamka's own take on Orientalism. While scholars such as Sijbrand acknowledge the Orientalists' contribu-tions in correcting some Western academics' mistaken ideas about Sufism, Hamka's

---

[11] For a discussion of this, see Charles Le Gai Eaton, *Islam and the Destiny of Man* (Albany: State University of New York, 1985), 39.

[12] Hamka, *Tasauf: Perkembangan dan Pemurniannya*, 60–61.

[13] Nile Green, *Sufism: A Global History* (Oxford: Wiley-Blackwell, 2012), 21.

[14] Hamka, *Tasauf: Perkembangan dan Pemurniannya*, 63.

[15] Ibid., 60.

[16] Linda Sijbrand, "Orientalism and Sufism: An Overview," in *Orientalism Revisited: Art, Land and Voyage*, ed. Richard Netton (London: Routledge, 2013), 103.

appraisal of Orientalism tended to be reductionist, essentialist, and, at times, disparaging. He gave his readers the impression that there was really nothing to be gained from Orientalist scholarship on the subject of Sufism. Such radical anti-Orientalism was characteristic of many Muslim writers in the Malay world during Hamka's era—the age of decolonization, from the 1940s into the 1980s—when they cast Western scholarship on Islam in negative terms as a means to vindicate their own reading of Muslim intellectual legacies and contributions in history.[17] The fact remains that many leading Orientalists, too, doubted the theory that Sufism originated from non-Islamic sources. As early as 1947, the French Orientalist René Guénon had written authoritatively on the origins of Sufism, which he regarded "as Arab as the Koran itself, in which it has its direct principles."[18]

But when did Sufism actually begin? Hamka traced it to the lifetime of Prophet Muhammad and his companions in the seventh century. Elements of Sufistic doctrines can be found in the ascetic life of these early Muslims, who were inspired by the Qur'an:

> When read aloud by a person with a mesmerizing and beautiful voice and heard by those who are absorbed in the art of knowing God, the Qur'an initiates a person into becoming a Sufi ascetic, ready to abandon a life full of deception, accepting whatever little they are given with *redha* [contentment]. The message of the Qur'an seeped into Muhammad's soul, who was given the option of becoming a rich prophet like Solomon, or a pauper such as the Prophet Job, but he chose to starve one day and be full on another. . . . Hence it is clear from my research that Sufism derived its roots from the Qur'an and the Hadith.[19]

Unlike the modernist reformers during Hamka's time who would rely only on *shahih* (authentic) Hadiths as sources of reference on religious matters, Hamka accepted the use of *dhaif* (weak) Hadiths to elucidate his theory that Sufism had begun in earnest during the lifetime of the Prophet of Islam. This method of using weak Hadiths, according to Carl Ernst, was common among the Sufis, and it brought them severe criticism from many Muslim scholars.[20] Hamka, however, saw no real problem in using such Hadiths to encourage noble deeds. However, he admonished his readers that the same Hadith must not be used to justify *ibadah* (acts of worship). Hadiths that were *maudhu* (fabricated) were to be totally rejected and should not be considered at all in any discussions on the origins of Sufism and Sufi practices.[21]

Though inventive within the context of the Malay world, Hamka's interpretation of the origins of Sufism is barely original. A number of Muslim scholars have traced

---

[17] See Mona Abaza, *Debates on Islam and Knowledge in Malaysia and Egypt* (London: Routledge Curzon, 2002), 90; Georg Stauth, *Politics and Cultures of Islamization in Southeast Asia* (Bielefeld, Ger.: Transcript Verlag, 2002), 187–228; and Sadiq Jalal Al-'Azm, "Orientalism and Orientalism in Reverse," in *Forbidden Agendas: Intolerance and Defiance in the Middle East*, ed. Jon Rothschild (London: Saqi, 1984), 349–76.

[18] René Guénon, *Insights into Islamic Esoterism and Taoism*, trans. Henry D. Fohr (New York: Sophia Perennis, 2004), 4.

[19] Hamka, *Tasauf: Perkembangan dan Pemurniannya*, 207–8.

[20] Carl Ernst, *Words of Ecstasy in Sufism* (Albany: State University of New York, 1985), 118.

[21] Hamka, *Hamka Membahas Kemusykilan Agama* (Shah Alam, Malaysia: Pustaka Dini, 2009), 441–43, and Hamka, *Tasauf Modern*, 2.

the beginnings of Sufism in almost the same manner as Hamka did. Ibn Khaldun (1332–1406), for example, wrote in his *Al-Muqaddimah*, "Sufism is based on [the assumption] that the method of those people [who later on came to be called Sufis] had always been considered by the important early Muslims, the men around Muham-mad and the men of the second generation, as well as those who came after them, as the path of truth and right guidance."[22] Many scholars in the wake of Ibn Khaldun have also noted that it took many centuries for Sufism to be formalized and institu-tionalized as a distinct form of practice.

Hamka, however, brought that definition to another level by giving illustrative examples of Sufistic practices of the Prophet and his companions. He explicated the Prophet's piety and charitable acts even though he lived in poverty. Many Hadiths pro-vide evidence of the Prophet's habit of waking up in the early hours of the morning to offer his prayers. The Prophet was recorded to have asked for forgiveness from Allah more than seventy times a day. He was patient in the face of extreme adversity. And, in one authentic Hadith, the Prophet emphasized that his followers should "be aloof from the world and Allah will love you. Be aloof from what the people possess and the people will love you."[23] In Hamka's retrospective formulation, the Prophet was a Sufi par excellence even though he did not use the term "Sufi" to describe himself. To be a Sufi, therefore, was to follow the injunctions of the Qur'an and the Spiritual Way of the Prophet as documented in the Hadith.

The Prophet's Sufistic life was not unique to himself. Hamka stressed that, to understand the origins of Sufism, one must also factor in the ascetic lives of Muham-mad's companions. Islam's first caliph, Abu Bakar, had only one garment when he held office. Umar was so humble and austere that even his appointment as the caliph did not make him forget his duties toward God. Even though endowed with a great deal of wealth, Uthman bin Affan was a spiritual man. Ali wore patched clothes through-out his life. The Prophet's other significant companions included those who stayed in the mosques and were deeply committed to the worship of God. They, Hamka wrote, "did not have families and wealth, and all of these did not steer them away from Allah. They were not disheartened because they received little of this world, and what pleased them was spiritual wealth because they were certain of victory in the days to come."[24] It is obvious here that Hamka drew heavily on the Sufi hagiographical tradi-tion, which tended to embellish the Prophet's companions as the earliest and greatest examples of mystical piety in Islam.[25]

There are two implications that follow from Hamka's discussion of the origins of Sufism. By stressing that Sufism began with the Prophet himself and not the later gen-erations, Hamka was indirectly dismissing the argument made by Muslim reformists and modernists that Sufism was a belated invention in Islamic history and an innova-tion within Islam.[26] Sufism, to Hamka, was neither an invention nor an innovation. Its seeds were planted by God in his Prophet through the gradual revealing of the

---

[22] Ibn Khaldun, *Al-Muqadimmah*, trans. Franz Rosenthal (Princeton: Princeton University Press, 1967), 76.

[23] An-Nawawi, *40 Hadith*, trans. Jamal Zarabozo (Denver: Al-Basheer Publications, 1999), 925.

[24] Hamka, *Tasauf: Perkembangan dan Pemurniannya*, 35.

[25] Mahmoud M. Ayoub, *Islam: Faith and History* (Oxford: Oneworld Publications, 2004), 121.

[26] See, for example, *Al-Munir* 2, no. 8 (1912).

Figure 6 Masjid Agung Al-Azhar, where Hamka used to give his weekly lectures.
Collection of the author.

Qur'anic verses. The failure of reformists and modernists to see this point had made them unfairly dismissive of Sufism.

Hamka's ideas on the origins of Sufism had implications for the Sufis as well. By tracing Sufism back to the Prophet and his companions and asserting that true Sufism must be in line with Prophetic traditions, Hamka limited the interpretive possibilities of what Sufism was and should be. Claims made by the Sufis that they were following a variant of Sufism other than what had been shown by the Prophet and his companions would be erroneous and deviant if measured against the yardstick of Hamka's interpretations. In other words, what Hamka indirectly sought to achieve by tracing Sufism back to the Prophet was to send a strong message to his Sufi readers that the early Muslims must be their primary source of reference and inspiration, rather than the practices, beliefs, and doctrines of the later Sufis and saints that might not necessarily be in line with orthodox Islam.

THE PARAMETERS OF SUFISM

Defining Sufism lay at the center of Hamka's restoration of that spiritual dimension of Islam. He saw the work of clearly demarcating what Sufism was and should be as necessary because there was a tendency among the Malays to confuse or conflate authentic Sufi practices with those of other pre-Islamic and supra-Islamic rituals. This was most palpable in Java and Sumatra, where Hamka lived. Mystical beliefs were all too often intertwined with sorcery and magic.[27]

---

[27] Hamka, *Perkembangan Kebatinan di Indonesia* (Jakarta: Bulan Bintang, 1971), 11–14. See also Margaret J. Kartomi, *Musical Journeys in Sumatra* (Urbana: University of Illinois Press, 2012), 323, and Mohammad Damami, *Tasawuf Positif dalam Pemikiran Hamka* (Yogyakarta, Indonesia: Fajar Pustaka Baru, 2000), 121.

The exercise of setting the parameters of Sufism was, of course, not peculiar to Hamka or to scholars in the Malay world. William Chittick, for example, notes that Sufism has been subjected to so many different definitions and conceptualizations in different contexts and periods throughout Islamic history and society that a scholar must be precise about his or her definition of the term.[28] This task was especially urgent in Hamka's eyes because, as Deliar Noer observes,

> In Sufism, many of the traditionalists often fell into practices that were close to *sjirk*, associating God with beings and objects. They venerated *keramat* (shrines, graves of saints), gave offerings to spirits, held *slametan* or *kenduri* (feasts) as offerings, and used *azimat* or charms to protect themselves from evil genii or bad luck—which all in all resulted in the watering down, at least, of *tauhid*, the oneness of God.[29]

Hamka conceived of authentic Sufism (*tasauf sejati*) as a branch of the shari'a that aimed to "cleanse the soul, educate and refine the emotions, enliven the heart to be in constant prayer, and ennoble the character; suppressing greed and gluttony, battling excessive lust that goes beyond what is needed to achieve calmness."[30]

In another passage, Hamka extended his definition of Sufism as a path that Muslims took

> to seek the pleasure of Allah, so as not to be swayed by materialism, and through the passage of time, this deep spirituality became a means toward a more noble, powerful, and profound end. That is, to unveil the face of God, to witness the beauty of eternal life. But the aim to unveil the face of God would then become unsatisfying. Those who wished to rise above that, to reach an even higher spiritual station [*maqam*], in other words, annihilation of the self [*fanaa*] and achieve union with God [*ittihad*], would do so through constant inner striving [*mujahadah*] and spiritual practices [*riyadhah*]. From this, there emerged a spiritual way of life that is systematic of a religious philosophy that touches on matters pertaining to the soul. It became known as Sufism.[31]

The pure form of Sufism, Hamka added, must be in line with laws governing rituals and daily conduct and not above and beyond them.

Hamka's ideas of Sufism as a branch of the shari'a were derived primarily from the works and sayings of renowned Sufi mystics and scholars such as Junaid Al-Baghdadi (830–910), Abu Talib Al-Makki (unknown–996), Al-Qushayri (986–1072), Al-Ghazali, and Ibn Qayyim—all of whom he cited in his writings. He agreed with these mystics and scholars that following the shari'a is the first step on the path to perfection in faith.

---

[28] William Chittick, *Faith and Practice of Islam: Three Thirteenth Century Sufi Texts* (Albany: State University of New York, 1992), 173–76.

[29] Deliar Noer, *The Modernist Muslim Movement in Indonesia, 1900–1942* (Kuala Lumpur: Oxford University Press, 1978), 300–301.

[30] Hamka, *Tasauf Modern*, 11.

[31] Hamka, *Tasauf: Perkembangan dan Pemurniannya*, 20.

Hamka then distinguished the various branches of Sufism. The pristine form is concerned primarily with the refinement of character, or what has been termed by scholars as "Ethical Sufism."[32] Hamka held the view that the purpose of Sufism is to realize the *akhlaqul karimah* (noble character). A person's character consists of two dimensions: *batin* (inner) and *zahir* (outer). By inner character, he meant training the heart to constantly seek forgiveness from God while beseeching His mercy. Training the inner character also involves thinking of things that would bring one closer to knowing the divine and reminding oneself of the eternal life in heaven or hell. All of these can be achieved through deep meditation, attentiveness to rituals, reciting chants, fasting, and searching for beneficial knowledge. Hamka used the terms *tasfiyah qulub* (the cleansing of the heart), *tazkiah al-nafs* (self-purification), and *riyadhah al-nafs* (self-discipline) to describe this process while arguing that the heart is the seat of all diseases.[33] The training of one's inner character is thus crucial because through it one may develop *habluminallah* (a strong relationship with Allah). In time, the Sufi votary would internalize the meanings of *zuhud* (asceticism), *syukur* (gratefulness), *tawakkal* (trust in God), *khauf* (fear), *qanaah* (contentment), *ikhlas* (sincerity), *raja'* (hopefulness), *taqwa* (piety), and *tafakkur* (contemplation). This would in turn shape one's behavior and enable that person to change from a vile character into a praiseworthy one.[34]

Hamka wrote several books, one of which is titled *Akhlaqul Karimah*, to elaborate on a person's outer character.[35] Good character was, to him, one of the essential foundations not only of Sufism but also of what it means to be a true Muslim. People with a noble character have *adab* (manners). They are sensitive to their surroundings and are polite to everyone regardless of age, descent, or background. They refrain from saying or doing things that would be seen as immoral in the eyes of the public. But what is regarded as good character is also subject to change. In this, Hamka offered a dynamic view of *akhlaqul karimah* that evolves in accordance with changing contexts. For example, if society is heading toward adopting wrongful practices that clearly contravene Islamic precepts, politeness and niceties must be dispensed with to put things right. The Sufis of the past, Hamka asserted, were noble in their character, but they did not hesitate to rise against the tide of disbelief and waywardness and were harsh when they needed to be.[36]

At the peak of one's ability to refine his or her inner and outer character is the eventual achievement of becoming *Al-Insanul Kamil* (the Perfect Man). Here Hamka drew heavily from the works of the Andalusian scholar and Sufi Ibn Arabi, who first wrote about the doctrine of the perfect man.[37] Agreeing with Ibn Arabi, Hamka maintained that very few persons, even among those who are steeped in Sufistic thought and practice, can actually achieve perfection in their lifetimes. When they do,

---

[32] Daphna Ephrat, *Spiritual Wayfarers, Leaders in Piety: Sufis and the Dissemination of Islam in Medieval Palestine* (Cambridge, MA: Harvard University Press, 2008), 105. See also William Chittick and Sachiko Murata, *The Vision of Islam* (Cairo: American University in Cairo Press, 2006), 304.

[33] Hamka, *Pandangan Hidup Muslim*, 22–23.

[34] Hamka, *Tasauf Modern*, 8.

[35] Hamka, *Akhlaqul Karimah*.

[36] Hamka, *Pandangan Hidup Muslim*, 191–92.

[37] William C. Chittick, *Sufi Path of Knowledge: Ibn al-Àrabi Metaphysics of Imagination* (Albany: State University of New York Press, 1989), 46.

they are inevitably held in high esteem. They are often described as *waliyullah* (the saints of Allah) and are honored by God.[38]

Sufism also has a devotional aspect that deals with character and behavior. The devotional practices, according to Hamka, were based on the practices of the Prophet and his companions. The Sufis systemized the disparate practices of these early Muslims so as to make them more accessible to ordinary Muslims. The Sufi masters' main objective was to ease the path of their followers in recognizing the greatness of God and loving him wholeheartedly.[39] The devotional aspect of Sufism included two elements. Hamka prioritized adherence to the *fard* (obligatory) aspects of Islam over those that were *nawafil* (supererogatory). The Sufis, according to Hamka, stressed a strict implementation of the pillars of Islam that consisted of witnessing the oneness of Allah, praying five times daily, fasting, paying zakah, and hajj. Adherence to the pillars was to be followed by *fadhail 'amal* (supererogatory practices), such as charity, nightly prayers, and *zikir* (repetitive recitations of litanies). The highest form of devotion within Sufism was to achieve a state of *khalwat* (solitude), that is, "to be in a state of reflection, thinking, and retrospection with and about oneself. To avoid being in the company of many people, especially those who are aimless. Because too much companionship leads to too much talk that contravenes what is necessary."[40]

Sufis who were able to practice all those devotions would eventually attain true happiness in this life and the hereafter. They would become fully cognizant of the oneness of God and the oneness of all creation, leading them toward the unveiling (*kashf*) of the secrets of the unseen.[41] The influence of the book *Revelation of the Veiled* (*Kashf al-Mahjub*), by the tenth-century Sufi master Ali bin Usman Hujwiri (990–1077), influenced Hamka's views about the unseen in Sufi thought.[42] Hamka was critical, however, of a few offshoots of Sufism that he saw as destabilizing Muslim spirituality from within, such as philosophical Sufism (*tasauf filsofis*). By this he meant "a form of philosophical inquiry that seeks to unravel the barrier between the outer and inner aspects of life. The search for what is hidden behind the screen."[43] Al-Suhrawardi al-Maqtul (1154–91), Ibn Arabi, and Mansur Al-Hallaj (858–922) were among the figures who spearheaded this strain within Sufism.

In Hamka's view these were a select group of Sufis who were influenced by Neoplatonism, as well as by mystical ideas emanating from Persia, India, and the Christian world. Through their prose, poetry, and treatises, philosophical Sufis promoted the notion of *Wahdatul Wujud*, which connotes the unity between God and mankind. They also believed in the concept of *Nur Muhammad* (the light of Muhammad), or *Alhaqiqatul Muhammad* (the essence of Muhammad), as the source of all deeds and knowledge. Above all, these Sufis held on to the idea that all religions are similar, differing only in name. These ideas were actually products of extreme reasoning and speculation on the one hand and being overwhelmed by mystical experiences on the other. As a result, philosophical Sufis fell into the error of declaring that they themselves were

---

[38] Hamka, *Falsafah Hidup*, 58.

[39] Hamka, *Tasauf: Perkembangan dan Pemurniannya*, 85.

[40] Ibid., 99.

[41] Hamka, *Pandangan Hidup Muslim*, 30.

[42] Ali bin Usman Hujwiri, *Revelation of the Unseen*, trans. R. A. Nicholson (New York: Pir Press, 1999).

[43] Hamka, *Tasauf: Perkembangan dan Pemurniannya*, 137.

God, as seen in the case of Al-Hallaj, or propounding theories about God and about the religions and religiosity that departed from the teachings of Prophet Muhammad.[44]

Although Hamka disagreed with the philosophical Sufis' ideas and methods of reasoning, he was sympathetic to their goals. The philosophical Sufis transcended the dissension and endless arguments among scholars who were interested only in matters pertaining to laws and the superiority of their respective schools of thought. They sought to move away from those petty squabbles toward an emphasis on metaphysical issues, which, they felt, could bring Muslims closer to God.[45] One can detect here Hamka's oblique criticism of the reformists and modernists whom he regarded as overly preoccupied with jurisprudential debates and differences. Still, Hamka saw that if taken too far and permitted to become dominant in any given setting, philosophical Sufism was an ideology that could bring its followers beyond the parameters of what Sufism really was, thereby weakening the Malay-Muslims. Hamka cited the case of Hamzah Fansuri (died in 1590), a sixteenth-century Acehnese philosophical Sufi who, in Hamka's, estimation, "went too far."

> He [Hamzah Fansuri] was an adherent of the teachings of al-Hallaj's *Ana al-haqq* [I am the truth]. His *tariqa* [Sufi order] was called the *Wujudiyyah,* promoting the unity between Creator and creature. The followers of this doctrine lost the spirit of struggle, which was in contrast with the spirit of *jihad* in Islam that was badly needed in Aceh at that time. . . . In the end Hamzah was killed because his doctrine was regarded as dangerous. His teachings, however, flourished in Java and become accepted by the followers of "Kawula Gusti."[46]

Hamka's sympathy for philosophical Sufism is, however, not evident in his approach to extremist Sufis and popular Sufism. Extremist Sufis (*Sufi yang ta'asub*) were those who submitted their lives totally to their *syaikhs* (masters). They called themselves *murids* (novices) who held the syaikhs as intercessors for prayers, as guides in spiritual matters, and as avenues by which the greatness and love of God could be experienced. The murids, therefore, lost themselves completely in their syaikhs. This was a train of thought that Hamka totally opposed in many of his writings on Sufism and his exegesis of the Qur'an. He advocated the use of reason on the part of Sufis and urged them not to be driven by their emotions in displaying unacceptable reverence for the syaikhs.[47]

Hamka further argued that the Prophet had enjoined Muslims to develop a direct connection with God without any intermediaries. The terms *wasilah* (means of approach) and *rabithah* (relationship forged with a spiritual guide) had been wrongly understood by the Sufis to require submitting one's life to a person in the form of the syaikh or a saint, either dead or alive. In Indonesia, the inordinate love for syaikhs

---

[44] Ibid., 150.

[45] Ibid., 110–11.

[46] Hamka, *Sejarah Umat Islam,* 914. Hamka was referring here to the ideology of Jumbuhing Kawula Gusti (union with God), which was popular among Javanese Muslims who were influenced by the writings of Hamzah Fansuri. Followers of such a belief have it that human beings could attain spiritual unions with God through chants, meditation, and mystical experience. For more see Andreas Yumarma, *Unity in Diversity: A Philosophical and Ethical Study of the Javanese Concept of Keselarasan* (Rome: Editrice Pontificia Universita Gregoriana, 1996), 58.

[47] Wan Sabri, "Hamka's 'Tafsir Al-Azhar,'" 209.

and saints had given rise to the worship of graves and tombs—Hamka described the Malay world as having a "hub of graveyards" that a Muslim would frequently visit to pray for the dead and ask for anything he or she wished.[48] Alternatively, Hamka stressed that the acceptable form of wasilah was to seek help from a learned or pious person regarding how to pray for oneself. In Hamka's rendering of Sufism, syaikhs were merely guides to be sought after if one required their assistance, but they were not to be revered beyond what had been stipulated in Islam. These ideas bear striking parallels to those of Ibn Taymiyya.[49]

Popular Sufism, in turn, referred to the *kebatinan* (the search for inner truth) movements in Indonesia.[50] These movements were a product of Javanese mysticism, which, with the coming of Islam, incorporated various ideas of Sufism into their beliefs and practices. Popular Sufism was fostered under colonial rule and flowered during the time of the New Order government, from the 1960s to the 1980s. Some of these kebatinan had gone to the extent of receiving *wahyu* (revelation from God) above and beyond what had already been revealed to Prophet Muhammad.[51] Hamka saw this as a symptom of the superficial understanding of Islam among many Javanese. He was also aware that the kebatinan groups were attracting people who had been alienated from Islam by the reformists, as well as those interested in a modern framing of spirituality.[52]

Unlike many modernist thinkers, such as H. Mohamed Rasjidi (1915–2001) and Abdul Mukhti Ali (1923–2004)—who launched an all-out effort to discredit the kebatinan movements—Hamka called for a mild and intellectually driven approach. He explained that kebatinan movements had persisted for many reasons, including the Dutch divide-and-rule policies in Indonesia, Javanese resistance to accepting orthodox Islam, and the schemes of many shamans who employed a combination of magic, trickery, and Islamic idioms to win the masses over to their own selfish ends.[53] Kebatinan movements could not be changed overnight or through sharp criticisms; instead, they should be approached in a respectful manner, and dialogues should be

---

[48] Hamka, *Pelajaran Agama Islam,* 241; Hamka, Mengembalikan Tasawuf Ke Pangkalnya (Jakarta: Pustaka Panjimas, 1973), 40–41, and Hamka, *Perkembangan Kebatinan di Indonesia,* 11.

[49] See Jon Hoover, *Ibn Taymiyya's Theodicy of Perpetual Optimism* (Leiden, Neth.: Brill, 2007), 206, and Hamka, *Tafsir Al-Azhar,* 6:1723.

[50] They were also known as *kejawen* (Javanism), *kejiwaan* (inner soul), and *aliran kepercayaan* (streams of thought). A detailed and remarkable study on this is found in Suwardi Endaswara, *Mistik Kejawen: Sinkrestime, Simbolisme dan Sufisme dalam Budaya Spiritual Jawa* (Yogyakarta: Penerbit Narasi, 2006), and Paul R. Stange, "Legitimate Mysticism in Indonesia," *Review of Indonesian and Malaysian Affairs* 22, no. 2 (1986): 76–117.

[51] Julia D. Howell, "Muslims, the New Age and Marginal Religions in Indonesia: Changing Meanings of Religious Pluralism," *Social Compass* 52, no. 4 (2005): 472–93, and Bianca J. Smith, "When *Wahyu* Comes through Women: Female Spiritual Authority and Divine Revelation in Mystical Groups and *Pesantren* Sufi Orders," in *Gender and Power in Indonesian Islam: Leaders, Feminists, Sufis and Pesantren Selves,* ed. Bianca J. Smith and Mark Woodward (London: Routledge, 2014), 87–88.

[52] Hamka, *Perkembangan Kebatinan di Indonesia,* 8, and Abd. Mutholib Ilyas and Abd. Ghofur Imam, *Aliran Kepercayaan & Kebatinan di Indonesia* (Surabaya, Indonesia: Amin, 1988).

[53] Hamka, *Perkembangan Kebatinan di Indonesia,* 53–55, and Harry Benda, "Christiaan Snouck Hurgronje and the Foundations of Dutch Islamic Policy in Indonesia," *Journal of Modern History* 30, no. 4 (1958): 338–47.

held so as to realize the aim of Restoring Sufism (*Mengembalikan Tasauf kepada Pangkal-nya*), which was the title of another one of Hamka's books.

Hamka held tariqas in high regard as long as they adhered to the teachings of the Qur'an and the Sunnah. In this regard, his position comes close to that of another Malay-Islamic scholar, Syeikh Ahmad Khatib Al-Minangkabawi. Michael Laffan states that Ahmad Khatib "was also receptive to the notion of a properly respected Sufi tariqa, provided that it accorded with attested practice, and that the attributes of God were not to be imputed to the Prophet or the saints."[54] To be sure, Sufi orders were to Hamka excellent platforms for *da'wah* (the preaching of Islam). The Sufis also "established the *Tariqa* movements with the intent of training the self to live moderately and to focus their aims toward seeking Allah so as to free oneself from the lure of worldly wealth."[55]

Hamka paid tribute to the Sanusiyyah tariqa in Libya for its role in resisting colonial rule and reforming society for many centuries, and he cited the contributions of the Tijaniyyah movement in the spread of Islam in North Africa. The tariqas maintained the pristine form of Sufism. Hamka, however, also highlighted the waywardness of those tariqas that fused Islamic teachings with un-Islamic practices, folk beliefs, and superstitions. This was evidenced in the Maulawiyah (or Mevlevi), who incorporated dances and whirling in their devotional practices. Another case in point was the Rifai'iyah Sufi order in Aceh and Banten, which taught its followers to believe that they were invulnerable. These cults existed in parts of the Malay world until the 1980s, but, in Hamka's eyes, "none of these are acceptable in Islamic missionary work, for they are merely entertainment."[56] Drawing on the works of Al-Ghazali, Hamka stated that the study and practice of Sufism through the tariqas must come after achieving a deep understanding of *tauhid* (the oneness of God) and the laws of Islam as enshrined in the shari'a, "so that we are not swayed by our emotions, outside the bounds of knowledge."[57]

Still, Hamka maintained that belonging to a Sufi order was not a necessary precondition for anyone who wished to tread the spiritual path. He advocated the idea of *tawawuf tanpa tarekat* (Sufism without tariqa), a version of Sufism that was unprecedented in the history of Sufism in the Malay world. Julia Howell rightly describes this version of Sufism as an enabling factor for "modern Muslims to cultivate a sense of closeness to God, and possibly even experience a lifting of the veils of earthly perception, without, however, getting involved in a Sufi order or using the Sufis' meditative rituals such as collective zikir."[58] I would go even further and argue that Hamka's promotion of Sufism without tariqa democratized the practice of Sufism in the Malay world. One of the impacts of his writings was a decline in reliance on the syaikhs of Sufi orders as mediums and guides in the spiritual life of ordinary Muslims. In line with his cosmopolitan reform, what Hamka achieved through his writings on Sufism

---

54 Laffan, *The Makings of Indonesian Islam*, 180.

55 Hamka, *Prinsip dan Kebijaksanaan Da'wah Islam* (Kuala Lumpur: Pustaka Melayu Baru, 1981), 210.

56 Ibid., 222.

57 Ibid. See also Hamka, *Hamka Membahas Kemusykilan Agama*, 548.

58 Julia D. Howell, "Revitalised Sufism and the New Piety Movements in Islamic Southeast Asia," in *Routledge Handbook of Religions in Asia*, ed. Bryan S. Turner and Oscar Salemink (London: Routledge, 2015), 282.

was to encourage Muslims to be deeply spiritual without being beholden to one particular dogma, leader, or thinker in Islam.

TASAWUF AS A CONSTRUCTIVE FORCE IN THE MALAY WORLD

From the discussion above, it is clear that Hamka acknowledged the importance of Sufism within Islam. He went even further to maintain that Sufism and Sufis had been among the crucial agents in the making and remaking of Muslim societies and civilization. They must and would continue to do so by "inculcating the spirit of determination in every task at hand. Deep spirituality brings forth dynamism and passion, giving rise to sincerity and honesty."[59] To Hamka, it was almost unthinkable for Malay-Muslims to ignore Sufism as one of their frames of reference. But the task of restoring Sufism in the Malay world did not stop there. For Sufism to persist as a constructive force in the lives of Muslims, Hamka proposed a number of ideational reforms. It is here that we see a part of Hamka that was akin to the reformists and modernists of his time. The point to him was not only to document what true Sufism was but also to change the present state of Islamic mysticism to make it congruent with modernity.

First, emphasis must be placed on the positive interpretations of Sufism (*tasawuf positif*) as opposed to the negative interpretations (*tawawuf negatif*), which must be eradicated.[60] Hamka directed his attention to a number of key concepts in Sufi cosmology that had been wrongly conceptualized by Muslims. Zuhud had been described as a retreat from worldly life by secluding oneself from society, but Hamka regarded such an understanding as selfish and egoistic.[61] He discussed this at length and offered a reinterpretation of the concept:

> There are so many Islamic teachings that are still written and read till today but are least understood because of the imbalance in knowledge. For example, the idea of *Zuhud*. When the religious spirit fades, *Zuhud* is wrongly understood. It signifies revulsion toward worldly life, revulsion toward wealth, revulsion toward status. Thus grew a self-deceiving predisposition that is an upshot of misconceptions. The world therefore escapes from one's grasp because one is taught to detest it. But this world is a place to sow, and the hereafter a place to reap. Detesting wealth leads to poverty, so much so that even a mosque could not be built. . . . We accuse the West of being materialistic, and the East we call, Idealist. But our pure teachings enjoin the seeking of as much wealth as we can so that the commandments of Allah can be upheld. [We are] enjoined to struggle and uphold Allah's path, foremost with wealth, then with our lives. Muslims are commanded to work hard so they can amass great wealth, so as to assist society with the wealth that they yield.[62]

---

[59] Hamka, *Pelajaran Agama Islam*, 34.

[60] A detailed analysis of Hamka's tasawuf positif is found in Mohammad Damami, *Tasawuf Positif dalam Pemikiran Hamka* (Jakarta: Fajar Pustaka Baru, 2000).

[61] Hamka, *Said Djamaluddin Al-Afghany: Pelopor Kebangkitan Muslimin* (Jakarta: Penerbit Bulan Bintang, 1970), 59.

[62] Hamka, *Empat Bulan di Amerika*, 2:65.

For Hamka, the proper interpretation of zuhud was summarized by the following words of Imam Ahmad bin Hanbal: "Seeking that which is permitted but to a degree that is necessary, without being excessive."[63]

Two other concepts that had been wrongly interpreted by Sufis in the Malay world, according to Hamka, were qanaah and tawakkal. These two terms had been used interchangeably by some Sufis to mean that Muslims should accept their fates, be mediocre at work, and leave it to God to change their destinies. Hamka was totally opposed to such misunderstandings, believing that they encouraged a culture of laziness among many Muslims. For Sufism to be a positive and empowering factor in Muslim life, Hamka redefined the word *qanaah* as the state of feeling satisfied with whatever one has achieved. Similarly, tawakkal was not about leaving everything to God but about struggling hard before leaving the outcomes of one's efforts to the mercy of the divine. Hamka derived this from the famous Hadith of the Prophet, who was reported to have said, "Tie the camel first and then put your trust in Allah."[64]

The second ideational reform that Hamka called for was the modernization of Sufism. He used the term *tasawuf moden* (or *tasauf moderen*, modern Sufism), in contrast to *tasawuf tradisional* (traditional Sufism). Tasawuf tradisional basically means a form of Islamic spirituality that is blemished with innovations, superstition, and the worship of anyone other than God. The practitioners of tasawuf tradisional were also averse to changes around them while insisting that to be a Sufi was to live as the Sufis of the past had done. Modern Muslims were shying away from Sufism because of this attitude, and Hamka saw this as tragic. The educated class of Muslims in particular, Hamka wrote, "feel that to be spiritual is to be old-fashioned."[65] Hamka was not wrong in making this argument, for studies have shown that Sufism in the Malay world suffered from a brief decline before World War II and in the immediate postwar period.[66]

Tasawuf moden is thus sensitive to the needs of the emerging generation, forward-looking, and dynamic. It is centered around the creation of spiritually conscious, morally upright, and socially connected Muslims who keep up with the demands of modern life. The main goal of tasawuf moden is the realization of total happiness, both in this life and the hereafter. In this regard, Hamka was clearly influenced by Al-Ghazali's book, *Kimiyah Al-Sa'adah* (The Alchemy of Happiness).[67] He divided happiness that could be gained through the practice of tasawuf moden into five parts—happiness in terms of wealth, happiness through kinship relations, happiness gained from social status, happiness from one's lineage and background, happiness in the form of bodily health, and happiness obtained from following the path of God. Such happiness would serve as the catalyst and inspiration for Muslims to adapt

---

[63] Hamka, *Prinsip dan Kebijaksanaan Da'wah Islam*, 222. See also Hamka, *Hamka Membahas Kemusykilan Agama*, 548.

[64] Hamka, *Tasauf Modern*, 169.

[65] Hamka, *Filsafat Ketuhanan*, 21.

[66] See Mark Sedgwick, *Saints and Sons: The Remaking of the Rashidi Ahmadi Sufi Order* (Leiden: Brill, 2005), 183, and Julia Day Howell, "Modulations of Active Piety: Professors and Televangelists as Promoters of Indonesian 'Sufisme,'" in *Expressing Islam: Religious Life and Politics in Indonesia*, ed. Greg Fealy and Sally White (Singapore: ISEAS, 2008), 41.

[67] Al-Ghazali, *The Alchemy of Happiness*, trans. Claud Field (Lahore, Pakis.: Sh. Muhammad Ashraf, 1987).

in an ever-changing world.[68] In other words, to Hamka, embracing modernity would not erode Islamic spirituality but rather enhance it further. A Sufi is foremost a Muslim, and a modern Sufi is inevitably a modern Muslim. What Hamka tried to explain to his readers was that there was no need to decouple Sufism from modernity. Sufism provided the spiritual ballast that modern Muslims needed.

Hamka also agitated for the cleansing of Sufism from *tahyul dan dongengan* (myths and legends) and the embrace of reason and intellectualism. Sufism in the Malay world had been led by "syaikhs of tariqas with their special flags; filled with superstition and wayward beliefs. And not least are the many layers of trickery [that come with them]. Not least also are the shamans, the soothsayers, the sorcerers, and the fortune tellers."[69] Rulers and Sufis kept these myths and legends alive to ensure the blind obedience of the masses. These stories often contradicted the laws of life and the Qur'an. Examples stories included the conversion of kings by Prophet Muhammad himself through dreams, the figure of Alexander in pre-modern Malay texts that was purported to be Iskandar Zulkarnain, and the miraculous feats of the nine saints of Java.[70]

True Sufism departs from the machinations of the "corruptors of Sufism."[71] Hamka exhorted his readers to use their God-given power of reasoning (*kekuatan akal*) in charting a spiritual life and battling their inner desires. The use of critical reasoning does not, however, entail the abandonment of imagination, esotericism, and mysticism. Hamka's true Sufism is one that "does not reject knowledge, true Sufism does not reject reality."[72] He furthered this point by stressing that true Sufism encourages Muslims to use their minds. "The mind is the motor of life. A healthy reasoning moves between the mind and the desires. The mind is at the top, desires are at the bottom, and reasoning is at the center."[73] Put differently, to be a modern Sufi is to strike a balance between the intellect, the emotions, and the will to love God and his creation.

Hamka also questioned the separation of spirituality from secular life. This dichotomy was made possible by Muslims who were impressed by the ideologies of secularism promoted by the West. Hamka gave the examples of Kamal Atartuk (in Turkey) and Syeikh Abdul Raziq (in Egypt), both of whom divorced politics from religion and spirituality from public life, hence falling into the fallacy of thinking about life in dualistic terms.[74] As an alternative, Hamka called for the coming together of the spiritual and the secular, with Sufism as a medium. "Let us be Sufis in confronting the demands of everyday life, even in commerce, even in politics, Sufi in business, Sufi in nurturing and teaching."[75]

---

[68] Hamka, *Tasauf Modern*, 130–33.

[69] Hamka, *Pelajaran Agama Islam*, 33.

[70] Hamka, *Dari Perbendaharaan Lama* (Kuala Lumpur: Penerbit Pustaka Antara, 1981), 202–43.

[71] Hamka, *Falsafah Hidup*, 50.

[72] Ibid., 54.

[73] Hamka, *Tasauf Modern*, 91.

[74] Hamka, *Pengajian Islam* (Kelantan, Malaysia: Pustaka Aman Press, 1977), 155.

[75] Hamka, *Pandangan Hidup Muslim*, 52.

A cursory survey will show that the discourses about Sufism in the Malay world today are saturated with Hamka's thought. His concepts of *tasawuf positif* and *tasawuf moden* have inspired several monographs on the subject.[76] His books on Sufism have sold by the hundreds and have been reprinted more than a dozen times by scores of publishers in Singapore, Malaysia, and Indonesia. The celebrated Indonesian intellectual Nurcholish Madjid underlined this point by stating that it has become almost impossible to begin or end any discussion of Sufism in Indonesia without a passing reference to Hamka's extensive oeuvre.[77] Hamka's project of restoring Sufism as a style of thought and a mode of piety that ought to be in line with the shari'a and purified from the many external influences has also gained him many followers who now adopt a universalist, inclusive, individualized, deritualized, and nonsectarian form of Islamic spirituality. So persuasive has Hamka been that many members of the Muhammadiyah have become more open to Sufism and Sufis in Indonesia and as a result have taken a more reformist and modernist path in their practice of Islam.[78]

In assessing the long shadow that Hamka has cast over Sufism in the Malay world, one wonders what it is that makes his works so alluring. The key to explaining Hamka's popularity may be found in the structure of his writings. He was deeply aware of his audience and wrote primarily for adherents of Sufism and their enemies, without forgetting those readers who might have been exposed to but were not actually adherents of either of those groups. As a result, Hamka's works on Sufism became accessible to all within an increasingly diverse and polarizing Muslim society, just as he touched on issues that affected everyone. Indeed, if it is to be accepted that Islam in the Malay world is characterized by its ability to syncretize many different strands of thought into a unique version of a cosmopolitan and inclusive Islam, Hamka may be seen as the offspring of that tradition.

---

[76] See Ahmad Najib Burhani, ed., *Manusia Menimba Allah: Renungan Tasawwuf Positif* (Jakarta: Penerbit Hikmah, 2002); C. Ramli Bihar Anwar, *Bertasawuf Tanpa Tarekat: Aura Tasawuf Positif* (Jakarta: Penerbit IIMan, 2002); and Sudirman Tebba, *Tasawuf positif: Manfaat Tasawuf Dalam Kehidupan Sehari-Hari* (Jakarta: Pustaka irVan, 2008).

[77] Nurcholish Madjid, *Tradisi Islam: Peran dan Fungsinya dalam Pembangunan di Indonesia* (Jakarata: Paramadina, 1997), 123–32.

[78] Martin van Bruinessen, "Controversies and Polemics Involving the Sufi Orders in Twentieth-Century Indonesia," in *Islamic Mysticism Contested: Thirteen Centuries of Controversies and Polemics,* ed. Frederick de Jong and Bernd Radtke (Leiden: Brill, 1999), 729.

CHAPTER SIX

HISTORY AS A TOOL
OF REFORM

Hamka dedicated much of his energy to writing histories that are still widely read among Muslims in the Malay world. His corpus includes well-trodden themes such as the global history of Islam, great Muslim personalities, and the history of spiritual movements in Islam. All of his works were reprinted several times because of their popularity. These works are particularly worthy of scrutiny because his historical writings have now become a source of reference for professional historians in the Malay world working on similar topics.[1] A leading scholar of Indonesian studies, Sartono Kartodirdjo, has perceptively noted that in Indonesia popular history books written by writers such as Hamka "often vastly exceed the influence of academic works, since [their] publication[s are] more widespread and possess great appeal among the people."[2] Jeffrey Hadler, in turn, stressed that Hamka's writings are acknowledged as sources of reference for both the general public and esteemed scholars such as Harry Benda, Anthony Reid, Taufik Abdullah, Deliar Noer, and Azyumardi Azra, among others.[3] This distinctive trait of Hamka's works is striking because he single-handedly bridged the gaps between academic and popular historians in Indonesia.

How then can we best characterize writers such as Hamka, who balanced his roles as cleric, preacher, and educator with his commitment to writing such influential histories? To my mind, Hamka is best described as a cosmopolitan public historian. He wrote what Benjamin Filene has termed influential "passionate histories" covering themes that are often neglected or downplayed by historians based in academia. Filene argues, however, that public historians, or what he calls "outsider history-makers," tended to be driven by instinct in their selection of historical themes, while professional historians were steered by the intellect.[4] Such distinctions, in my view, do not accurately represent either public or professional historians. Both place a great deal of importance on instinct and intellect. What differentiates one from another is the primary audience at which their respective works are directed. Cosmopolitan public historians such as Hamka sought to make history accessible to the general public, while professional historians place a high degree of importance in addressing the scholarly community and expanding the frontiers of the historical discipline in academe.

Cosmopolitan public historians go a step further in that they fuse their individual experiences with the collective memories of others in their historical narratives.

---

[1] Jeffrey Hadler, "Home, Fatherhood, Succession," 125.

[2] Sartono Kartodirdjo, *Indonesian Historiography* (Yogyakarta, Indonesia: Kanisius, 2001), 25–26.

[3] Hadler, "Home, Fatherhood, Succession," 125.

[4] Benjamin Filene, "Passionate Histories: 'Outsider' History-Makers and What They Teach Us," *Public Historian* 34, no. 1 (2012): 12–14.

Rather than suspending their own subjective positions toward the past, they state their biases openly, their preferences avowedly, and their agendas clearly in order to enliven history for the consumption of the general public. Pierre Nora in his influential essay "Between Memory and History" argued that the advent of public historians like Hamka was a result of the disintegration of the age-old distinction between history and memory since the 1950s. According to Nora, a new type of historian emerged, "who unlike his precursors, is ready to confess the intimate relation he maintains to his subject. Better still, he is ready to proclaim it, deepen it, make of it not the obstacle but the means of his understanding."[5]

Hamka clearly proclaimed his individual agendas and purposes while using his historical works as tools of cosmopolitan reform. His histories are thus best described as "reformist histories." These works were guided by the belief that history could be utilized as an instrument to reconstruct the minds of ordinary Malay-Muslims. History fulfilled a practical function for Hamka. He did not merely narrate facts through the use of conventional methods of historical research; instead, he presented facts to challenge conventional and commonplace assumptions about the Islamic past in order to bring about changes in the everyday life and ways of thinking of Muslims in the Malay world.[6] In other words, Hamka as cosmopolitan public historian did not just inform his Muslim audience about past events, societies, and movements; he inspired his readers to draw lessons from the past—lessons that could be put to use in the present and the future.

Writing mainly in the vernacular language to reach his primary audience, Hamka hoped that Muslims would become cognizant of the achievements of their ancestors and therefore believe that they too could construct a flourishing civilization by learning how their forebears succeeded and by understanding the factors that led to their downfall. Through this, he hoped that Muslims would recover the legacy of cosmopolitanism embedded in their own traditions just as they would become more cosmopolitan in their views of the world around them and of Islam as a religion. He wrote on themes that encouraged Muslims to be open to their coreligionists of different backgrounds and also to non-Muslims in the Malay world. This was a legacy of Muslim history, notably the history of the Malay world, which Hamka sought to capture and popularize to his readers in his effort to reform their minds.[7]

This chapter critically examines a few strands of Hamka's reformist histories. These histories compellingly describe the vastness of Islamic civilization while connecting its disparate and fragmented strands. By linking the Arab world of Islam with other centers of the faith in Africa, Asia, and Europe into one seamless and synergistic whole, as evinced in *Sejarah Umat Islam*, Hamka sought to reform the self-identity of Malay-Muslims into a feeling of belonging to a millennium-old civilization.[8] Another strand of Hamka's reformist histories underscores the agency of grassroots reformers in determining the course of Muslim history and the lessons that can be learned from their attempts to overcome the odds that were stacked against them. In his books on the celebrated reformer Sayyid Jamaluddin Al-Afghani and a personal account of his own father's struggles, Hamka hoped to convince readers

---

[5] Pierre Nora, "Between Memory and History: *Les Lieux de Mémoire*," *Representations* 26 (1989): 18.

[6] Hamka, *Antara Fakta dan Khayal "Tuanku Rao"* (Jakarta: Penerbit Bulan Bintang, 1974), 288.

[7] Hamka, *Sejarah Umat Islam*, 2.

[8] Ibid.

to see these men as dedicated individuals who sought to reform their societies through their writings and the institutions that they established. In Hamka's formulation, they were archetypes for later generations of Muslims to emulate in their endeavor to realize a modernized society that was freed from foreign domination. Their life stories are signposts for Muslims trying to cope with change and reform in their societies.[9]

Last, Hamka's reformist histories underlined how a proper understanding and practice of social justice had led to positive outcomes in Muslim societies. Social justice that was enforced during the age of Islamic empires had led to the creation of flourishing civilizations in which Muslim learned and worked together with non-Muslims. He faulted the Muslims of his time for jettisoning their own noble pasts. The fact that the pasts had been forgotten and laid aside contributed to rampant injustice in Muslim societies, especially toward non-Muslim minorities. The problems of individualism and the culture of greed and irreligiosity defined contemporary Muslim societies.

Before proceeding to discuss these three strands of Hamka's histories in detail, a note about the general landscape of Muslim historiography as well as the other overlapping contexts is needed here in order to explain why Hamka was so active in history writing from the 1950s to the 1980s and the circumstances that have made his historical works so appealing even today. The years following the end of the Second World War witnessed the growth of a new trend in historiography throughout the Muslim world that was driven by the ideals of Islamic resurgence. Muslims of varying backgrounds and professions took on the essential task of writing new Muslim histories to achieve several purposes, such as galvanizing Muslims to unite under the framework of nation-states, critiquing and offering alternatives to Orientalist writings about Muslim histories, providing new perspectives on the forgotten struggles of Muslims against colonial rule, and celebrating the achievements of Muslims prior to the ascendance of the West.[10]

The group of fledgling writers who helped to expand the postwar Muslim historiography included clerics. For instance, the Pakistani cleric Maulana Abul A'la Maududi's book *A Short History of the Revivalist Movement in Islam* enjoyed immediate commercial success on its initial publication in Urdu in 1963. It was translated into English and other languages in the following decades.[11] Sharing similar success was the Egyptian don Ahmad Shalabi (1925–?), who also wrote popular Muslim history books that enjoyed widespread admiration. After being dismissed from the Dar al-Ulum (House of Sciences) in Cairo, Shalabi taught for several years at the Islamic University of Indonesia (1955–63). Shalabi's book *The History of Islam and Its Culture* (first published in Arabic in 1970) enjoyed a wide reception throughout the Muslim world and was reprinted several times in the Malay language.[12]

A similar trend in historical writings within the wider Muslim world was also evident in the Malay world. Muslim historiography received an encouraging boost

---

[9] Hamka, *Said Djamaluddin Al-Afghany*, and Hamka, *Ayahku*.

[10] Yvonne Haddad, *Contemporary Islam and the Challenge of History* (Albany: State University of New York Press, 1982).

[11] Maulana Abul A'la Maududi, *A Short History of the Revivalist Movement in Islam* (Karachi: Islamic Publications, 1963).

[12] Aḥmad Shalabi, *Sejarah dan Kebudayaan Islam* (Singapore: Penerbitan Pustaka Nasional, 1970).

Figure 7 University Hamka in Jakarta is one of the accredited universities in the country today.
Collection of the author.

during the period of decolonization, thanks to students who were trained in Western and Islamic universities.[13] Hundreds of new histories of Islam were published
to inspire the public with the splendors of the precolonial era. The spread of mass

---

[13] Sulasman, "Kiyai and Pesantren in the Islamic Historiography of Indonesia," *TAWARIKH:
International Journal for Historical Studies* 4, no. 1 (2012): 71–73.

education and literacy and the advent of publishing companies resulted in the mass production of books, journals, and magazines, which further enhanced the consumption of these popular books on Islamic history. In Indonesia from the 1960s onward, reformist Muslims organized conferences and wrote new Muslim histories that would indirectly challenge the official national histories produced by the Indonesian state.[14]

Hamka was at the crest of this new wave of Muslim historiography in addition to participating in various efforts to reform the Muslim community in the Malay world. He strove to popularize the reformist ideas from the Middle East and South Asia within the Malay world context. His project of Islamic reform was directed toward exposing his readers to the developments in the global Muslim community as a whole while at the same time addressing problems and issues in the local context. Such an outlook was in part inspired by one of his mentors, Agus Salim.[15] Indeed, what clearly distinguished Hamka from other writers in the Malay world in his time was not only that he wrote in the vernacular language or that he focused on Islamic history. Rather, his importance comes from the fact that his historical works obliquely addressed immediate challenges and also exposed his audience to the cosmopolitan reforms that he sought to promote.

Uppermost on Hamka's list of concerns was the rapid growth of secularism among Muslims in Indonesia. Secularist thinking came in a variety of forms: from those who advocated a privatization of religion, separate from public sphere, to those who envisioned the creation of socialist state to the proponents of militant communism. The mass executions of communists in Indonesia in the 1960s sent shock waves through the Muslim community, not only because of the brutality of the state but also because of the spread of communism in that country.[16] One thread that bound these different strands of secularist thinking was the reinterpretation of the importance of Islam in the lives of ordinary Indonesians. Since the 1960s, this secular trend had troubled many Indonesian clerics and Muslim activists, including Hamka.[17] To combat secularism, he advocated a modernized Islamic education. Hamka was part of the Muhammadiyah modernist movement, which was critical of the backwardness of the traditional ulama and their adherence to old interpretations of Islamic history that did not appeal to the emerging class of educated Muslims. The Muhammadiyah movement founded schools that taught modern subjects along with the Islamic sciences. Students were also taught world history as part of the movement's efforts to keep them abreast of the developments in the larger ummah.[18]

Among the other germane issues—as seen chapter 5—was the mushrooming of heretical Sufi cults in the country and, with it, the rise of anti-Sufi thinking among many mainstream Muslims. In the 1970s, for example, Javanese mystical groups

---

[14] Michael Wood, *Official History in Modern Indonesia* (Leiden, Neth.: Brill, 2005), 165–66.

[15] Hamka, "Haji Agus Salim sebagai Sastrawan dan Ulama," in *100 Tahun H. Agus Salim*, ed. Panitia 100 Tahun (Jakarta: Sinar Harapan, 1984): 252–65.

[16] Robert Cribb, "Genocide in Indonesia," *Journal of Genocide Research* 3, no. 2 (2001): 219–39.

[17] Nader Hashemi, *Islam, Secularism and Liberal Democracy* (New York: Oxford University Press, 2009): 159, and Lutfi Assyaukanie, *Islam and the Secular State in Indonesia* (Singapore: ISEAS Press, 2009), 149.

[18] Robert W. Hefner, "Social Legacies and Possible Futures," in *Indonesia: The Great Transition*, ed. John Bresnan (Lanham, MD: Rowman & Littlefield, 2005), 92.

agitated for official recognition of their heterodox practices, a move that gained the ire of major Muslim organizations such as the Muhammadiyah. The divide between Sufis and anti-Sufis became so marked during this period that some Sufi groups were accused by their adversaries of being closet communists, or at least of providing shelter for former communists.[19] History writing was thus one avenue that Hamka used to remind the Muslims about their shared heritage and the need to preserve it and remember those persons who had worked toward the restoration of Islamic brotherhood. This could also explain why Hamka's historical works continue to remain popular. They touched on issues that are still very much alive and vigorously debated in the Malay world.[20]

Because Hamka's historical writings dealt with these pertinent challenges, he and many other clerics with similar approaches broadened their appeal and made "significant contributions to public discourses . . . even in setting the terms for such discourses."[21] By the 1930s, Hamka's books were already found in libraries of local schools. His ardent followers were school students and young adults. Mesmerized by his historical works, a notable group of young scholars went on to do research on many topics about the history of Islam in Malay world.[22] It is to these works, which he used as tools of reform, that we now turn.

CONNECTED HISTORIES OF THE UMMAH

Hamka's historical works are marked by their enticing prose and unconventional arguments that were employed to describe the vastness and connectedness of Muslim history, as shown in *Sejarah Umat Islam*. A monumental work that resulted from two decades of research (from 1939 to 1961), this book was the first global history of the Muslim peoples to be written in the Malay language.[23] Divided into seven parts and thirty-nine chapters, the book begins, like most histories of Islam, with pre-Islamic Arab society and the conditions that gave rise to the first Muslim, Muhammad. His approach to the life of the Prophet is innovative because he utilizes not only traditional sources such as the Hadiths but also the works of non-Muslim scholars whom he found to be objective and reliable. This is followed by the period of the Righteous Caliphs (*Khulafa Rashidun*), the Umayyads, the Abbasids, and the Muslim kingdoms in Spain, Africa, Persia, South Asia, and Turkey. The last chapter of the book traces

---

[19] Mark Woodward, *Java, Indonesia and Islam* (New York: Springer, 2011), 26, and Martin van Bruinessen, "Saints, Politicians and Sufi Bureaucrats: Mysticism and Politics in Indonesia's New Order," in *Sufism and the "Modern" in Islam*, ed. Martin van Bruinessen and Julia Day Howell (New York: I.B. Tauris, 2007), 98.

[20] For debates over Islamic issues that Hamka mentioned in his histories, see Carool Kersten, *Islam in Indonesia: The Contest for Society, Ideas and Values* (New York: Oxford University Press, 2015).

[21] Muhammad Qasim Zaman, *The Ulama in Contemporary Islam* (Princeton: Princeton University Press, 2002), 2.

[22] A. Suryana Sudrajat, *Ulama pejuang dan ulama petualang: Belajar kearifan dari Negeri Atas Angin* (Jakarta: Penerbit Erlangga, 2006), 14; Mohammad Redzuan Othman, "Sumbangan HAMKA dalam Penulisan Sejarah Melayu di Alam Melayu," in *Pemikiran Hamka*, ed. Siddiq Fadzil (Kuala Lumpur: Dewan Bahasa dan Pustaka, 2008), 115–29, and Wood, *Official History in Modern Indonesia*, 165.

[23] Sulasman M. Hum, "Rethinking Islamic Historiography in Indonesia," *Journal of Social Sciences* 2, no. 4 (2013): 201, and Hamka, *Sejarah Umat Islam*, i.

the history of Islam in the Malay world up to the seventeenth century. As a form of reformist history, *Sejarah Umat Islam* manifests some interesting features that enabled it to shape the thinking of the masses.

Hamka wrote in a style that evoked emotions and provided historical facts with a sense of contemporary and contextual relevance. *Sejarah Umat Islam* incorporates the use of all four types of plotting strategies in historical writing described by Hayden White (romance, comedy, tragedy, and satire) throughout the book.[24] This style of writing history is, of course, not unique to this particular work by Hamka or to him alone. It is a style that distinguishes many public and popular histories in Indonesia and beyond. Simon Schama called such a style of writing the "poetic connexion" in that historians strive to "persuade our readers or our viewers to suspend their disbelief; to spend a while imagining they are indeed in a world akin, I suppose, to dreams or memories, a fugitive universe."[25] From this, it follows that Hamka's structuring of the book makes Muslim history applicable to the present while being a basis for reflection and further action. The Muslim past, from this position, is not a foreign country; it is instead a living trove of wisdom and a mirror of introspection, which Muslims are called on to empathize with, reflect on, and draw on to understand their own circumstances and to strive toward the construction of a better future.

A few examples will suffice to illustrate Hamka's evocative, persuasive, and advocacy-oriented writing style. He explained, for example, that the chapter on the life of Prophet Muhammad was written for the sole reason of providing "lessons for my people who are at the nascent stages of awakening."[26] A few pages later, in a preamble for the chapter on Andalusia, Hamka stressed that readers would encounter "with much sadness the expulsion of Muslims from Spain. . . . Hence you will witness the never-ending struggle and reach the conclusion that Islam has gone through so many tribulations. It fell asunder too often! But it rose again, and stood firm and moved on. Islam will not succumb!"[27] A third example is found in the pages on the Abbasid caliph Al-Mu'tazz (847–69). Hamka portrayed the caliph as an unpopular king whose tyranny, lust for power, and love for worldly wealth led to his assassination and the ceding of power to Turkish mercenaries. Writing in a hyperbolic way to warn his readers about the dangers of following in the footsteps of Caliph Al-Mu'tazz, Hamka wrote, "Thus came to an end the life of a human being who traversed all avenues for position. The Turks become more powerful as a result of this, distributing the monies from the state treasury to fill up their stomachs."[28]

The second reformist aspect of *Sejarah Umat Islam*, which at the same time reflects Hamka's cosmopolitan outlook, is its presentation of the vast history Islam and Muslims in an interconnected and comparative way, rather than in separate, distinct regional or national units. Notably, Hamka's approach is in line with his contemporary, the pathbreaking Islamicist Marshall Hodgson (1922–68). Hodgson maintained that

---

[24] Hayden White, *Metahistory: The Historical Imagination in Nineteenth-Century Europe* (Baltimore: Johns Hopkins University Press, 1973), 10.

[25] Quoted in Justin Champion, "Seeing the Past: Simon Schama's 'A History of Britain' and Public History," *History Workshop Journal* 56, no. 1 (2003): 166.

[26] Hamka, *Sejarah Umat Islam*, 2.

[27] Ibid., 3.

[28] Ibid., 283.

"Islamic civilization should be studied not only in the several regions where it flour-ished, but also as a historical whole, as a major element in forming the destiny of all mankind. The vast Islamic society certainly has been this."[29] Hamka made frequent comparisons between the societies and histories of the Arab-Muslim world and those of their African, Turkish, and Malay counterparts. As a cosmopolitan public historian who was not bound by the rules of academic history, he went further to move effort-lessly across time and space in two main ways.

In the first place, Hamka sought to draw similarities and parallels between occurrences that took place in one Muslim context with those of another. This approach to the narration of Muslim history is employed throughout the book. One interesting example is the section on Arab society before the coming of the Prophet. Here Hamka explained the differences between the language of the people of Hijaz and that of the Yemenites in the sixth century. Such differences, in his view, could be closely compared to the variations between the Malay language in Indonesia and that in Malaysia in the 1960s.[30] Later, in a section on the caliph Al-Mustakfi (905–949), who reigned for less than a year before he was deposed, Hamka com-pared the fate of this Abbasid caliph to that of the Ottoman sultan Abdul Majid II, who was deposed and exiled by Kamal Ataturk after reigning for less than two years (November 1922–March 1924).[31]

Aside from drawing parallels between different contexts, in his writing Hamka traveled from one time zone to another to show recurrences within one geographical area. Frederick Cooper has criticized such an approach, branding it "leapfrogging lega-cies." By this he meant a historian's fallacy of showing connections between events in two different time periods without explaining the processes that took place in between and the circumstances that might explain these recurrences.[32] For cosmopolitan pub-lic historians like Hamka, leapfrogging legacies are a source of strength rather weak-ness because such an approach engenders more alluring historical narratives. The history of the city of Tripoli in modern-day Libya is a case in point. Hamka discussed how and why Tripoli had been continuously subjected to foreign colonization, the lon-gest duration of which was under the Turks in the sixteenth century. Many hundreds of years later, in 1912, the same city was again subjected to colonial rule, this time by Italy. Hamka did not discuss what happened between these two different time periods or why Tripoli was prone to foreign invasion.[33]

In a similar way, Hamka narrated what he viewed as an unbroken chain of bat-tles between Muslims and the Crusaders. Although mainstream historians main-tain that the Crusades ended in the thirteenth century, Hamka argued otherwise. For him, the spirit of the Crusades remained in the hearts of the European imperi-alists for several centuries, only to reemerge in the twentieth century. "During the First World War," he wrote, "Palestine was taken over by the English. Lord Allenby, the commander of the English forces, was obviously not able to suppress what was

---

[29] Marshall Hodgson, *Rethinking World History: Essays on Europe, Islam and World History* (New York: Cambridge University Press, 1993), 171.

[30] Hamka, *Sejarah Umat Islam*, 19–20.

[31] Ibid., 290.

[32] Frederick Cooper, *Colonialism in Question: Theory, Knowledge, History* (Berkeley: University of California Press, 2005), 17–18.

[33] Hamka, *Sejarah Umat Islam*, 325.

embedded in his heart when he exclaimed, 'Now the Crusades have formally ended with this conquest of Palestine!'"[34]

One other reformist feature of Hamka's *Sejarah Umat Islam* is its heavy emphasis on Malay-Islamic history. The attention given to the Malay world was a marked departure from the emphasis in most textbooks and surveys of the global history of Islam that were published from the 1930s to the 1960s. Until the late twentieth century, the Malay world was always marginalized within the field of Islamic studies because the beliefs and practices of Muslims in that region were presumed to be derivatives of Middle Eastern Islam.[35] Hamka filled this lacuna in the literature by dedicating one-third of his nine hundred-page book to describing the evolution of Islam in the Malay world, covering topics such as the Hindu-Buddhist legacies, the theories of Islamization, the spread of Islam in different kingdoms throughout the region, the impact of colonialism, and early Muslim resistance toward colonial rule. Hamka's approach to sources and revisionist elucidations of the Islamization of the Malay world vividly demonstrate the book's reformist character.

In terms of sources, Hamka afforded a balanced and thoughtful view of Orientalists and their studies of Islamic history at a time when most Muslim writers were cynical toward Orientalism.[36] Muslims in the Malay world, Hamka urged, should be open-minded and not be so swayed by *tekanan-tekanan politik* (political pressures) that they became biased against the works of non-Muslim scholars.[37] Orientalist writings about Islam and Muslims were to be critiqued and corrected when interpretive errors got in the way of accurate representations of Muslim pasts. The works of Orientalists must, however, be credited when they exhibited a perceptive and in-depth understanding of Muslim societies. Hamka acknowledged the scholarly interventions of Thomas Arnold (1795–1842), Gustave Le Bon (1841–1931), Rudolf Kern (1873–1958), and Nicholas Johannes Krom (1883–1945), whose writings on Islam tended to be fair and objective. He was more circumspect toward Dutch Orientalists because of a sense that imperialistic and missionary ends might have colored their research. Hamka's methodological position was thus analogous to that of another prominent Malay world historian, Syed Naquib Al-Attas, who also acknowledged the contributions of Dutch Orientalists with a guarded awareness of their biases and prejudices.[38] In the opening pages of *Sejarah Umat Islam*, Hamka wrote,

> Finally, we must be thankful toward the Dutch scholars who researched the history of Muslim kingdoms during their periods of greatness. A reading of the research of the Dutch scholars provides us with many sources on the evolution of Islam and its growth in Indonesia. They were the ones who propounded the theories of history and the attendant facts, to the point of the minutest details. . . . But the findings of these scholars should not to be accepted

---

[34] Ibid., 367.

[35] Robert W. Hefner, "Islam in the Era of Nation-States: Politics and Religious Renewal in Muslim Southeast Asia," in *Islam in the Era of Nation-States*, ed. Robert W. Hefner (Honolulu: University of Hawai'i Press, 1997), 9.

[36] See, for example, A. L. Tibawi, "English Speaking Orientalists," *Islamic Quarterly* 8 (1964): 25–64.

[37] Hamka, *Sejarah Umat Islam*, 666.

[38] Syed Muhd Khairudin Aljunied, "Transcending Orientalism: Syed Muhammad Naquib Al-Attas and the History of Islam in the Malay World," *Tafhim* 6, no. 1 (2014): 1–21.

uncritically. There are two issues, which they could not distance themselves from fully, and their historical writings may be tainted by these "hidden agendas." They are: First of all, colonial and hegemonic interests. Second, the Christian missionizing ends.[39]

However, Hamka did not dwell on a drawn-out critique of Orientalism; to do so would have given too much attention to the very knowledge that he hoped to deconstruct. He sought instead to transcend the limitations of these works by providing his own revisionist interpretation of the Islamization of the Malay world. Hamka criticized Orientalists who attributed the spread of Islam in the Malay world to missionaries from India, thus postdating the arrival of the religion to the eleventh and twelfth centuries.[40] He instead pointed to evidence from Chinese, Arab, and Persian records that suggested that Muslim missionaries and traders had already set foot in the Malay world as early the seventh century, during the period of the Umayyads.[41] From the seventh century onward, Arabs established colonies in the region, and these Arabs converted the Hindu-Buddhist Malays to Islam and introduced a new religious life and worldview among them.

Hamka acknowledged the roles of other Muslim missionaries from India, China, and Persia and the agency of the Malays themselves in furthering what the Arabs had achieved. These later Muslim missionaries gradually propagated Islam in the region, making the Malay world one of the most populous Muslim regions in the world. How did they achieve this? Hamka proposed a seven-stage periodization framework that was designed to encourage his readers to rethink how Islam had developed in the Malay world within the context of the global evolution of the faith.[42]

Encyclopedic and, in many respects, a tour de force, *Sejarah Umat Islam* suffered from one glaring limitation: the bulk of the text covers the history of statesmen and caliphs, their intrigues, successes, and failures. It would be too far-fetched simply to label the book a political history because Hamka devoted many pages to cultural, intellectual, and social developments within various Muslim societies, along with geographical details of many parts of the Muslim world. In a passage within the text, he stated that "only the kings fell, Islam itself did not. If in the past the kings were the bastions of Islam, in the years that ensued, the bastions of Islam were the hearts of ordinary Muslims."[43] We can only surmise that Hamka saw that a history of such length and scope could be made simpler and more accessible to his lay readers by focusing on powerful figures that influenced the shape of events in the Muslim world. His method of addressing the limitations of his own magnum opus was to write his own biographies of Muslim reformers.

---

[39] Hamka, *Sejarah Umat Islam*, 5.

[40] See, for example, G. W. J. Drewes, "New Light on the Coming of Islam to Indonesia," *Bijdragen tot de Taal-, Land- en Volkenkunde* 124, no. 4 (1968): 433–59, and R. O. Windstedt, "The Advent of Muhammadanism in the Malay Peninsula and Archipelago," *Journal of the Royal Straits Branch of the Royal Asiatic Society* 77 (1917): 171–75.

[41] Hamka, *Sejarah Umat Islam*, 685–86.

[42] Ibid. 697–701.

[43] Ibid., 820.

ON THE AGENCY OF GRASSROOTS REFORMERS

The grassroots reformers who became the subjects of Hamka's sharp pen were Sayyid Jamaluddin Al-Afghani and Hamka's own father, Abdul Karim Amrullah. I use the term "grassroots reformers" because it captures Hamka's description of these two figures as *tokoh pergerakan dan tajdid*, which can be translated as "social movement and renewal personalities." The two figures were involved in the intellectual reform of Muslims at the same time that they were active in collectives that endeavored to change various aspects of the Muslims' social, educational, and economic conditions. Born in Afghanistan, Al-Afghani traveled across the Middle East, South Asia, and Europe to promote Pan-Islamic unity, Islamic modernism, and resistance against the West during the heydays of European colonialism.[44] While Al-Afghani was involved in transnational causes and promoting the creation of a global Muslim identity, Abdul Karim Amrullah had his eyes centered on the reformation of the local Indonesian community by advocating the abolition of *bid'ah* (innovations in Islam) and the adoption of modern forms of education. The two seemingly overlapping projects of these reformers are reflected in the titles of the books, namely, *Said Djamaludin Al-Afghany: Pelopor Kebangkitan Islam* (Said Djamaludin Al-Afghany: The Pioneer of Islamic Revivalism) and *Ayahku: Riwayat Hidup Dr. H. Abdul Karim Amrullah dan Perjuangan Kaum Agama di Sumatera* (My Father: A Biography of Dr. H. Abdul Karim Amrullah and the Struggle of Religious Groups in Sumatra). These two books ought to be analyzed together rather than separately, since they are similar in several ways.

Both books followed the same narrative structure, tracing the indelible impact that Western colonialism and Muslim lack of development had on the formative years of these two grassroots reformers. Hamka went on to explicate the forms of resistance that the two men faced both inside and outside Muslim society. He examined the ways in which these reformers transformed Muslim minds in order to prepare them to cope with the challenges of Western modernity. Undergirding these biographies is the emphasis given to the strategic alliances that these men forged with equally talented and committed persons to further their reformist goals. The books, from this perspective, differed significantly from most Western biographies, in which "a biographer usually focuses on his or her subject's individuality, those aspects, attitudes, and abilities that separate the subject from the masses."[45] Al-Afghani and Abdul Karim Amrullah were not necessarily distinct from the Muslim masses. Hamka showed how many individuals and groups in their milieu had aided their causes while molding their worldviews and ideas.

Both books also reflect Paula Backscheider's point that most "decisions to write a biography of a specific person have an element of intellectual or personal passion."[46] Personal passion drove Hamka to write the biography of his father, who was, as Harry

---

[44] One of the best studies of Jamaluddin Al-Afghani is by the late Nikki R. Keddie. See *An Islamic Response to Imperialism: Political and Religious Writings of Sayyid Jamal al-Din al-Afghani* (Berkeley: University of California Press, 1968).

[45] R. Keith Schoppa, "Culture and Context in Biographical Studies: The Case of China," in *Writing Biography: Historians & Their Craft*, ed. Lloyd E. Ambrosius (Lincoln: University of Nebraska Press, 2004), 28.

[46] Paula R. Backscheider, *Reflections on Biography* (Oxford: Oxford University Press, 1999), 31.

Benda succinctly put it, "one of the most impressive and influential representatives of Indonesian reformism."[47] Hamka maintained that one of the factors that spurred him to work on the biography was the fact that, since he was "the eldest child and was able to observe him [his father] up close, I knew more about his aspirations, his acquaintances, his likings, his passions, and his idiosyncrasies as a human being."[48] Intellectual motivations, in turn, encouraged him to write the biography of Al-Afghani. He praised the European, American, and Muslim scholars who had all recognized the long shadow that Al-Afghani had cast in the history of revivalism in Asia and Africa, so much so that no study of Islam would be complete without a reference to him. His biography thus adds to a growing body of work on Al-Afghani that was being written in the Malay language.[49]

But Hamka's authorial motivations were guided not only by personal passions, familial connections, and intellectual curiosities. A close reading of these biographies reveals that he was also driven by other aims that were in line with his vocation as a cosmopolitan engaged in the writing of history as a tool of reform. Above all, he hoped that these biographies would instill a sense of pride in the hearts of Muslim youths—a group to which he directed most of his works throughout his writing career.[50] By telling the life stories of Al-Afghani and Abdul Karim Amrullah, Hamka hoped to make Muslim youths realize the importance of piety, fortitude, and determination in any person's attempt to reform his society. Ignorance of these virtues could result in the creation of a generation of Muslims whose "spirits are diminished" (*berjiwa kecil*) and who would forget that they were once a great people.[51] Hamka specifically targeted Muslim youths as his main audience because this group had played the most important role in expanding the appeal of the Islamic reformism that was pioneered by both Al-Afghani and Abdul Karim Amrullah. In Sumatra and Java, where Abdul Karim Amrullah spent most of his life spreading the message of Islamic reformism, the youths from Muslim schools helped to recruit many Muslims to join reformist organizations such as the Muhammadiyah.[52]

Second, the study of important persons served to remind Muslims in the Malay world of the need to see themselves as belonging to a genealogy of struggles for freedom and reformation.[53] The life journey of Al-Afghani, according to Hamka, and the multitude of obstacles and opportunities that he had undergone were not unique; rather, they were typical of the kinds of experiences that would be faced by any Muslim who sought to follow his path. Abdul Karim Amrullah faced setbacks that were similar to those encountered by Al-Afghani. In fact, one chapter of the biography of Abdul Karim Amrullah was devoted to a discussion of the fates of Al-Afghani and his followers in the Arab world and the Malay world, by way of showing not only that the reformist project was global in reach but also that the life of one Muslim reformer

---

[47]   Harry J. Benda, "Southeast Asian Islam in the Twentieth Century," in *The Cambridge History of Islam*, vol. 2A, ed. P. M. Holt, Ann K. S. Lambton, and Bernard Lewis (Cambridge: Cambridge University Press, 1979), 189.

[48]   Hamka, *Ayahku*, i.

[49]   Hamka, *Said Djamaluddin Al-Afghany*, 11.

[50]   Peter Riddell, *Islam and the Malay-Indonesian World*, 268.

[51]   Hamka, *Said Djamaluddin Al-Afghany*, 26.

[52]   Hamka, *Ayahku*, 113–50.

[53]   Hamka, *Said Djamaluddin Al-Afghany*, 11.

would inevitably reflect or at least mirror that of another. Hamka also admonished his readers to avoid arguing about Al-Afghani's nationality in the closing pages of the biography: "We are not concerned with whether he [Al-Afghani] is Iranian or Afghan. What is clear is that he belongs to the entire Muslim world. Indonesia is his homeland too. His portraits are hung in Indonesia but not in Afghanistan or even in Iran. The history of the reformist movement in Indonesia begins with the diffusion of the ideas and teachings of Djamaluddin and Abduh into Indonesia, at around 1906AD/1326M."[54]

Third, the two biographies served as launching pads for the critique of selected social groups in society. Hamka singled out the umara and the ulama as groups that had been the source of hindrance to critical thought, stifling the ability of Muslim societies to adapt to modern life. These two groups schemed against reformers to protect their status and positions. Ideally, the leaders and religious scholars were supposed to be the torchbearers of development, unity, and intellectualism. But in the case of Al-Afghani, the reverse held true; these groups rejected him. Writing in an emotive way, Hamka explained, "The biggest obstacle to Muslim unity . . . was not anyone else but the kings. And they were supported by a group called the ulama! The kings exploited the common people, oppressing them, making them ignorant, and the ulama supported the kings! Both of these obstacles must be removed. First by way of enhancing the energies of the common people, eradicating their ignorance. And more importantly by breaking the ropes of taqlid. That is to follow blindly."[55] Abdul Karim Amrullah, by Hamka's account, faced the same resistance from state-sponsored ulama in his society. Among his father's staunch enemies were Sufi scholars who labeled him and his followers *orang-orang sesat* (deviant people).[56]

In the last analysis, the biographies that Hamka wrote are but a reflection of who he was. Or, in the words of Shirley Leckie, "all biography is, in part, autobiographical."[57] Through the absorbing life stories of these two men, Hamka as a cosmopolitan public historian pursued his own ideas of reforms without necessarily making these ideas too explicit in his narratives. One reform that he pursued was a movement beyond partisan histories. Hamka was critical of the sort of histories that were clouded by sectarian divisions within Islam. He stressed that Al-Afghani should not be seen as belonging to a given sect, Shiite or Sunni. He was the pride of the whole world of Islam.[58] Hamka drove home the point that partisan histories obscured a more comprehensive and fair view of the Muslim pasts. His own narrative was thus reformist in that he sought to promote an alternative method that transcended Muslim ethnic parochialism, sectarian fanaticism, and ideological bias in the writing of history.

MUSLIMS AND SOCIAL JUSTICE

In chapter 3 I discussed Hamka's lengthy deliberations of the nature, purposes, and enablers of social justice from the Islamic perspective. As a cosmopolitan public

---

[54] Ibid., 175.

[55] Ibid., 11.

[56] Hamka, *Ayahku*, 290–92.

[57] Shirley A. Leckie, "Biography Matters: Why Historians Need Well-Crafted Biographies More Than Ever," in Ambrosius, *Writing Biography*, 2.

[58] Hamka, *Said Djamaluddin Al-Afghany*, 175.

historian, Hamka asked a related question: Have Muslims lived up to their ideals of social justice? His answer to this question was in the affirmative. For Hamka, the fact that Muslims embodied the Islamic conception of social justice was evidenced in the millennium-long history of Islam. The most ideal manifestation of social justice occurred during the time of Prophet Muhammad and his companions. Prophet Muhammad was guided by revelation and taught to his contemporaries the sanctity of human life, the freedom of all human beings, respect for women and children, the virtue of charity, the evils of exploitation, and the notion that no needy person should be denied assistance. These teachings revolutionized Arab society in the decades following the Prophet's demise, changing a community that had been rampantly unjust into a civilization that was defined by the spirit of universal brotherhood.

Many remnants of prejudiced practices during the age of ignorance, Hamka wrote, persisted in Arab society. But the balance sheet of history showed the Prophet and his companions had, by addressing the stark inequalities in society, created a powerful civilization that was admired by others. Hamka buttressed this point by quoting the famed British writer Ronald Victor Courtenay Bodley (1892–1970), who wrote in his long biography titled *The Messenger: The Life of Mohammed* that true socialism could be found in the teachings of Islam. This was realized during the time of the Prophet. The Prophet shunned injustice. According to Bodley, he was the arch defender of the poor and the underclass in his setting.[59]

Using the Prophet and his companions as his yardstick, Hamka sharply observed that, for much of Islamic history, many Muslim rulers had departed from the examples shown by the first generation of Muslims. There were, however, enlightened rulers such as Umar Abdul Aziz (682–720), Salahuddin Al-Ayyubi (1137–1193), Muhammad Al-Fatih (1432–1481), Akbar the Great (1556–1605), and Mansur Shah (1456–1477). Nonetheless, his study of the global Muslim past revealed that there were countless episodes in which social justice had been breached by Muslim rulers and their underlings. The most vivid example of this occurred during the nineteenth century, when the Muslim empires were at their lowest ebb. Most rulers during this period were concerned largely with their self-preservation. They were in cahoots with the colonialists in making use of the common people to accumulate wealth and to maintain their statuses. Because of this, Muslims became pawns in the chessboards of Christian missionaries and European colonizers.[60]

This brings us to Hamka's contemporaneous assessment of the state of social justice in the Malay world. He was firm about the reality of manifold injustice in Muslim societies in the Malay world and the Muslim world as a whole. In the Malay world more specifically, Hamka highlighted the maltreatment of Muslim women in the family and in the many other areas of life. He also brought to the fore the problem of poverty that characterized Malay-Muslims, leading to the rise of social ills such as prostitution, petty crimes, and other criminal activities. Even though many countries in the Malay world and elsewhere had achieved independence by the 1960s, Hamka held that the ruling states had done little to the alleviate class divisions and tensions between the rich and the poor. If anything, the leaders of postcolonial Muslim

---

[59] Hamka, *Sejarah Umat Islam*, 199. See Ronald Victor Courtenay Bodley, *The Messenger: The Life of Mohammed* (New York: Doubleday, 1946).

[60] Hamka, *Cara Zending dan Missi Menyerang Aqidah Kita.*

states exercised their hegemony over the masses by maintaining colonial policies and exploitative structures, or what Hamka termed "the scraps of colonialism."[61]

At the heart of all these injustices was the heedlessness toward Islam and the Islamic conception of justice by Muslims themselves:

> Economics [ought to be] guided by ethics. It is forbidden for the rich to do anything they like with their wealth, for pleasure and liquor, and for betting on horses and so forth. The affluent are enjoined to give part of their wealth to help the poor and destitute, those that are swept by the wave of society. If these teachings are realized, the class struggles that we have now will surely vanish, [along with] the endless expressions of vengeance. There will no longer be those who are excessively wealthy, those who are downright poor, but a fine rope binds the rich and the poor, a rope of service to God for society. Generally, Muslims have long forgotten such teachings, to the extent that what is left is merely in writing without anyone practicing it. Happiness in the life of a Muslim can only be reclaimed if that person returns to those teachings.[62]

Hamka further stressed that while heedlessness of faith had made Muslims unjust, the loss of personal character had sealed their fates. Muslims had succumbed to a few evil traits: *riya* (arrogance), *tamak* (greed), and *dengki* (envy). Riya had caused Muslims to look with disdain at their own coreligionists and others. They regarded the people around them only as means to these ends. Arrogant and greedy persons, Hamka added, were addicted to praise and admiration from others. They were also envious of anyone who was doing well and would find ways to outdo and cripple the efforts of their competitors. They cheated in their business dealings, lied when they spoke, and betrayed the trusts given to them. The effects of these traits, which had plagued Malay-Muslims from various backgrounds, were animosity, dishonesty, and hypocrisy, as well as disunity in Muslim societies, which paved the way to the continued manipulation by European countries.[63] Or, to put it differently, a dog-eat-dog environment reigned supreme in which even efforts that at first appeared to be for the benefit of society become launchpads for the self-absorbed.[64]

The fact that Muslims were heedless of their own faith and displayed bad character had made them susceptible to the machinations of persecutors. Hamka gave the examples of the Zionist occupation of Palestine and the annexation of many Muslim settlements in Mindanao, Philippines. All these cases of victimhood were linked to social injustices committed by the Muslims themselves.[65] But Hamka was not a negativist. He was optimistic that Muslims in the Malay world would be torchbearers of social justice if they strove to recover the ideals and practices that had been cast aside.

Hamka's histories have widened public knowledge and appreciation of the past in ways that are not so easily achieved by professional historians. The reasons for this

---

[61] Hamka, *Hak Asasi Manusia dalam Islam dan Deklarasi PBB*, 188.

[62] Hamka, *Keadilan Sosial Dalam Islam*, 135.

[63] Ibid., 82.

[64] Hamka, *Akhlaqul Karimah*, 177–81.

[65] Hamka, *Di Bawah Gema Takbir* (Kuala Lumpur: Utusan Melayu Berhad, 1976), 65.

are quite obvious. He could move freely across different themes without having to meet the demands of specialization. He was also able to write narratives that were wide-ranging in scope while taking occasional leaps across time and space, feats that are impossible for those who are bound by the conventions of scholarship. The emotive prose and journalistic style that Hamka utilized to structure his histories also give these works the power to motivate readers to read about the past in the same gratifying way as they would read works of fiction. More crucially, the calls to action that are so often embedded within Hamka's histories are appealing to readers who prefer to view history not merely as an account of past happenings but as a model for reform that is relevant in everyday life.

In 1991 Graeme Davison summed up the various strands of public history using a fashion metaphor: 'People's History is history in blue jeans; Public History is history in a tweed jacket; Applied History is history in a grey flannel suit.'[66] I would add that Hamka's historical works are best described as "history in flamboyant robes," written by a cosmopolitan reformer whose presentation and representation of the past piqued the interest of the masses in the Malay world. Indeed, Hamka's historical works were his tools to reform the minds of Muslims. History served as a useful instrument by which Hamka could make Muslims more aware of their pasts in the road to reconstruct their understanding of Islam into becoming one that is more more inclusive, humanistic and, most importantly, so that they could learn to understand Islam as a religion that is inclusive, humanistic, and—most important—cosmopolitan.

---

[66] Graeme Davison, "Paradigms of Public History," *Australian Historical Studies* 24, no. 96 (1991): 12.

CONCLUSION
Thinking with Hamka

The advent of the twentieth century ushered in a new chapter for Muslims in the Malay world as the community of believers confronted the destabilizing effects of modernity. The Malay feudal order had already been weakened by the colonial powers. The masses, now under European rule, were exposed to secular influences that crept into almost all aspects of Muslim life. These rapid changes were soon met by responses from the proponents of traditionalism, Sufism, Salafism, and Islamic reformism, all of whom held that Muslims must choose between total subservience to the West and charting their own path toward self-determination. It did not take long before the advocates of these disparate ideologies were on a collision course. Such skirmishes did much to divide Muslims in the region into different splinters, with each group asserting that only its vision of Islam would be best for society. From the 1930s until the last days of decolonization in the 1970s, Islam in the Malay world became an arena of conflict between the communities of believers and between Muslims and non-Muslims. "The old world," as a noted historian explained, "was gradually being swept away by the new modes of Islamic thinking. Traditional authority structures were being challenged, as was the right of Sufi approaches to hold center stage on the Malay theological arena."[1]

Hamka was at the center of these stormy currents. He witnessed one ideological battle after another among Muslims from a variety of backgrounds. He saw how anxieties about the future of Islam had led some Muslims to become insular and chauvinistic. Although Hamka admired the courage many movements and intellectuals showed in planting the seeds of reformism and in urging social change, he recognized that there was a need to move beyond polemics and divisive rhetoric. He was cognizant that, left unresolved, the divisions among Muslims would stifle the renewal of Islamic thought and practice.[2] His method of reconstructing Muslim minds was unique. It was a fresh variant of reform that manifested tolerance, moderation, positivity, and inclusiveness and embraced an array of influential ideas stemming from Islam and other intellectual traditions. Hamka did not live to describe neatly the new brand of reform that he was promoting. He would not have done so after all, preferring the *angkatan baru* (new generation) of *pemuda* (youthful) Muslims to think, reflect, and build on the rich legacy of works that he and his generation of reformers were leaving behind.[3] I term Hamka's innovative approach to reconstructing Muslim thought in the Malay World cosmopolitan reform.

---

[1] Riddell, *Islam and the Malay-Indonesian World*, 215.

[2] Hamka, *Teguran Suci dan Jujur Terhadap Mufti Johor*, 43.

[3] Hamka, *Lembaga Hidup*, 253, and Hamka, *Pribadi*, 164.

Hamka blended and appropriated relevant ideas from many streams of Islamic thought to breathe new life into Malay-Muslims' understanding of their faith. To him, every school of thought in Islam had particular strengths from which modern Muslims could benefit. The rapid changes in the modern world required Muslims to be pluralistic and open to other ways of thinking about Islam rather than partisans of a single paradigm. Toward that end, he called on them to utilize ideas from the millennium-old genealogy of Islamic scholarship. Muslim societies, he argued, could achieve great heights in all areas of life if they moved beyond disputes over microreligious issues and focused on matters that affected all Muslims, as well as humanity at large.[4]

Furthermore, Hamka believed that to actualize cosmopolitan reform Muslims must be receptive to the ideas of non-Muslims as well. He encouraged his coreligionists to be abreast of new developments in philosophy, in the sciences, and in other branches of modern knowledge. He stressed that all Muslims must be informed in as many disciplines as possible and develop expertise in every field of knowledge. As an example he pointed to the lives of medieval Muslim philosophers and scientists whose expertise in various sciences that they learned from other civilizations had transformed Islam into a faith that was respected and envied by all. It was the developments in scientific and philosophical thought in the Muslim world that ushered in the Enlightenment, the founding of great universities, and the advent of modernity in Europe.[5] At the same time, to be absorbed in the study of sciences hailing from other nations and cultures required Muslims in the Malay world to move beyond prejudices as well as racialist and intolerant tendencies that had imprisoned their minds for too long. Hamka was certain that Muslims could transcend these obstacles if they addressed a number of long-standing crises in thought and action.

The first step toward actualizing cosmopolitan reform began with the reclamation of guided reason. This was a form of reason that eschewed taqlid and overreliance on the suppositions of preceding generations without taking into consideration the radical transformations that came with modernity and globalization. Guided reason was, to Hamka, a form of reasoning guided by the Qur'an and Hadith, by good character, and by changing contexts, as well as by the introduction of new knowledge to redefine and reinvigorate how Islam was to be lived and practiced. By applying this form of reasoning, scholars and ordinary Muslims alike would use the study of Islam to offer fresh solutions to contemporary problems.[6] While guided reason provided Muslims with the intellectual tool kit to enable them to cope with the ever-changing world, a wholesome approach to life and faith required moderation in all things. Moderation, from Hamka's point of view, was an antidote to the extremism and fanaticism that had plagued Muslims for many generations. It was also a potent defense against negative media and scholarly portrayals of Muslims as a community that was predisposed to zealotry.

Hamka believed that guided reason and moderation would not be enough to orient Muslims toward a more nuanced attitude regarding knowledge and the practice of everyday life. Another aspect of reform that Muslims severely needed was the upholding of social justice. The idea of social justice in Muslim societies, Hamka wrote, suffered from the corruptive sway of materialist and partisan ideologies. These

---

4 Hamka, *Pengaruh Muhammad Abduh di Indonesia*, 18.

5 Hamka, *Pelajaran Agama Islam*, 259.

6 Hamka, *Tafsir Al-Azhar*, 8:2360.

interpretations of social justice failed to ensure equality globally. Hamka's alternative was to reclaim the Islamic conceptions of social justice, which were guided by the practical concepts of khalifatullah fil'ard, amanah, shura, and maslahah. The Islamic conception of social justice could flourish only when good leaders and responsible institutions appreciated and implemented its requirements. Hamka gave hope to the masses by insisting that the weakest in society be justly treated. Among the weakest in Muslim societies during Hamka's lifetime were women.

Women in the twentieth-century Malay world were victims of all forms of oppression. Hamka wrote against such tyranny and sought to uproot it by waging an intellectual battle against hegemonic gendered paradigms. Through his novels and other writings, he questioned various dominant understandings of the roles, functions, and responsibilities of women in Islam and societies across the Malay world while offering new discourses regarding women's empowerment. In his view, the dire state of women mirrored Muslims' outlook toward spirituality. Attitudes toward women and Sufism were tainted with Orientalist and wrongful misinterpretations of Islam and had been muddled by irrationality and superstition. Hamka's cosmopolitan reform was directed at restoring Sufism in the Malay world by offering fresh readings of the geneses, boundaries, and objectives of Islamic spirituality. The reform of Sufism, as Hamka saw it, must be carried out alongside the reform of the state of women because both aspects were necessary for the vitality of the social and spiritual dimensions of modern Muslim life.

The last facet of Hamka's cosmopolitan reform centered on rewriting Muslim history. He used history to inform Malay-Muslims of the achievements of their ancestors and to show that they could chart their own achievements. Hamka's reformist histories tracked the global connections that Muslim societies had had prior to colonialism and the connections that were reestablished by reformers such Al-Afghani and Hamka's own father. What Islam had to offer historically was the making of a socially just global society. This could be reenacted and relived only if Muslims knew about their past and if they learned from other cultures and acted on the lessons of history.

Still, it is important to recognize that despite Hamka's tolerance and breadth in thinking, he worked for the most part within the modernist and Sunni body of thought. A product of his intellectual environment, Hamka used Sunni modernism as his primary frame of reference to articulate his ideas of reform. He was, however, open to premodern ideas and drew heavily from the writings of thinkers outside the Sunni fold. For Hamka, no strain of thinking was perfect. No school of thought should be regarded as absolute. Cosmopolitan reformers, therefore, need not be free-floating intellectuals without any ideological base or attachment to any systems of thought. Instead, Hamka showed that they could be firmly located within a particular intellectual tradition but still be organic, constantly questioning and relentlessly reconstructing the very intellectual traditions they belonged to.

Was Hamka alone in the call for cosmopolitan reform? Certainly not. A quick survey of Islamic reformist thought in the twentieth century reveals a long list of thinkers who followed a course similar to Hamka's. One could include Mahmud Shaltut, Malek Bennabi, Muhammad Iqbal, and Ali Syariati, among many others, who called for reforms in Muslim thought and for Muslims to be impartial in their attitudes regarding matters of faith and piety. Taken together, these cosmopolitan reformers changed the manner in which Islam had been interpreted while paving the way for the development of new institutions and causes that promoted rethinking the place of reason, moderation, social justice, women, Islamic spirituality, and the historiography of Muslim countries across the globe. What sets Hamka apart from many of these scholars and intellectuals is that he was able to delve into so many cognate disciplines in Islam while making inroads even in the areas of fiction and poetry. This was a remarkable accomplishment unsurpassed by most of his peers that has made Hamka so difficult to ignore.

It is therefore unfortunate that even after close to half a century of wide recognition in the Malay world, Hamka's ideas have yet to make a deep impact outside the region he called home. The cosmopolitan reform he championed has touched the hearts of millions, but little is known about him in the wider Muslim world. This neglect of Hamka may be partly attributed to the limitations of language. He wrote in the Malay-Indonesian language, while the rest of the Muslim world is more exposed to Islamic writings in the Arabic and European languages. Beyond the linguistic factor, Islam in the Malay world has been relatively marginalized since the last century in discussions regarding intellectual reforms in the Muslim world as a whole. Indeed, despite the rapid expansion of publications on Islam and Muslims in the Malay world, a problematic tendency persists.

Malay-Islamic thought has often been cast as peripheral to the large story of the spread of Islam in world history. Scholars working within such a paradigm argue that much of the Islamic scholarship produced in the Malay world is more often than not a mere imitation or derivative of "superior" and "developed" versions of Islam found in the Arab countries. From this, it follows that more attention should therefore be given to scrutinizing how Islam from the Arab world has been appropriated in the Malay world rather than the other way around. Very little work, if any, has been done in showing the novelty of reformist ideas in the Malay world and how these ideas can inform the study of Islam elsewhere. The idea that Arab Islam is more advanced and developed than Malay Islam, and that Islam in the Malay world is but a distillation of Arab Islam, has contributed much to scholarly amnesia toward luminaries such as Hamka in the Arab and Western-speaking worlds.

Hamka's cosmopolitan reform clearly shows that Malay-Muslim intellectuals and scholars have much to offer in the realm of Islamic thought. His ideas reflect the globalization of Muslim intellectual life—a process whereby twentieth-century Muslim intellectuals globally delved into hermeneutical engagements with ideas coming both from within Islam and from the West.[7] Sensitive to the vagaries of local, regional, and global developments and always in dialogue with a wide range of Muslim thinkers and activists, Hamka had an intellectual vision that was ambitious, broad-ranging, and distinctive. His prodigious scholarship has left us with fresh questions about how Muslims could reform their societies.

Elsewhere I have argued that Islam in the Malay world is marked by its pluralistic and inclusive character, or what could be termed "Muslim cosmopolitanism."[8] Undoubtedly, Hamka is an embodiment of it. His cosmopolitan reform induced Muslims of his time and our time to adopt a style of thought, a habit of seeing the world, and a way of living that is rooted in the central tenet of Islam, which is that everyone is part of a common humanity accountable to God and that we are morally responsible

---

[7] Cemil Aydin, "Globalizing the Intellectual History of the Idea of the 'Muslim Worlds,'" in *Global Intellectual History*, ed. Samuel Moyn and Andrew Sartrori (New York: Columbia University Press, 2013), 180.

[8] Aljunied, *Muslim Cosmopolitanism*.

toward one another. To embrace cosmopolitan reform is to exhibit a high degree of receptiveness to universal values, to be at ease with one's own Islamic and cultural identities while maintaining and embracing a tolerant attitude toward people of other backgrounds. Indeed, if there is one thing that Muslims and non-Muslims all over the world can learn from Hamka, it is a new way of thinking about Islam that makes the faith more inclusive, more cosmopolitan, and more universal than what it was before his day and age.

Perhaps the last word should go to Hamka. Writing in August 1943, at a moment when Muslim activists across the Malay world felt that all hope of freedom was lost while they were in the hands of a brutal colonizer, Hamka urged his readers to recognize their pitfalls. His tone was one of optimism—so relevant in our time in calling Muslims to embrace reform and craft a new destiny for themselves through the strength of faith and a deep commitment to Islam:

> Recognize the mistakes of our forebears,
> Change our fates promptly,
> What is past let it wither,
> Chart a new history here and now.
>
> Cast off the faint zeal,
> Embolden the weak soul,
> Strengthen the passion, reinforce the conviction,
> The future beckons with hope.[9]

---

[9] Hamka, "Di-atas runtohan Melaka lama," in *Karangan Bunga dari Selatan*, ed. Abu Zaki Fadzil (Kuala Lumpur: Jambatanmas, 1963), 59.

GLOSSARY

adab   manners
adat   traditional customs
al-ghazwul fikr   the war of ideas
Al-Insanul Kamil   The Perfect Man
akal   intellect
akal fikiran   faculty of reasoning
akhlaqul karimah   noble character
amanah   sacred trust
batin   inner
bid'ah   innovations in Islam
da'wah   the preaching of Islam
dhaif   weak
fanaa   annihilation of the self
fard   obligatory
fatwas   religious edicts
fikiran   thinking
ghaib   supernatural
ghirah   justifiable jealousy
hajj   pilgrimage to Mecca
halal   permissible
Hadith   Prophetic sayings
hikmah/hikma   wisdom
ibadah   acts of worship
ijma'   scholarly consensus
ijtihad   independent reasoning
ikhlas   sincerity
i'tidal   equilibrium
ittihad   union with God
jahil   ignorance
jahiliyyah   state of ignorance
kafir   disbelief
kafirun   disbelievers
kebatinan   the search for inner truth
khalifatullah fil'ard   vicegerents of God on earth
khalwat   solitude
khatibs   those who deliver religious sermons
khauf   fear
kashf   unveiling
kyai   religious teachers
maqam   spiritual station

maslahah   general welfare
maudhu   fabricated
mufti   expounder of Islamic laws
mujahadah   striving
mujtahid   scholar who does *ijtihad*
mu'minun   true believers of Islam
murids   novices
murshids   spiritual guides
nafs   desires
nawafil   supererogatory
qanaah   contentment
rabithah   relationship forged with a spiritual guide
raja'   hopefulness
riyadhah   spiritual practices
sesat   wayward
shahih   authentic
shari'a   Islamic legal and ethical code
shura   mutual consultation
Sunnah   words and acts of Prophet Muhammad
syaikhs   masters
syukur   gratefulness
tafakkur   contemplation
ta'lim   teaching
taqdir   fate
taqlid   blind obedience
taqwa   piety
tarbiyah   cultivating
tariqa   Sufi order
tauhid   the oneness of God
tawakkal   trust in God
ulama   Muslim scholars
ummah   global Muslim community
umara   leaders
usul fiqh   principles of Islamic jurisprudence
Wahdatul Wujud   the unity between God and mankind
wahyu   revelation from God
waliyullah   the saints of Allah
wasat   balance
wasilah   means of approach
zakah   compulsory tax
zahir   outer
zikir   repetitive recitations of litanies
zindiq   heretic
zuhud   asceticism
zulm   injustice

BIBLIOGRAPHY

Abaza, Mona. *Debates on Islam and Knowledge in Malaysia and Egypt.* London: Routledge Curzon, 2002.

Abd. Mutholib Ilyas and Abd. Ghofur Imam. *Aliran Kepercayaan & Kebatinan di Indonesia.* Surabaya, Indonesia: Amin, 1988.

Abdul Rahman Abdul Aziz. *Pemikiran Etika Hamka.* Kuala Lumpur: Utusan Publications, 2002.

Abdul Rauf. *Tafsir Al-Azhar: Dimensi Tasawwuf.* Selangor, Malaysia: Piagam Intan, 2013.

Abdullah Saeed. *Interpreting the Qur'an: Towards a Contemporary Approach.* London: Routledge, 2006.

Abrahamov, Binyamin. "Ibn Taymiyya on the Agreement of Reason with revelation." *Muslim World* 82, nos. 3–4 (1992): 256–73.

Addas, Claude. "Ibn 'Arabī's concept of *ahl al-bayt.*" *Journal of the Muhyiddin Ibn 'Arabi Society* 50 (2011). Accessed on July 10, 2017. http://www.ibnarabisociety.org/articles/muhammadan-house.html.

Adeeb Khalid, Islam. *After Communism: Religion and Politics in Central Asia.* Berkeley: University of California Press, 2007.

Ahmad Burhani. "Liberal and Conservative Discourses in the Muhammadiyah: The Struggle for the Face of Reformist Islam in Indonesia." In *Contemporary Developments in Indonesian Islam: Explaining the "Conservative Turn,"* edited by Martin van Bruinessen, 105–44. Singapore: ISEAS, 2013.

———, ed. *Manusia Menimba Allah: Renungan Tasawwuf Positif.* Jakarta: Penerbit Hikmah, 2002.

Aḥmad Shalabi, *Sejarah dan Kebudayaan Islam.* Singapore: Penerbitan Pustaka Nasional, 1970.

Al-Albani, M. Nashiruddin, *Ringkasan Shaḥiḥ al-Bukhari.* Translated by Abdul Hayyie al-Kattani dan A. Ikhwani. Vol. 3. Jakarta: Gema Insani, 2008.

Al-Alwani, Taha Jabir. Introduction to *Imam Al-Shatibi's Theory of the Higher Objectives and Intents of Islamic Law,* by Ahmad Raysuni. Herndon, VA: International Institute of Islamic Thought, 2006.

Al-'Azm, Sadiq Jalal. "Orientalism and Orientalism in Reverse." In *Forbidden Agendas: Intolerance and Defiance in the Middle East,* edited by Jon Rothschild, 349–76. London: Saqi, 1984.

Al-Faruqi, Ismail R. "On the Raison D'Etre of the Ummah." *Islamic Studies* 2, no. 2 (1963): 159–203.

Al-Ghazali. *The Alchemy of Happiness.* Translated by Claud Field. Lahore, Pakis.: Sh. Muhammad Ashraf, 1987.

——. *On Disciplining the Soul*. Translated by T. J. Winter. Cambridge: The Islamic Texts Society, 1995.

Al-Hadi, Syed Shaikh. *Kitab Ugama Islam dan Akal*. Penang: Jelutong Press, 1931.

Ali bin Usman Hujwiri. *Revelation of the Unseen*. Translated by R. A. Nicholson. New York: Pir Press, 1999.

Alfian. *Muhammadiyah: The Political Behavior of a Muslim Modernist Organization under Dutch Colonialism*. Yogyakarta, Indonesia: Gadjah Mada University Press, 1989.

Aljunied, Khairudin. "Edward Said and Southeast Asian Islam." *Journal of Commonwealth and Postcolonial Studies* 11, nos. 1–2 (2004): 159–75.

——. *Muslim Cosmopolitanism: Southeast Asian Islam in Comparative Perspective*. Edinburgh: Edinburgh University Press, 2017.

——. *Radicals: Resistance and Protest in Colonial Malaya*. Dekalb: Northern Illinois University Press, 2015.

——. "Transcending Orientalism: Syed Muhammad Naquib Al-Attas and the History of Islam in the Malay World." *Tafhim*, 6, no. 1 (2014): 1–21.

Allen, Roy F. "Social Theory, Ethnography and the Understanding of Practical Islam in South-East Asia." In *Islam in South-East Asia*, edited by M. B. Hooker, 50–91. Leiden, Neth.: Brill, 1983.

Andaya, Barbara. *The Flaming Womb: Repositioning Women in Early Modern Southeast Asia* (Honolulu: University of Hawai'i Press, 2006).

An-Nawawi. *40 Hadith*. Translated by Jamal Zarabozo. Denver: Al-Basheer Publications, 1999.

Arskal Salim. *Challenging the Secular State: The Islamization of Law in Modern Indonesia*. Honolulu: University of Hawai'i Press, 2008.

Asma Asfaruddin. "Mawdudi's 'Theo-Democracy': How Islamic Is It Really?" *Oriente Moderno* 87, no. 2 (2007): 301–25.

Aydin, Cemil. "Globalizing the Intellectual History of the Idea of the 'Muslim Worlds.'" In *Global Intellectual History*, edited by Samuel Moyn and Andrew Sartrori, 159–86. New York: Columbia University Press, 2013.

Ayoub, Mahmoud M. *Islam: Faith and History*. Oxford: Oneworld Publications, 2004.

Azra Aryumardi. *Historiografi Islam Kontemporer: Wacana, Aktualitas dan Actor Sejarah*. Jakarta: Gramedia Pustaka Utama, 2002.

——. *Menuju Masyarakat Madani: Gagasan, Fakta dan Tantangan*. Bandung, Indonesia: Remaja Rosadakarya, 1999.

——. *The Origins of Islamic Reformism in Southeast Asia: Networks of Malay-Indonesian and Middle Eastern "Ulamā" in the Seventeenth and Eighteenth Centuries*. Honolulu: University of Hawai'i Press, 2004.

Backscheider, Paula R. *Reflections on Biography*. Oxford: Oxford University Press, 1999.

Badawi, Abdel Latif Awad. "The Moderation of Islam." *Islamic Quarterly* 7, no. 3–4 (1963): 83–89.

Badran, Margot. *Feminism in Islam: Secular and Religious Convergences* (Oxford: Oneworld Publications, 2009).

Benda, Harry J. "Christiaan Snouck Hurgronje and the Foundations of Dutch Islamic Policy in Indonesia." *Journal of Modern History* 30, no. 4 (1958): 338–47.

——. "Southeast Asian Islam in the Twentieth Century." In *The Cambridge History of Islam*. Vol. 2A, edited by P. M. Holt, Ann K. S. Lambton and Bernard Lewis, 182–209. Cambridge: Cambridge University Press, 1979.

Bennabi, Malek. *Islam in History and Society*. Translated by Asma Rashid. New Delhi: KitabBhavan, 1999.

Berger, Mark T. "Decolonisation, Modernisation and Nation-Building: Political Development Theory and the Appeal of Communism in Southeast Asia, 1945–1975." *Journal of Southeast Asian Studies* 34, no. 3 (2003): 421–48.

Blackburn, Susan, ed. *First Indonesian Women's Congress of 1928*. Clayton, Aus.: Monash University Publishing, 2008.

——. *Women and the State in Modern Indonesia*. New York: Cambridge University Press, 2004.

Bodley, Ronald Victor Courtenay. *The Messenger: The Life of Mohammed*. New York: Doubleday, 1946.

Brown, Jonathan A.C. *Hadith: Muhammad's Legacy in the Medieval and Modern World*. Oxford: Oneworld Publications, 2009.

Buruma, Ian, and Margalit, Avishai. *Occidentalism: The West in the Eyes of Its Enemies*. New York: Penguin, 2004.

Cecep Ramli Bihar Anwar. *Bertasawuf Tanpa Tarekat: Aura Tasawuf Positif.* Jakarta: Penerbit IIMan, 2002.

Champion, Justin. "Seeing the Past: Simon Schama's 'A History of Britain' and Public History." *History Workshop Journal* 56, no. 1 (2003): 153–74.

Chittick. William C. *Faith and Practice of Islam: Three Thirteenth Century Sufi Texts*. Albany: State University of New York Press, 1992.

——. *Sufi Path of Knowledge: Ibn al-Àrabi Metaphysics of Imagination*. Albany: State University of New York Press, 1989.

Chittick, William C., and Murata, Sachiko. *The Vision of Islam*. Cairo: American University in Cairo Press, 2006.

Cribb, Robert. "Genocide in Indonesia." *Journal of Genocide Research* 3, no. 2 (2001): 219–39.

Cooper, Frederick. *Colonialism in Question: Theory, Knowledge, History*. Berkeley: University of California Press, 2005.

Crouch, Melissa. *Law and Religion in Indonesia: Conflict and the Courts in West Java*. London: Routledge, 2014.

Davison, Graeme. "Paradigms of Public History." *Australian Historical Studies* 24, no. 96 (1991): 4–16.

de Venne, Marie-Sybille. *Brunei: From the Age of Commerce to the 21st Century*. Singapore: NUS Press, 2015.

Durkheim, Emile, *Rules of Sociological Method*. New York: Free Press, 1982.

Deliar Noer. *The Modernist Muslim Movement in Indonesia, 1900–1942*. Kuala Lumpur: Oxford University Press, 1973).

———. "Yamin and Hamka: Two Routes to an Indonesian Identity." In *Perceptions of the Past in Southeast Asia*, edited by Anthony Reid and David Marr, 249–62. Singapore: Heinemann, 1979.

Drewes, G. W. J. "New Light on the Coming of Islam to Indonesia." *Bijdragen tot de Taal-, Land-en Volkenkunde* 124, no. 4 (1968): 433–59.

Dumas *fils*, Alexandre. *Margaretta Gauthier*. Translated by Hamka. Bukit Tinggi, Malaysia: Nusantara, 1940.

Eaton, Charles Le Gai. *Islam and the Destiny of Man*. Albany: State University of New York Press, 1985).

el Fadl, Khaled Abou. *The Place of Tolerance in Islam*. Boston: Beacon Press, 2002.

Ephrat, Daphna. *Spiritual Wayfarers, Leaders in Piety: Sufis and the Dissemination of Islam in Medieval Palestine*. Cambridge, MA: Harvard University Press, 2008.

Ernst, Carl. *Words of Ecstasy in Sufism*. Albany: State University of New York Press, 1985.

Esposito, John L. *What Everyone Needs to Know about Islam*. New York: Oxford University Press, 2002.

Etin Anwar. *Gender and Self in Islam*. London: Routledge, 2006.

Fauzan Saleh. "The Belief in *al-Qada'* and *al-Qadr* in Indonesian Islamic Discourse." *Studia Islamika* 8, no. 3 (2001): 125–55.

———. *Modern Trends in Islamic Theological Discourse in Twentieth Century Indonesia*. Leiden, Neth.: Brill, 2001.

Fazlur Rahman. *Major Themes in the Qur'an*. Chicago: University of Chicago Press, 2009.

Federspiel, Howard M. *Sultans, Shamans, and Saints: Islam and Muslims in Southeast Asia*. Honolulu: University of Hawai'i Press, 2007.

Feener, R. Michael. *Muslim Legal Thought in Modern Indonesia*. Cambridge: Cambridge University Press, 2007.

———. "A Re-examination of the Place of al-Hallaj in Southeast Asian Islam." *Bijdragen tot de Taal-, Land-en Volkenkunde* 154, no. 4 (1998): 571–92.

Filene, Benjamin. "Passionate Histories: 'Outsider' History-Makers and What They Teach Us." *Public Historian* 34, no. 1 (2012): 12–14.

Goodman, Lenn Evan. "Did Al-Ghazali Deny Causality?" *Studia Islamica* 47 (1978): 83–120.

Green, Nile. *Sufism: A Global History*. Oxford: Wiley-Blackwell, 2012.

Guénon, René *Insights into Islamic Esoterism and Taoism*. Translated by Henry D. Fohr. New York: Sophia Perennis, 2004.

Haddad, Yvonne. *Contemporary Islam and the Challenge of History*. Albany: SUNY Press, 1982.

Haddad, Yvonne Y., and John L. Esposito. *The Islamic Revival since 1988: A Critical Survey and Bibliography*. Westport, CT: Greenwood Press, 1997.

Hadler, Jeffrey. "Home, Fatherhood, Succession: Three Generations of Amrullahs in Twentieth-Century Indonesia." *Indonesia* 65 (1988): 122–54.

———. *Muslims and Matriarchs: Cultural Resilience in Indonesia through Jihad and Colonialism*. Ithaca: Cornell University Press, 2008.

Hairus Salim HS. "Indonesian Muslims and Cultural Networks." In *Heirs to World Culture*, edited by Jennifer Lindsay and Maya H. T. Liem, 76–89. Leiden, Neth.: KITLV Press, 2012.

Hallaq, Wael. "Was the Gate of Ijtihad Closed?" *International Journal of Middle East Studies* 16, no. 1 (1984): 3–41.

Hamka. *Adat Minangkabau Menghadapi Revolusi*. Djakarta: Firma Tekad, 1963.

——. *Akhlaqul Karimah*. Jakarta: Pustaka Panjimas, 1992.

——. *Antara Fakta dan Khayal "Tuanku Rao."* Jakarta: Penerbit Bulan Bintang, 1974.

——. *Ayahku: Riwayat Hidup Dr. H. Abdul Karim Amrullah dan Perjuangan Agama di Sumatera*. Djakarta: Djajamurni, 1967.

——. *Beberapa Tantangan terhadap Ummat Islam Dimasa Kini: Secularisme, Syncritisme dan Ma'shiat*. Djakarta: Penerbit Bulan Bintang, 1970.

——. *Berkisah Nabi dan Rasul*. Kuala Lumpur: Pustaka Melayu Baru, 1982.

——. *Cara Zending dan Missi Menyerang 'Aqidah Kita*. Kuala Lumpur: Pustaka Melayu Baru, 1979.

——. *Dari Hati ke Hati: Bercakap Soal Agama, Sosial-Budaya Dan Politik*. Selangor, Malaysia: Pustaka Dini, 2009.

——. *Dari Lembah Chita-Chita*. Kuala Lumpur: Pustaka Melayu Baru, 1968.

——. *Dari Perbendaharaan Lama*. Kuala Lumpur: Penerbit Pustaka Antara, 1981.

——. "Di-atas runtohan Melaka lama." In *Karangan Bunga dari Selatan*, edited by Abu Zaki Fadzil, 57–59. Kuala Lumpur: Jambatanmas, 1963), 57–59.

——. *Di Bawah Gema Takbir*. Kuala Lumpur: Utusan Melayu Berhad, 1976.

——. *Di Bawah Lindungan Ka'bah*. Jakarta: Bulan Bintang, 1983.

——. *Doktrin Islam yang Menimbulkan Kemerdekaan dan Keberanian*. Jakarta: Idayu Press, 1977.

——. *Empat Bulan di Amerika*. 2 vols. Djakarta: Tintamas, 1954.

——. *Falsafah Hidup*. Kuala Lumpur: Pustaka Antara, 1977.

——. *Filsafat Ketuhanan*. Melaka, Malaysia: Toko Buku Abbas Bandong, 1967.

——. *Ghirah dan Tantangan Terhadap Islam*. Djakarta: Pustaka Panjimas, 1982.

——. "Haji Agus Salim sebagai Sastrawan dan Ulama." In *100 Tahun H. Agus Salim*, edited by Panitia 100 Tahun, 252–65. Jakarta: Sinar Harapan, 1984.

——. *Hak Asasi Manusia dalam Islam dan Deklarasi PBB*. Selangor, Malaysia: Pustaka Dini, 2010.

——. *Iman dan Amal Saleh*. Jakarta: Pustaka Panjimas, 1982.

——. *Keadilan Sosial Dalam Islam*. Kuala Lumpur: Pustaka Antara, 1966.

——. *Kedudukan Wanita dalam Islam*. Selangor, Malaysia: Pustaka Dini, 2009.

——. *Kenangan kenangan-ku di-Malaya*. Singapore: Setia Darma, 1957.

——. *Kenang-kenangan Hidup*. Shah Alam, Malaysia: Pustaka Dini, 2009.

——. *Kerana Fitnah*. Djakarta: Balai Pustaka, 1938.

——. *Khutbah Iftitah Ketua Umum Majelis Ulama Indonesia*. Jakarta: Sekretariat Majelis Ulama Indonesia, 1978.

——. *Khutbah Pilihan Buya HAMKA: Juma'at, Idul Fitri & Idul Adha*. Jakarta: Pustaka Panjimas, 2005.

——. *Lembaga Budi: Perhiasan Hidup Cemerlang*. Shah Alam, Malaysia: Pustaka Dini, 2008.

——. *Lembaga Hidup*. Djakarta: Widjaya, 1958.

——. *Lembaga Hikmat*. Kuala Lumpur: Pustaka Antara, 1967.

——. *Membahas Kemusykilan Agama*. Selangor, Malaysia: Pustaka Dini, 2009.

——. *Mengembalikan Tasawuf Ke Pangkalnya*. Jakarta: Pustaka Panjimas, 1973.

——. *Merantau ke Deli*. Kuala Lumpur: Pustaka Antara, 1966.

——. *Muhammadiyah di Minangkabau*. Jakarta: Yayasan Nurul Islam, 1974.

——. *1001 Soal-Soal Hidup*. Djakarta: Penerbit Bulan Bintang, 1961.

——. *Pandangan Hidup Muslim*. Djakarta: Bulan Bintang, 1984.

——. *Pelajaran Agama Islam*. Kelantan, Malaysia: Pustaka Aman Press, 1967.

——. *Pemimpin dan Pimpinan*. Kuala Lumpur: Pustaka Melayu Baru, 1973.

——. *Pengaruh Muhammad Abduh di Indonesia; Pidato Diutjapkan Sewaktu Akan Menerima Gelar Doctor Honoris Causa Dari Universitas al-Azhar di Mesir Pada Tgl. 21 Djanuari 1958*. Jakarta: Tintamas, 1961.

——. *Perkembangan Kebatinan di Indonesia*. Jakarta: Bulan Bintang, 1971.

——. *Pribadi*. Kuala Lumpur: Pustaka Antara, 1965.

——. *Prinsip dan Kebijaksaan Da'wah Islam*. Kuala Lumpur: Pustaka Melayu Baru, 1981.

——. *Renungan Tasauf*. Jakarta: Pustaka Panjimas, 2002.

——. *Revolusi Agama*. Djakarta: Pustaka Antara, 1949.

——. *Said Djamaluddin Al-Afghany: Pelopor Kebangkitan Muslimin*. Djakarta: Penerbit Bulan Bintang, 1970.

——. *Sejarah Umat Islam*. Singapore: Pustaka Nasional, 1994.

——. *Tafsir Al-Azhar*. 30 vols. Singapore: Pustaka Nasional, 1982.

——. *Tasauf Modern*. Medan, Indonesia: Tokobuku Islamijah, 1939.

——. *Tasauf: Perkembangan dan Pemurniannya*. Jakarta: Pustaka Panjimas, 1983.

——. *Teguran Suci & Jujur Terhadap Mufti Johor*. 1958; repr., Selangor, Malaysia: Pustaka Dini, 2009.

——. *Terusir*. Selangor, Malaysia: Pustaka Dini, 2007.

——. *Tuan Direktur*. Kuala Lumpur: Pustaka Antara, 1966.

——. *Tuntutan Puasa, Tarawih dan Salat Aidilfitri*. Selangor, Malaysia: Pustaka Dini, 2009.

——. *Umat Islam menghadapi tantangan Kristenisasi dan Sekularisasi*. Jakarta: Pustaka Panjimas, 2003.

Hefner, Robert W. "Islam in the Era of Nation-States: Politics and Religious Renewal in Muslim Southeast Asia." In *Islam in the Era of Nation-States*, edited by Robert W. Hefner, 3–42. Honolulu: University of Hawai'i Press, 1997.

——. "Social Legacies and Possible Futures." in *Indonesia: The Great Transition*, edited by John Bresnan, 75–136. Lanham, MD: Rowman & Littlefield, 2005.

Henk, Maier. *We Are Playing Relatives: A Survey of Malay Writing*. Leiden, Neth.: KITLV Press, 2004.

Hilliard, Marion. *A Woman Doctor Looks at Love and Life*. New York: Doubleday, 1957.

———. *Women and Fatigue: A Woman Doctor's Answer*. New York: Doubleday, 1960.

Hodgson, Marshall, *Rethinking World History: Essays on Europe, Islam and World History*. New York: Cambridge University Press, 1993.

Hooker, Virginia. *Writing a New Society: Social Change through the Novel in Malay*. Honolulu: University of Hawai'i Press, 2000.

Hourani, Albert. *Arabic Thought in a Liberal Age*. Cambridge: Cambridge University Press, 1983.

Hoover, Jon. *Ibn Taymiyya's Theodicy of Perpetual Optimism*. Leiden, Neth.: Brill, 2007.

Howell, Julia D. "Indonesia's Salafist Sufis." *Modern Asian Studies* 44, no. 5 (2010): 1029–51.

———. "Modulations of Active Piety: Professors and Televangelists as Promoters of Indonesian 'Sufisme.'" In *Expressing Islam: Religious Life and Politics in Indonesia*, edited by Greg Fealy and Sally White, 40–62. Singapore: ISEAS, 2008.

———. "Muslims, the New Age and Marginal Religions in Indonesia: Changing Meanings of Religious Pluralism." *Social Compass* 52, no. 4 (2005): 472–93.

———. "Revitalised Sufism and the New Piety Movements in Islamic Southeast Asia." In *Routledge Handbook of Religions in Asia*, edited by Bryan S. Turner and Oscar Salemnik, 276–92. New York: Routledge, 2015.

Hunter, Shireen T., ed. *Reformist Voices of Islam: Mediating Islam and Modernity*. London: M.E. Sharpe, 2009.

Ibn Khaldun, *Al-Muqadimmah*. Translated by Franz Rosenthal. Princeton: Princeton University Press, 1967.

Ibn Qayyim. *On Taqlīd: Ibn al Qayyim's Critique of Authority in Islamic Law*. Translated by Abdul Rahman Mustafa. Oxford: Oxford University Press, 2013.

Ibn Tufayl. *Hayy Ibn Yaqzan: A Philosophical Tale*. Translated by Lenn Evan Goodman. Chicago: Chicago University Press, 2009.

Ibrahim Abu Bakar. *Islamic Modernism in Malaya: The Life and Thought of Sayid Syakh Al-Hadi, 1867–1934*. Kuala Lumpur: University of Malay Press, 1994.

Ibrahim M. Abu-Rabi, ed. *The Blackwell Companion to Contemporary Islamic Thought*. Malden, UK: Blackwell, 2006.

Iik Arifin Mansurnoor. "Islam in Brunei Darussalam: An Analysis of their Interaction." In *Islam in the Era of Globalization*, edited by Johan Meuleman, 51–71. London: Routledge, 2002.

Ilyas Ba-Yunus. "Ideological Dimensions of Islam: A Critical Paradigm." In *Interpreting Islam*, edited by Hastings Donnan, 99–109. London: Sage, 2002.

Irfan Hamka. *Ayah: Kisah Buya Hamka*. Jakarta: Republika, 2013.

Jones, Gavin. *Marriage and Divorce in Islamic South-east Asia*. Kuala Lumpur: Oxford University Press, 1994.

Junus Amir Hamzah. *Hamka sebagai Pengarang Roman*. Djakarta: Megabookstore, 1964.

Kartomi, Margaret J. *Musical Journeys in Sumatra*. Urbana: University of Illinois Press, 2012.

Keddie, Nikki R. *An Islamic Response to Imperialism: Political and Religious Writings of Sayyid Jamal al-Din al-Afghani.* Berkeley: University of California Press, 1968.

——. "Pan-Islamism as Proto-Nationalism." *Journal of Modern History* 41, no. 1 (1969): 17–28.

Kersten, Carool. *Islam in Indonesia: The Contest for Society, Ideas and Values.* New York: Oxford University Press, 2015.

Khadduri, Majid. *Islamic Conception of Justice.* Baltimore: Johns Hopkins University Press, 1984.

Kuhn, Thomas S. *The Structure of Scientific Revolutions.* Chicago: University of Chicago Press, 2012.

La Capra, Dominic. *Rethinking Intellectual History: Texts, Contexts, Language.* Ithaca: Cornell University Press, 1983.

Laffan, Michael Francis. *Islamic Nationhood and Colonial Indonesia: The Umma below the Winds.* New York: Routledge, 2003.

——. *The Makings of Indonesian Islam: Orientalism and the Narrations of a Sufi Past.* Princeton: Princeton University Press, 2011.

Lamia Rustum Shehadeh. *The Idea of Women under Fundamentalist Islam.* Gainesville: University of Florida Press, 2003.

Leccese, Francesco Alfonso. "Islam, Sufism, and the Postmodern in the Religious Melting Pot." In *Routledge Handbook of Islam in the West*, edited by Roberto Tottoli, 441–54. London: Routledge, 2015.

Leckie, Shirley A. "Biography Matters: Why Historians Need Well-Crafted Biographies More Than Ever." In *Writing Biography: Historians & Their Craft*, edited by Lloyd E. Ambrosius, 1–27. Lincoln: University of Nebraska Press, 2004.

Lee, Dwight E., and Robert N. Beck. "The Meaning of 'Historicism.'" *American Historical Review* 59, no. 3 (1954): 568–77.

Loeb, Edwin M. *Sumatra: Its History and People.* Vienna: Institut fur Volkerkunde der Universitat Wien, 1935.

Lutfi Assyaukanie. *Islam and the Secular State in Indonesia.* Singapore: ISEAS Press, 2009.

Kurzman, Charles, ed. *Modernist Islam: A Sourcebook, 1840–1940.* New York: Oxford University Press, 2002.

M. Alfan Alfian. *Hamka dan Bahagia: Reaktualisasi Tasauf Di Zaman Kita.* Bekasi, Indonesia: Penjuru Ilmu Sejati, 2014.

M. Yunan Yusuf. *Corak Penafsiran Kalam: Tafsir al-Azhar.* Jakarta: Pustaka Panjimas, 1990.

Mahmoud Ayoub. *The Qur'an and Its Interpreters.* Vol. 1. Albany: State University of New York Press, 1984.

Mahmud Shaltut. *Al-Islam: 'Aqidah wa Shari'ah.* Cairo: Dar al-Syuruq, 2001.

Martin, Richard C., and Mark R. Woodward, with Dwi S. Atmaja. *Defenders of Reason in Islam: Mu'tazilism from Medieval School to Modern Symbol.* Oxford: Oneworld Publications, 2003.

Martyn, Elizabeth. *The Women's Movement in Post-Colonial Indonesia: Gender and Nation in a New Democracy.* London: Routledge, 2005.

Maududi, Abul A'la. *Economic System of Islam* (Lahore, Pakis.: Islamic Publications, 1984.

———. *A Short History of the Revivalist Movement in Islam*. Karachi, Pakis.: Islamic Publications, 1963.

Mcgregor, Katharine E. "Confronting the Past in Contemporary Indonesia: The Anticommunist Killings of 1965–1966 and the Role of the Nahdatul Ulama." *Critical Asian Studies* 41, no. 2 (2009): 195–224.

Mohammad Sidin Ahmad Ishak, ed. *Pemikiran dan Perjuangan Hamka*. Kuala Lumpur: Angkatan Belia Islam Malaysia, 2001.

Moch. Nur Ichwan. "*Ulama*, State and Politics: Majelis Ulama Indonesia after Suharto." *Islamic Law and Society* 12, no. 1 (2005): 45–72.

Milhan Yusuf. "Hamka's Method in Interpreting Legal Verses." In *Approaches to the Qur'an in Contemporary Indonesia*, edited by Abdullah Saeed, 42–66. Oxford: Oxford University Press, 2005.

Miller, David. *Principles of Social Justice*. Cambridge, MA: Harvard University Press, 1999.

Mohammad Damami. *Tasawuf Positif dalam Pemikiran Hamka*. Yogyakarta, Indonesia: Fajar Pustaka Baru, 2000.

Mohammad Hashim Kamali. *The Middle Path of Moderation in Islam*. Oxford: Oxford University Press, 2015.

———. *Shari'ah Law: An Introduction*. Oxford: Oneworld Publications, 2008.

Mohammad Redzuan Othman. "Sumbangan Hamka dalam Penulisan Sejarah Melayu di Alam Melayu" In *Pemikiran Hamka*, edited by Siddiq Fadzil, 115–29. Kuala Lumpur: Dewan Bahasa dan Pustaka, 2008.

Mohd Asri Zainul Abidin. "Pesan Hamka: Panggil saya Muslim." June 8, 2014. Accessed June 6, 2017. https://m.malaysiakini.com/columns/265033.

Moosa, Ebrahim. *Ghazali and the Poetics of Imagination*. Chapel Hill: University of North Carolina Press, 2005.

Mortimer, Rex. *Indonesian Communism under Sukarno: Ideology and Politics*. Ithaca: Cornell University Press, 1974.

Muhammad Natsi. *Islam sebagai Ideologie*. Jakarta: Penjiaran Ilmu, 1950.

Muhammad Qasim Zaman. *Modern Islamic Thought in a Radical Age*. New York: Cambridge University Press, 2012.

———. *The Ulama in Contemporary Islam*. Princeton: Princeton University Press, 2002.

Muhsin Mahdi. *Alfarabi and the Foundation of Islamic Political Philosophy*. Chicago: Chicago University Press, 2001.

———. "The Rational Tradition in Islam." In *Intellectual Traditions in Islam*, edited by Farhad Daftary, 43–65. London: I.B. Tauris, 2000.

Mun'im Sirry. *Scriptural Polemics: The Qur'an and Other Religions*. New York: Oxford University Press, 2014.

Muslim Ibn al-Hajjaj al-Qusayri. *Sahih Muslim: Being Traditions of the Sayings and Doings of the Prophet Muḥammad as Narrated by His Companions and Compiled under the Title al-Jāmi' al-ṣaḥīḥ*. Translated by Abdul Hamid Siddiqui. Vol. 4. Lahore, Pakis.: Sh. Muhammad Ashraf, 1976.

Nader Hashemi. *Islam, Secularism and Liberal Democracy*. New York: Oxford University Press, 2009.

Nadirsyah Hosen. "Behind the Scenes: Fatwas of Majelis Ulama Indonesia (1975–1998)." *Islamic Studies* 15, no. 2 (2004): 147–79.

Nani Soewondo. "Organisasi2 Wanita dan Pekerdjaanja." *Madjalah Kedudukan Wanita Indonesia* 1, no. 1 (1959): 39–41.

Nasr, Seyyed Vali Reza. *Maududi and the Making of Islamic Revivalism*. Oxford: Oxford University Press, 1996.

Nina Nurmila. "Feminist Interpretation of the Qur'an." *Journal of Qur'an and Hadith Studies* 2, no. 2 (2013): 155–66.

Nora, Pierre. "Between Memory and History: *Les Lieux de Mémoire*." *Representations* 26 (1989): 7–25.

Nurcholish Madjid. *Tradisi Islam: Peran dan Fungsinya dalam Pembangunan di Indonesia*. Jakarta: Paramadina, 1997.

Nyazee, Imran Ahsan. *Theories of Islamic Law: The Methodologies of Ijtihad*. Kuala Lumpur: The Other Press, 2002.

Plato. *The Republic*. Translated by Tom Griffith. Cambridge: Cambridge University Press, 2003.

Rahmat Nur Hakim. "Lewat Islam, Hamka dan Pramoedya Ananta Toer pun Berdamai." June 29, 2016. Accessed June 6, 2017. http://nasional.kompas.com/read/2016/06/29/05050041/Lewat.Islam.Hamka.dan.Pramoedya.Ananta.Toer.pun.Berdamai.

Ramadan, Tariq. *Radical Reform: Islamic Ethics and Liberation*. Oxford: Oxford University Press, 2009.

Rawls, John. *A Theory of Justice*. Rev. ed. Cambridge, MA: Harvard University Press, 1999.

Sanday, Peggy Reeves. "Androcentric and Matrifocal Gender Representations in Minangkabau Ideology." In *Beyond the Second Sex: New Directions in the Anthropology of Gender*, edited by P. R. Sanday and R. G. Goodenough, 139–68. Philadelphia: University of Pennsylvania Press, 1990.

Riddell, Peter. *Islam and the Malay-Indonesian World: Transmission and Responses*. Singapore: Horizon Books, 2001.

Rosen, Lawrence. *Varieties of Muslim Experience: Encounters with Arab Political and Cultural Life*. Chicago: University of Chicago Press, 2008.

Rosnani Hashim. *Educational Dualism in Malaysia: Implications for Theory and Practice*. Kuala Lumpur: Oxford University Press, 1996.

——. "Hamka: Intellectual and Social Transformation of the Malay World." In *Reclaiming the Conversation: Islamic Intellectual Tradition in the Malay Archipelago*, edited by Rosnani Hashim, 187–205. Kuala Lumpur: The Other Press, 2010.

Rumadi. *Islamic Post-Traditionalism in Indonesia* (Singapore: ISEAS Press, 2015).

Rush, James R. *Hamka's Great Story: A Master Writer's Vision of Islam for Indonesia*. Madison: University of Wisconsin Press, 2016.

Rusydi Hamka. *Hamka: Pujangga Islam Kebanggaan Rumpun Melayu* (Selangor, Malaysia: Pustaka Dini, 2002).

Ruthven, Malise. *Islam in the World*. New York: Oxford University Press, 2006.

Said, Edward. *Covering Islam: How Media Experts Determine How We See the World*. New York: Vintage, 1997.

——. *The World, the Text and the Critic*. Cambridge, MA: Harvard University Press, 1983.

Saliba, George. *Islamic Science and the Making of the European Renaissance*. Cambridge, MA: MIT Press, 2007.

"Sambutan rakyat Indonesia terhadap Dr Hamka" (editorial). *Al-Islam* 9 (1974): 12–13.

Samira Haj. *Reconfiguring Islamic Tradition: Reform, Rationality and Modernity*. Stanford: Stanford University Press, 2009.

Sartono Kartodirdjo. *Indonesian Historiography*. Yogyakarta, Indonesia: Kanisius, 2001.

Schoppa, R. Keith. "Culture and Context in Biographical Studies: The Case of China." In *Writing Biography: Historians & Their Craft*, edited by Lloyd E. Ambrosius, 27–52. Lincoln: University of Nebraska Press, 2004.

Sedgwick, Mark. *Saints and Sons: The Remaking of the Rashidi Ahmadi Sufi Order*. Leiden, Neth.: Brill, 2005.

Shamsul Nizar. *Membincangkan Dinamika Intelektual dan Pemikiran Hamka tentang Pendidikan: Seabad Buya Hamka*. Jakarta: Kenchana, 2008.

Shepard, William. *Sayyid Qutb and Islamic Activism: A Translation and Critical Analysis of Social Justice in Islam*. Leiden, Neth.: Brill, 1996.

Shukri Ahmad. *Pengaruh Pemikiran Ulama di Semenanjung Malaysia Abad Ke-20*. Kedah, Malaysia: UUM Press, 2011.

Sidek Baba, ed. *Pemikiran Hamka*. Kuala Lumpur: Dewan Bahasa dan Pustaka, 2008.

Sijbrand, Linda. "Orientalism and Sufism: An Overview." In *Orientalism Revisited: Art, Land and Voyage*, edited by Richard Netton, 98–114. London: Routledge, 2013.

Skinner, Quentin. *Visions of Politics*. Vol. 1. Cambridge: Cambridge University Press, 2002.

Smith, Bianca J. "When *Wahyu* Comes through Women: Female Spiritual Authority and Divine Revelation in Mystical Groups and *Pesantren* Sufi Orders." In *Gender and Power in Indonesian Islam: Leaders, Feminists, Sufis and Pesantren Selves*, edited by Bianca J. Smith and Mark Woodward, 87–88. London: Routledge, 2014.

Soh, Byungkuk. "Ideals without Heat: Indonesia Raya and the Struggle for Independence in Malaya, 1920–1948." *Wacana: Jurnal Ilmu Pengetahuan Budaya* 7, no. 1 (2005): 1–30.

Solichin Salam. *Hadji Agus Salim: Hidup dan Perdjuangannja*. Djakarta: Djajamurni, 1961.

Soroush, Abdolkarim. *Reason, Freedom, and Democracy in Islam*. Oxford: Oxford University Press, 2000.

Souaiaia, Ahmed. *Contesting Justice: Women, Islam, Law and Society*. Albany: State University of New York Press, 2008.

Stange, Paul R. "Legitimate Mysticism in Indonesia." *Review of Indonesian and Malaysian Affairs* 22, no. 2 (1986): 76–117.

Stauth, Georg. *Politics and Cultures of Islamization in Southeast Asia.* Bielefeld, Ger.: Transcript Verlag, 2002.

Steenbrink, Karel. "Hamka (1908–1981): A Mystical Teacher as Political Leader of Islam in Indonesia." Unpublished paper, IAIN (Institut Agama Islam Negeri) Syarif Hidayatullah, Indonesia, 1982.

——. "Hamka (1908–1981) and the Integration of the Islamic *Ummah* of Indonesia." *Studia Islamika* 1, no. 3 (1994): 119–47.

Stivens, Maila. "(Re)framing Women's Rights Claims in Malaysia." In *Malaysia: Islam, Society and Politics,* edited by Virginia Hooker and Noraini Othman, 126–47. Singapore: ISEAS Press, 2003.

Stowasser, Barbara. "Gender Issues and Contemporary Qur'an Interpretation." In *Islam, Gender and Social Change,* edited by Yvonne Yazbeck Haddad and John L. Esposito, 32–42. New York: Oxford University Press, 1998.

Sudirman Tebba. *Tasawuf Positif: Manfaat Tasawuf Dalam Kehidupan Sehari-Hari.* Jakarta: Pustaka irVan, 2008.

Sudrajat, A. Suryana. *Ulama Pejuang dan Ulama Petualang: Belajar kearifan dari Negeri Atas Angin.* Jakarta: Penerbit Erlangga, 2006.

Sulasman M. Hum. "Kiyai and Pesantren in the Islamic Historiography of Indonesia." *TAWARIKH: International Journal for Historical Studies* 4, no. 1 (2012): 71–73.

——. "Rethinking Islamic Historiography in Indonesia." *Journal of Social Sciences* 2, no. 4 (2013): 199–206.

Suwardi Endaswara. *Mistik Kejawen: Sinkrestime, Simbolisme dan Sufisme dalam Budaya Spiritual Jawa.* Yogyakarta, Indonesia: Penerbit Narasi, 2006.

Taufik Abdullah. "Adat and Islam: An Examination of Conflict in Minangkabau." *Indonesia* 2 (1966): 1–24.

——. "Hamka dalam Struktur dan Dinamik Keulamaan." In *Hamka di Mata Hati Umat,* edited by Nasir Tamara, Buntara Sanusi, and Vincent Djauhari, 399–419. Jakarta: Sinar Harapan, 1983.

Taylor, Jean Gelman. *Global Indonesia.* London: Routledge, 2013.

Teuuw, Adries. *Modern Indonesian Literature.* 's-Gravenhage, Neth.: Martinus Nijhoff, 1967.

Tibawi, Abdul Latif. "English Speaking Orientalists." *Islamic Quarterly* 8 (1964): 25–64.

Tilly, Charles, and Sidney Tarrow. *Contentious Politics.* Boulder: Paradigm Publishers, 2006.

Tripp, Charles. *Islam and the Moral Economy: The Challenge of Capitalism.* Cambridge: Cambridge University Press, 2006.

Tuozzo, Thomas M. *Plato's Charmides: Positive Elenchus in a Socratic Dialogue.* New York: Cambridge University Press, 2011.

Universiti Kebangsaan Malaysia. *Majlis Konvokesyen Kedua* (Bangi: UKM, 1975).

van Bruinessen, Martin. "Controversies and Polemics Involving the Sufi Orders in Twentieth-Century Indonesia." In *Islamic Mysticism Contested: Thirteen Centuries of*

Controversies and Polemics, edited by Frederick de Jong and Bernd Radtke, 705–28. Leiden: Brill, 1999.

———. "Ghazwul Fikri or Arabization? Indonesian Muslim Responses to Globalization." In *Southeast Asian Muslims in the Era of Globalization*, edited by Ken Miichi and Omar Farouk, 61–85. Basingstoke, UK: Palgrave Macmillan, 2014.

———. "The Origins and Development of Sufi Orders (*Tarekat*) in Southeast Asia." *Studia Islamika—Indonesian Journal for Islamic Studies* 1, no. 1 (1994): 1–23.

———, "Saints, Politicians and Sufi Bureaucrats: Mysticism and Politics in Indonesia's New Order." In *Sufism and the "Modern" in Islam*, edited by Martin van Bruinessen and Julia Day Howell, 92–112. New York: I.B. Tauris, 2007.

van Doorn-Harder, Pierternall. *Women Shaping Islam: Reading the Qur'an in Indonesia*. Urbana: University of Illinois Press, 2006.

Vaselou, Sophia. *Ibn Taymiyya's Theological Ethics*. New York: Oxford University Press, 2016.

Von der Mehden, Fred R. *Two Worlds of Islam: Interaction between Southeast Asia and the Middle East*. Gainesville: University Press of Florida, 1993.

Vu, Tiong. "Socialism and Underdevelopment in Southeast Asia." In *Routledge Handbook of Southeast Asian History*, edited by Norman G. Owen, 188–98. London: Routledge, 2014.

Wadud, Amina. *Qur'an and Woman: Rereading the Sacred Text from a Woman's Perspective*. New York: Oxford University Press, 1999.

Wan Sabri Wan Yusof. "Hamka's 'Tafsir al-Azhar': Qur'anic Exegesis as a Mirror of Social Change." PhD diss., Temple University, 1997.

———. "Religious Harmony and Inter-faith Dialogue in the Writings of Hamka." *Intellectual Discourse* 13, no. 2 (2005): 113–34.

Watson, Conrad William. *Of Self and Nation: Autobiography and the Representation of Modern Indonesia*. Honolulu: University of Hawai'i Press, 2000.

Wazir Jahan Karim. *Women and Culture: Between Malay Adat and Islam*. Boulder: Westview Press 1992.

White, Hayden. *Metahistory: The Historical Imagination in Nineteenth-Century Europe*. Baltimore: Johns Hopkins University Press, 1973.

Wieringa, Saskia. "Matrilinearity and Women's Interests: The Minangkabau of Western Sumatra." In *Subversive Women: Women's Movements in Africa, Asia, Latin America and the Caribbean*, edited by Saskia Wieringa, 241–69. London: Zed Books, 1995.

Windstedt, Richard O. "The Advent of Muhammadanism in the Malay Peninsula and Archipelago." *Journal of the Royal Straits Branch of the Royal Asiatic Society* 77 (1917): 171–75.

Wood, Michael. *Official History in Modern Indonesia*. Leiden, Neth.: Brill, 2005.

Woodward, Mark. *Java, Indonesia and Islam*. New York: Springer, 2011.

Young, Iris Marion. *Responsibility for Justice*. New York: Oxford University Press, 2011.

Young, Robert J. C. *Postcolonialism: A Historical Introduction*. Oxford: Blackwell, 2001.

Yudiono, K. S. *Pengantar Sejarah Sastra Indonesia*. Jakarta: Grasindo, 2010.

Yumarma, Andreas. *Unity in Diversity: A Philosophical and Ethical Study of the Javanese Concept of* Keselarasan. Rome: Editrice Pontificia Universita Gregoriana, 1996.

Yunus Amir Hamzah. *Hamka sebagai Pengarang Roman*. Jakarta: Puspasari Indah, 1993.

Zaim Rais. *Against Islamic Modernism: The Minangkabau Traditionalists' Responses to the Modernist Movement*. Jakarta: Logos Wacana Ilmu, 2001.

Zebiri, Kate. *Mahmud Shaltut and Islamic Modernism*. Oxford: Clarendon Press, 1993.

INDEX

CPSIA information can be obtained
at www.ICGtesting.com
Printed in the USA
LVHW100540051218
599323LV00014B/265/P

9 781501 724565